THE BAGHDAD AIR MAIL

THE BAGHDAD AIR MAIL

THE BAGHDAD AIR MAIL

WING COMMANDER RODERIC HILL

NONSUCH

First published 1929

Nonsuch Publishing Limited
The Mill, Brimscombe Port, Stroud, Gloucestershire, GL5 2QG
www.nonsuch-publishing.com

British Library Cataloguing in Publication Data.
A catalogue record for this book is available from the British Library.

ISBN 1-84588-009-9

Typesetting and origination by Nonsuch Publishing Limited
Printed in Great Britain by Oaklands Book Services Limited

CONTENTS

INTRODUCTION TO THE MODERN EDITION

In today's world we take the concept of air mail for granted, but it should not be forgotten that as late as the 1920s the main way of sending a letter was overland or by sea and that it could take literally weeks for a letter to reach its destination. At the end of World War One Britain was left with RAF squadrons based in Egypt, Palestine and Iraq. For a letter to reach Iraq from Britain by the land and sea route it had to go via Bombay and took an average of 28 days from London. The obvious solution to this problem was to take the mail by air, but with no civilian airlines working in the area the task fell to the RAF itself. So in June 1921 the RAF began the fortnightly Desert Airmail Service which reduced the overall time of mail delivery to just five days going via Cairo.

The aircraft which were used for this service were the D.H.10 and the Vickers Vimy and its derivative, the Vernon. Both the D.H.10 and the Vimy were twin-engined biplanes, developed as bombers for use in the war, but neither were developed in time to see much action. The Vimy type was renowned for its long distance flights, having been the plane used by John Alcock and Arthur Whitten Brown in the first non-stop flight across the Atlantic and so was perfect for its new role as a mail plane.

However, despite having the newest models in aircraft, in the 1920s navigation was still done using the compass, stars and visible landmarks. The part of the route which traversed the south Syrian desert was devoid of landmarks and so that pilots could find their way, but also so that they could be found if they were forced into an emergency landing, a track was marked with a plough and tractor across the stony landscape to guide them. Even with this visual guide the pilots faced major difficulties:

> The track was extremely difficult to follow in places. The strain of gazing to keep its continuity is very fatiguing. You have it one moment; and dare you but take your eyes away to gaze at an instrument and then look back, it has eluded you. … It is like reading faint and faded writing in an old book, or a story when you are half asleep, and keep losing the sense thereof.

At night they were left with the compass and the stars, and usually a healthy dose of luck, to guide their planes safely between airstrips, on which they took off and landed by the light of oil lanterns and flares. Yet, navigation was the least of worries these pilots faced. *Baghdad Air Mail* vividly describes the dangers of adverse weather conditions and forced landings due to engine and other mechanical failure. In an attempt to make sure no-one was lost in transit, the planes went out in twos, so that if one was lost along the way the other could land to help, or go on and report the position of the downed plane.

Despite the difficult and dangerous job that the pilots of the Air Mail service faced, that did not save them from criticism. In letters written by Gertrude Bell, archaeologist and Arabist, who was an advisor to Churchill when he was Colonial Secretary in 1921, she complains of delays to incoming and outgoing mail.

> Dec. 4. [1921] Baghdad. Dearest Father. We are now seeing the air mail from its less agreeable aspects. It doesn't work in wet weather and consequently, though we succeeded in getting off our mail last week,… they haven't been so fortunate from the other end, and there has been no incoming mail for 3 weeks and no prospect of one as yet, for the rain continues and our world has vanished in mud.

Despite these criticisms, the RAF played a vital role in the delivery of private and official mail to Iraq from the years 1921 to 1927, when the service was taken over by the commercial airline, Imperial Airways. Wing Commander Roderic Hill, who worked on the route from 1924 to 1926, provides a comprehensive history of the service and a personal insight into the dangers and delights of working on the Middle East's first major aerial postal service.

PREFACE

The purpose of this book is to present a series of personal narratives of flights over the Cairo-Baghdad Air Mail Route and elsewhere in Iraq. In the earlier part of the book I have written some chapters outlining the history and operation of the Air Mail Route. I do not pretend to have dealt exhaustively with the subject, and I have inserted such material only as I think will make my subsequent narratives interesting and intelligible to the reader who has no special knowledge of the route.

My narratives, being personal, are inevitably one-sided. If any other pilot sat down to write his experiences, I should not be surprised if the result were vastly different from mine. On the other hand, if my story conveys something of what one pilot felt when he flew over the desert, I shall feel that my labours have not been in vain.

For information about the history and working of the Air Mail Route I must acknowledge my indebtedness to a lecture given to the Royal Aeronautical Society by Air Vice-Marshal Sir Robert Brooke-Popham, and also to the writers of the Pilot's Handbook of the Cairo-Baghdad Route, which is of course an old friend of mine, and has naturally supplied me with copious information.

The Royal Aeronautical Society has kindly given me permission to publish certain of the photographs and parts of a lecture that I gave before the Society. I am also indebted to Flying Officer J.E. Davies for the photograph of H.M. King Faisal at Ramadi, to Colonel W. Dent, of Air Headquarters, Baghdad, for information about the tribes on the Air Mail Route, and to Lieut.-Colonel H. Burchall, of Imperial Airways, for his kindness in letting me have some notes on the operation of the civil air route. Finally I must express my appreciation of the permission accorded me by the Air Ministry to publish the book itself.

RODERIC HILL.

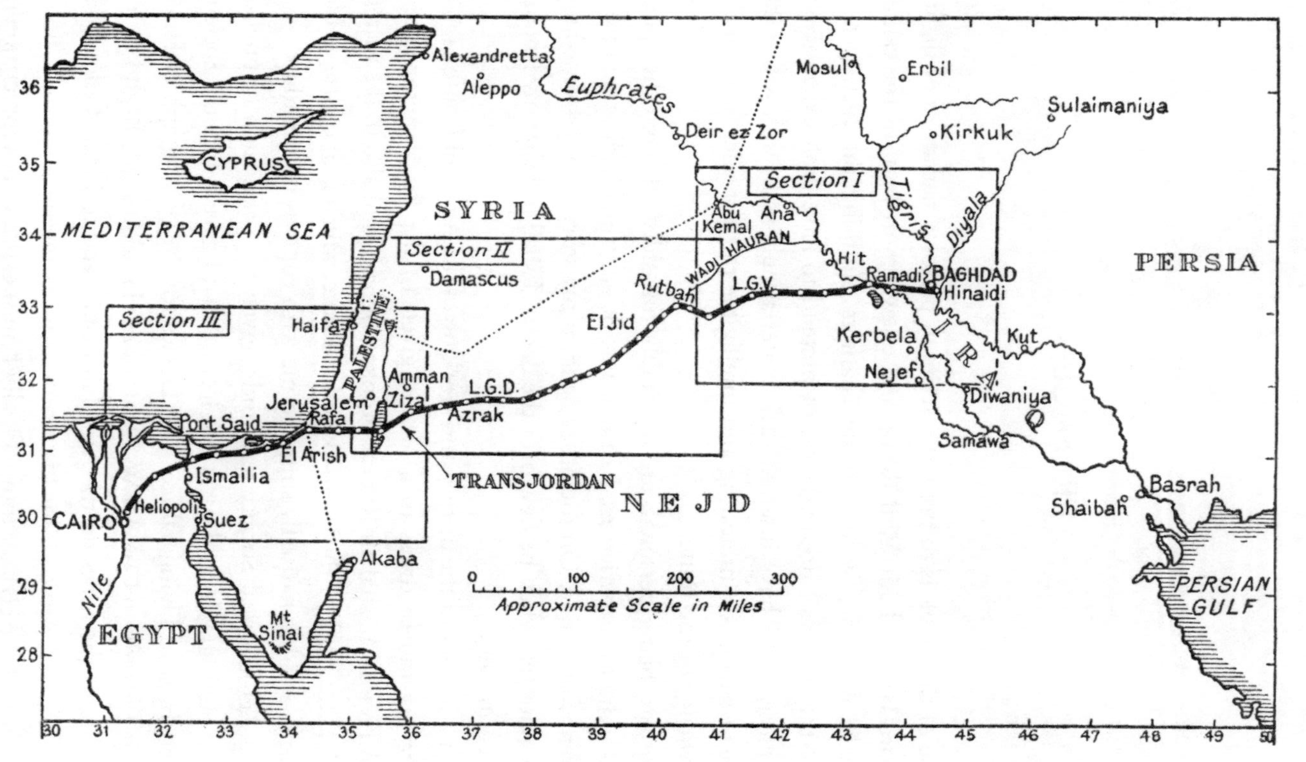

KEY MAP OF THE CAIRO-BAGHDAD AIR MAIL ROUTE

THIS SKETCH MAP SERVES AS A KEY TO THE THREE ENLARGED MAPS OF THE ROUTE MARKED SECTION I, II, III (AT THE BACK OF THE BOOK)

CHAPTER I

THE MAKING OF THE AIR MAIL ROUTE

After the War of 1914-1918 Great Britain found herself with a number of Royal Air Force squadrons in Egypt, Palestine and Iraq. The Turk had been expelled from the two latter countries, which had previously been under his dominion. By the Peace Treaty they were mandated to Great Britain. Egypt, on the other hand, had been garrisoned by British troops since 1882. During the War a British Protectorate was proclaimed. In 1922 this was abolished and Egypt was given her present limited independence.

One of the problems that confronted those who were responsible for restoring order out of the chaos of the shattered dominions of Turkey, was how to link up Egypt, Palestine and Iraq, countries which over 2,000 years ago Alexander the Great conquered and absorbed into his empire. As far as civilized communication was concerned, between Palestine and Iraq there existed an aching void. How was this to be bridged? The normal route from the Land of the Two Rivers to the Mediterranean was via the Euphrates to Damascus, where the stretch of open desert was shortest. As in olden times those who wished to make the crossing had to go on a camel or else walk it, the advantages of a route which ran out of touch with water for the minimum distance were only too apparent. As it happened, Syria was given to the French to take care of after the War, and the middle Euphrates-Damascus Route is therefore to a large extent out of the zone of British influence. Proposals were made to run a railway more or less direct across the desert from Baghdad to Palestine, but the cost of constructing it would be enormous, and it is doubtful whether it would in the end be a paying proposition.

What more natural than to turn to the new means of transport, the aeroplane, to find a solution of the difficulty. In March, 1921, there was held a conference at Cairo, at which were present the Secretary of State for the

Colonies, the Chief of the Air Staff and the local Army and Royal Air Force commanders, besides a number of people who had special knowledge of the Middle East. All sorts of problems were discussed, and among them was the question of an Air Route. At this conference the momentous decision was taken to open a desert route between Amman in Transjordan and Ramadi in Iraq. The commercial and strategic advantages of such a route were obvious, and comparable with those afforded by the opening of the Suez Canal fifty-two years before. It is interesting to reflect, too, that the inauguration of this route has gone a long way towards opening up a line of communication that has suffered for so many years from the discovery of a passage round the Cape and later from the construction of the Canal. The Air Route was intended as a link in the Imperial chain of communications, which it is hoped will one day run across India all the way to Australia. The route would combine the advantages of an Air Mail service with a means of training the pilots in long-distance flying. I think it is fair to say that the route could never have been pioneered by a civil organization. The first crossings had to be carried out in the way that a military expedition is undertaken. This was mainly because no one had any idea of what would be involved nor of what measures would be necessary to obtain adequate security.

To start with, anyone ignorant of the flying conditions in that part of the country might well ask, what is an Air Route? Aeroplanes sail along through the air and are not forced to bother about the ground as long as they do not come to a lofty mountain range that they cannot easily climb over. All the business of having a broad paved track with brightly coloured petrol pumps and frequent hotels is unnecessary. In fact all that an Air Route ought to be is a line on a map, with landing grounds where petrol and oil are available at suitable intervals, and perhaps sheds or hangars at the terminal points where the aircraft can be overhauled and polished up when they have done the trip and as it were come safely into port. That is true for flying over normal types of reasonably developed country, and a pilot could, as far as pure flying is concerned, fly the 470 odd miles from Amman to Ramadi by means of his compass. If he were flying in an easterly direction and made a mistake of a few degrees in his navigation, he would just have to go on until he hit the Euphrates. And he would have arrived. But at the time that the route was opened aero engines were not anything like so reliable as they are nowadays, and there was always the chance of an aeroplane being forced to land *en route* due to engine failure. Now if this happened to an aeroplane, even when fitted with wireless, it was about as easy to find in the vast uncharted spaces as a needle in a haystack; meanwhile the unfortunate pilot and passengers would be exposed to a lingering death, the horrors of which it is advisable not to think about. The twentieth-century pilot could not submit to the fatalism of the Bedouin, so well pictured by Hassanein Bey in his book, *The Lost Oases*: "… it is then that the Bedouin, when he has offered up his prayers to the Almighty Power for deliverance, when he has offered up his prayers and they have not been granted, it is then that he draws his jerd around him, and sinking down upon the sands awaits with astounding equanimity the decreed death. This is the faith in which the journey across the desert must be made."

Something a good deal more substantial was needed to provide for contingencies that might so easily lead to fatal results. The region between Amman and Ramadi, usually dismissed on the maps as the Syrian Desert and left at that, is, unlike the country between Amman and Cairo, peculiarly deficient in landmarks which a pilot can follow and thus check his position. Perhaps it is truer to say that though it does possess a multitude of landmarks, they are so easy to confuse with one another that for the most part they mislead instead of guiding. It therefore became necessary to create artificial land marks. Various suggestions were put forward for doing this cheaply and effectively, one of which was to make craters in the ground at short intervals by blowing up explosive charges. But an even simpler means was found, and this was the track of the wheels of a convoy of cars run over the desert, which made a continuous landmark that the pilot could keep in view the whole time. The pilot has only got to follow the track, and if he comes down anywhere, rescue aircraft go out along the track until they find him.

In addition to the above the aeroplanes were normally unable to fly the whole distance from Transjordan to Iraq on one fill of petrol, more especially in the reverse direction, that is from east to west, because of the prevailing wind. It was soon found necessary to instal special desert refuelling points located on the track, without which it would be nearly impossible to find them; so as it turned out the making of the track provided an adequate and economical method of ensuring safety and smoothness of working. Before describing the making of the track, I must give some idea of the country over which it was marked.

The land between the Euphrates and the Jordan is referred to on the maps as a desert. As a matter of fact it is not desert in the strict sense of the word. I looked the word "desert" up in Mr. Webster's dictionary and found that he described a desert as a "barren tract incapable of supporting any considerable population without an artificial water supply, and almost destitute of moisture and vegetation." The country we are dealing with is more accurately fitted by the definition of the word "steppe," which is given as "xerophilous grassland, usually treeless." This means a country covered with grass that likes growing in dry places. But it is the word "treeless" which gives the keynote. You can go on and on and on, and whatever else you may see, you may be certain that it will not be a tree. Yet until you come back to a land in which trees grow you hardly realize what you have been missing; and I think that it is the absence of trees that gives the peculiar empty look to the country, which I shall still obstinately go on calling desert, because "steppe" sounds pedantic. Who ever heard of anyone coming in and saying, "I've been out in the steppe to-day"?

The next thing about this "desert" is that it lies quite high above sea level; the average height is about 2,000 feet. Yet many of the desert uplands are so flat that you would never for a moment think that you were not somewhere near sea level; and the significance of this comes in when you are landing an aeroplane in the desert, as I shall explain later on. The desert, then, is a great upland plateau; and if you can imagine it as a block about 450 miles long tilted up towards its western edge, you will have a crude idea of what this section of the plateau looks like.

The Air Mail Route may be likened to the string of a bow with its back bent northwards and outlining the more fertile grasslands which lie between the mountains and the plains. The western edge of the plateau is tilted up because this is where the string joins the western end of the bow the eastern end of the route stops short of the eastern end of the bow which is formed by the foothills of the Persian mountains.

Let us now climb up on to the top of Mount Nebo, whence we are told that Moses was allowed to see the Promised Land before he died at the age of 120 years. To the westward of us lies the Jordan Valley, about 10 miles away, and stretching to the southward of it is the Dead Sea lying in its deep volcanic cleft, some 1,300 feet below the level of the Mediterranean, the "Great Sea" of olden times. To the south of us the gnarled ridges of the Hills of Moab rise up in an endless perspective. We are actually in the modern province of Transjordan, and 20 miles away to the north-east lies the town of Amman, its capital, where lives Abdullah, the ruling prince. He is the brother of King Faisal of Iraq, and his family, the Sharifian house, is descended from Hassari, the son of the famous Ali, cousin of Mahomet. The ancient city, built picturesquely into a green cleft in the hills beside a stream which was a tributary of the river Jabbok of the Old Testament, was called Raboth Ammon, the "City of Waters." In those times it belonged to the Ammonites, who were constantly fighting the Hebrews. King David sent his army under Joab to attack the citadel, the remains of which are still visible on a hill overlooking the present town. It was on the rugged slopes below the citadel that Joab, by the king's orders, put Uriah the Hittite "in the forefront of the hottest battle," that he might be got out of the way. In later years, soon after the death of Alexander the Great, a Greek city was founded on the site of Raboth Ammon, which was mostly in ruins, by Ptolemy Philadelphus, the second son of the first Ptolemy of Egypt; and it was called Philadelphia. It was subsequently garrisoned by the Romans, and became an important military headquarters. Perched on another hill that stands above the gorge is the aerodrome of Amman, a little natural piece of tableland. It is getting on for 3,000 feet above sea level. And this was the western end of the Air Mail Track.

Amman is situated on the western scarp of the desert plateau, which, a few miles east of the Dead Sea, rises at points to about 3,500 feet. This height, taken in conjunction with the depression of the Dead Sea, makes the western slope of the plateau, which is exceedingly precipitous, nearly 5,000 feet in all. The country of Transjordan, which is a strip of land lying to the east of the Jordan Valley, is chiefly marked by deeply cut gorges all ruffling westward towards the Jordan and the Dead Sea. The intervening hills look like nothing so much as a mass of giant barnacles, scarred and eroded, stark and gaunt. The biggest of these gorges is that of the Wadi Seil el Mojeb, the River Arnon of the Bible. The plateau itself is composed mostly of limestone rock, large areas of which are very thinly covered with an apology for surface soil. The soil is sufficient, however, to support a shabby growth of all sorts of grasses and scrub and bushes bearing sharp thin spines, called camel-thorn, which often reach a height of 3 and 4 feet. During the winter time, when it rains, the vegetation becomes quite vigorous and green looking, and affords good grazing for camels, but in the height of summer it withers to a faded drab colour. On the edge of civilization, such as the country round Amman, there is a settled agricultural population and there are fairly good-looking wheat-fields. The surface of the plateau consists of gently rolling uplands, with now and then a steepish cliff-side, or some sharp isolated hills. But the hardness of aspect of the desert does not come so much from its actual contours as from its barrenness. If, for instance, it were covered with soft green grass and sweet-smelling herbs, like Salisbury Plain, in many parts I hardly think you would be sensible of much difference.

If you go east from Amman, one of the first valleys that you come to is the valley of Azrak, the floor of which is 1,700 feet above sea level. Here there are a series of springs, which in winter time develop into quite a large lake. Azrak means "blue," and the name is an appropriate one. The quality of the blue of the pools of Azrak is that of lapis lazuli set in the pewter or amber hues of the valley floor. The fact that there is always water at Azrak is sufficient to make it a resting-place for the nomad inhabitants of the desert. In the spring there are some strips of green at Azrak; and the contrast of the place to a wanderer coming from the lands beyond would give him a vivid sense of the sublime words of the Twenty-third Psalm. Azrak is also a haunt of wild birds, and the duck-shooting is good enough to attract parties from a considerable distance. In these parts there are the remains of forts. They look Roman in origin and appear to run in a line eastwards from the Dead Sea. Their names are Kasr Azrak, Kasr Amra and Kasr Kharana. Perhaps they marked the Roman frontier at one time against the restless border tribes, and it is not unlikely that they were used by the Persians and later on by the Ommayad caliphs of Damascus.

Where there is no surface soil on the face of the desert, there is a covering of flinty gravel, with a good deal of quartz which glistens in the sun. East of Azrak there must be some sandstone mixed up with the limestone, for there are large patches of orange and red, which are repeated at intervals as you travel towards Mesopotamia. About 20 miles east of Azrak what is sometimes called the Basalt country is encountered. It is a belt 50 or 60 miles wide, running roughly north and south and cutting your direction of travel at right angles. The hills in this belt are capped with basalt, a very hard black volcanic rock. I once landed in this country for the night on a grey winter evening, and on the western horizon a tattered sunset still struggled with the gathering darkness. That place was the epitome of loneliness. All around the hills rose like odious flat-topped slag heaps, and filled me with a sinister foreboding. Originally the lava seems to have bubbled up in some great seismic convulsion, and spread itself as a hard crust over the limestone. Incidentally there are no signs of a volcano. In the course of time the basalt has been eroded except for those portions capping the hills, and has broken up into boulders which have rolled down into the valleys. These boulders, the black spilth of many thousand years, have paved the valley floors in such a way as to make them almost impassable for wheeled traffic. Some of them are embedded in loam, and hardly show. The first thing you know about one of them is that you have broken the tailskid of your aeroplane against it. In the middle of the basalt country there are three sharp-looking hills in a line which have the appearance of shark's teeth. Amongst the basalt boulders sparse thorn and scrub find a precarious existence.

In the basalt country you hardly ever see a living soul. The Bedou seem to avoid it and only move through its fringes. But sometime in the past it must have supported a settled or partially settled population. Most of the hilltops, especially those towards the western end, look as if they had been fortified. The remains of these fortifications consist of low walls of basalt boulders, which, while not very obvious from the ground, stand out distinctly when viewed from the air. The patterns they made reminded me of those books that people give you to write your name in and then fold together so as to blot the signature and its reversed image on the opposite page. In essence the fortifications are composed of a walled redoubt on the higher ground, with radiating walls running down the slopes, something like a sector of a spider's web. They seem on the whole to have been built to defend this region from aggressions coming from the west; for in some cases, at any rate, the redoubts face in a westerly direction and the radiating lines of walls spread out towards the east. The Bedou say that they were made by the "old men," which indicates a tradition of some prehistoric tribe. The idea is that flocks could be grazed in the valleys, and on the danger signal could be driven into the defended area with the help of the converging walls.

There is one more feature of the basalt country that requires description, and that is the presence of large and perfectly level areas called mud flats. These are not exclusive to the basalt region, but they are much more noticeable than elsewhere because of their sharp contrast to their grimy surroundings. The shallow depressions between the hills have become filled up with fine yellowish mud carried down in suspension by drainage water running off the hills. Some of them are nearly circular in shape, some roughly elliptical and some kidney-shaped. Their principal feature from the flying point of view is that their forms are individual and characteristic; and certain of them are easily recognizable when you get to know them well. When dry they make excellent landing grounds because their surface is absolutely flawless. But there is one important disadvantage. When the sun is shining on them they possess a surface almost like a mirror and reflect the glare in a dazzling way. Although a pilot likes to have a flat surface on which to land, he also likes to be able to see some features on it, such as tufts of grass or ruts, which assist his estimation of the nearness of the ground while he drops towards it. On the mud flats there is nothing. If you land on one in summer you have the feeling that you are dropping into vacancy, and unless you exercise considerable caution you are liable to misjudge the landing with disheartening results. Luckily there are ways of overcoming the difficulty. Then, again, it is essential to make sure that the mud is really dry. This can be gauged pretty well from the air by the colour. If the mud is wet, it is much darker than when dry. If the season has been very rainy, the mud flats occasionally become covered with water. A mud flat in the middle of the desert that holds within its confines a miniature of the sky gleaming like blue and white enamel is arrestingly beautiful.

If we continue our journey eastward from the basalt country, we emerge from the gloomy hills on to a plain about 120 miles broad. Its section where we cross it is convex; for example, when we leave the basalt we are 2,000 feet or so above sea level, when we are a little over half-way across we are at nearly 3,000 feet, and when we arrive at a nondescript range of hills at the other end of the plain we are slightly higher than when we started. This seems to belie my earlier statement that the plateau between the Jordan and the Euphrates is like a block tilted up towards its western edge; but the plain that is situated to the east of the basalt hills, and the hills themselves, are but minor features of the complete geometrical design which is on a much huger scale than they. After the end of this plain the ground drops away quite rapidly to the Euphrates: 2,000 feet in just over 200 miles. The nondescript hills that I have mentioned mark approximately the mid-point of the journey from Amman. In this neighbourhood are the wells of El Jid, cut deep in the limestone rock; and about 35 miles further on in a north-easterly direction are the wells of Rutbah, hewn into the floor of the Wadi Hauran which drains the hills and runs into the Euphrates Valley. The wells at El Jid and the wells at Rutbah are both situated in the same system of watercourses which wind about in the hills in a complex way and unite in the Hauran. In summer time the Wadi Hauran is dry on the surface, but in the rainy season the wadi itself and its numerous tributaries are streaked and fretted with pale blue. You will practically always see several dozen to several hundred of the dark goat-skin Arab tents pitched along the edge of the wadi now and then amongst the meaner tents you see a larger one which belongs to a sheikh. The tribes come to the Wadi Hauran for water and grazing, and not infrequently squabble about the wells and water-holes. This they have done since the beginning of time.

During our journey down the hill towards the Euphrates we keep crossing shallow north-eastward draining wadis which are all bent towards the Euphrates

RE-FUELLING AT THE DESERT TANK

THE ZIGGURAT AT AQQAR KUF

They are broader and less eroded than the wadis running into the Jordan cleft on the westward face of the great plateau. Soon after leaving Rutbah the Wadi Amej is crossed. You may then follow over the sloping plain for 40 miles till you come to a large elliptical mud flat around which as far as you can see grow bushes of prickly camel-thorn. Away to the south there have always been visible lines of low flat-topped hills, but as you continue towards the Mesopotamian plain they become less prominent. Just after you have passed through another range of quite low hills from which the Wadi Muhammadi drains towards the Euphrates, you may see far away on the north-eastern horizon the faint rim of dull green that marks the line of the river itself.

After sighting the Euphrates you come to two great black pools in the desert. These are the Bitumen Pools, lying like dark blots on the plain. When flying over them you can smell the acrid odour of the bitumen at a thousand feet above the ground. Finally you reach the Euphrates at the little market town of Ramadi, which has a settled population. It is the outpost of civilization in this direction. As far as the Mail Track is concerned it forms the eastern jumping-off point in the same way as Amman formed the western jumping-off point. When living in Baghdad I used to imagine Ramadi as the gateway of the desert through which the pilot passes out to new and exciting adventures. Beyond is the open desert with all its mysterious fascination; and few who behold it from the air as they are about to leave Ramadi on the westbound trip for the first time can fail to experience that slight catch of the breath which comes with the sudden view of the sea from a high place.

The desert seen thus gives the impression of a land with no ending; it has an unreal atmospheric quality comparable only with the sky. Perhaps that is why people call it the "Blue."

To the south-east of Ramadi there is a large lake called Habbaniyah, sometimes anglicized into "Have a Banana." The city of Baghdad is 6 miles away to the eastward. If you are flying to Baghdad you follow the Euphrates for about 25 miles till you come to Fellujah, another town on the river, and then jump across the intervening desert "strait" to the Tigris. As you approach Baghdad there lies on your left hand a wide depression, the Lake of Aqqar Kuf. Normally there is very little water in it, and you would be inclined to ask where the lake was, which you would never do about Lake Habbaniyah. It may be that the Lake of Aqqar Kuf was used as a reservoir to supply ancient Babylon by means of canals. Now it consists of a swamp and a few insignificant pools. On the southern borders of this so-called lake there rises out of the plain on a small mound a Ziggurat, or ancient temple tower. This tower is a prominent landmark, and is built of mud brick, the courses being interleaved with layers of bitumened straw which act as a kind of cement. The lapse of time has not been kind to it, and it is weathered and worn away by winds and dust storms till its original shape is unrecognizable. Now it is the refuge of birds and jackals. Yet I cannot look at it without being impressed by its solitary grandeur and without feeling a certain respect for this battered image of greatness. It has been given the suggestive name of "Dead Man's Finger."

From there onwards to the Tigris, you pass over areas of cultivation, which look miserable and unkempt compared with the cultivation of the Nile. Close by the river banks it is perceptibly richer; but as the fields stretch away into the desert they become poorer and poorer until they fade out altogether.

This short description of the plateau between Amman and Baghdad should dispel the idea that the country is a desert. Although water is not abundant, there are a number of places where it can be got, even in summer time, if you know where to go for it. On the other hand there are large areas which are waterless, and you always have to carry a good supply with you. There are few places where at any time of year you will not see vegetation of some kind or other, though it may be very fragile. In the wadi beds it secures a firmer hold, and you may find even a profusion of wild flowers. In these beds the vegetation tends to grow in transverse wavy lines, which from the air frequently give the appearance of the striped skin of an animal. Parts of the country have a tolerably smooth surface fit to drive an ordinary car over without much difficulty, if a careful watch for boulders is kept. It is simply necessary to pick one's way carefully and not to be in too much of a hurry. In practice you would probably follow one of the broad tracks used by the Bedou.

There are practically no roads in our sense of the word in Mesopotamia. When dry the mud surface of the ground makes a very fair road, almost as hard as the gravel of the plateau that I have described. The trouble comes in the rainy season, when the mud becomes a glutinous morass, a veritable Slough of Despond. The mud roads such as the one that covers the 6 miles between the cantonment of Hinaidi and Baghdad have to be closed; and wheeled traffic finds its way, if it can without sinking up to the axles and becoming derelict, along tracks which border the road on both sides The whole of Lower Mesopotamia consists of a flat plain of alluvial mud deposited by the action of the rivers; here and there the intense monotony of the landscape is relieved by some shapeless mounds that look like low hills. They may be natural or, on the other hand, the remains of some ancient city. There are various depressions, too, where the water collects and forms swamps.

The mud of the plain is a fine grey loam, and it is said that in places you could dig down to 150 feet with out coming to the bottom of it. In the dry weather the mud has a dusty surface which is blown up by certain winds. It is then that a dust storm rises, which, though it does not sting you like a sand storm because the particles of dust suspended in the air are smaller and not so gritty, gets into your eyes and throat, and may become so thick that visibility is reduced to a few yards. You can sometimes see the sun through it as a sullen tawny disc. At other times the dust clouds are sucked up into the air and float at some thousands of feet. Then, though it is possible to see quite a long way on the ground below, the whole sky is overcast with a malignant sort of haze. A dust storm may last with varying intensity for three or four days. The Air Mail Route is far freer from dust or sand storms than the Mesopotamian plain, which is bordered on the south-west by a soft sand belt. The gravel surface is too heavy to be blown up, and it helps to bind the soil. Nevertheless it is possible occasionally to encounter these storms, especially in the regions which slope down to the Euphrates. There is also enough loam on the plateau to make certain areas wet in addition to the mud flats proper in the rainy season. If a heavily laden aeroplane happens to land on a wet patch, there is a risk of its tipping up on its nose, or at any rate of its wheels sinking in so much that it cannot get up enough speed to rise into the air.

I have described the features of the ground along the Air Mail Route and in Mesopotamia in some detail because it is difficult to get a fair picture of what the ground parties that went out to make the track were up against, unless one can appreciate the conditions in which they had to work. In Mesopotamia the climate is continental and subject to extremes. It is very hot in summer and can be quite cold in winter, although in an average winter the worst cold does not amount to more than a light ground frost at night. The temperature is naturally modified by the height you are above sea level. The desert is so exposed that you feel the extremes of temperature far more than in sheltered places; as far as feeling the heat is concerned the dryness of the atmosphere causes one's skin to evaporate rapidly, and thus to keep cooler than if the humidity of the air were high. It is extremely unpleasant to do any hard work when exposed to the sun in the daytime, and it is better to fit your day's work into the early morning and the evening hours. In the heat of the day the only thing is to sit as still as you can and rig up some form of covering to afford shade. If you are the lucky possessor of an aeroplane, you can always crawl under its protecting wings.

Of such is made up the life in the desert. The men who set out into the unknown to mark the track had no light task before them. Courage and optimism were necessary, and they were not found wanting. Before the summer of 1921 no European, so far as is known, had been right across the plateau in an easterly or westerly direction, except along the well-known caravan route from Damascus to the Euphrates, which lay a long way north of the proposed crossing. Explorers like Miss Gertrude Bell had wandered over many parts of the desert, but nobody had a complete idea of what might be encountered in the central parts.

Somewhere about the time of the Cairo conference in March, 1921, that I referred to earlier, Major Holt with a convoy of Ford cars penetrated as far as the eastern edge of the basalt country from the Ramadi end, the return journey being about 800 miles. He was carrying out a preliminary reconnaissance for the Iraq railways. In the June of that year two car convoys set out, one from Amman on the west and the other from Ramadi on the east. They actually met at the wells of El Jid, about half-way across. The convoy from Amman consisted of two Rolls armoured cars, two Rolls tenders and six Crossley desert tenders, which had the frames raised to give greater clearance over the ground. The parties from both ends consisted of Royal Air Force personnel. The Amman party was accompanied by Dr. Ball, who surveyed the route as accurately as could be managed under the circumstances, and whose map subsequently formed the pilot's guide when flying across. Peake Pasha, who knew as much as any man about the country and its inhabitants, also went. Every night the position of the convoy was fixed by stellar observations, and the accurate time necessary for the calculations was received by means of a portable wireless set which the party took with them.

But the car convoy would have been blind to the unknown country ahead had it not been accompanied by a Flight of aeroplanes which co-operated with the men on the ground and kept reconnoitring ahead. From time to time an aeroplane would come back to the cars and land beside them when possible. The pilot would give a description of the country ahead and would indicate a favourable route for the cars to follow. This air reconnaissance was undoubtedly one of the principal factors in the success of the whole operation. The cars from the west were accompanied by D.H.9a aeroplanes of No. 47 Squadron based on Amman, while those from the east were escorted by similar aeroplanes of No. 30

Squadron at Baghdad. Major Holt went with the latter aircraft, and the previous experience that he had gained of the country was of the greatest help.

It was found that the track most visible from the air was that made by the wheels of the cars as they followed each other across the desert. Over certain portions of the route a Fordson tractor was used with a plough attached which made a plough track as well. Where the track twisted, for example to negotiate an obstinate wadi, an arrow would be ploughed for extra guidance. It was when the first eastbound party came to the basalt country that it was very nearly baffled. At one time the explorers were for giving up the job as hopeless; but pluck and determination won the day and they forced their way through in the end.

Landing grounds were marked at intervals of 15 to 30 miles all the way along the track. Over the greater part of the route it was not difficult to find pieces of ground suitable for landing grounds. The great advantage of these landing grounds is that in nearly all cases the approaches are quite open; and a piece of ground, even though gently undulating in contour, if it has a reasonably smooth surface, is good enough for the average requirements if it is not less than 500 yards square. Sometimes, on the other hand, it is possible to find a "T" or "L"-shaped area, the arms of which are 200 yards broad. An aeroplane has always to take off and land directly into a wind of any consequence; and with an "L"-shaped landing ground the pilot can normally select his run so that it is directly along one of the arms of the "L" or else slightly across, which gives him a little more room and allows him freedom to land and take off in any direction he pleases or as dictated by the direction of the wind. All that the ground parties did in marking the landing grounds on the Mail Route was to plough a circle about 20 yards in diameter in the desert and inside the circle plough a letter or number. In some cases they were able to make corner markings as well, which are a great help to a pilot unfamiliar with the ground; but the best thing to do at these desert landing grounds is to take no risks and land as near the circle as possible. In the basalt country it was much harder to find landing grounds other than the conspicuous mud flats, because of the profusion of basalt boulders. Circles and letters were therefore marked on certain mud flats which the track crossed, and further markings made on the smoothest patch that could be found on their edges, which might be used in case a mud flat was wet and therefore dangerous to land on.

The party from Amman lettered all the landing grounds that they marked, from "A" to "R," with the omission of "I" and "Q." The party from the other end numbered their landing grounds from "I" to "XI," which is not far from where the two parties met at the wells of El Jid. All the numbered landing grounds are marked in Roman numerals, except landing ground No. 8, which is marked as written. The landing grounds were always referred to by the Mail pilots as "*L.G.*" for short. Thus, landing ground No. VII would be talked about as *L.G.* VII. The landing ground by the Pools of Azrak is known as *L.G.* C. *L.G.* B, though not marked till much later, is by the old fort of Kasr Kharana, some miles west of the pools.

L.G. R marks a zonal division. As regards responsibility for salvage operations all landing grounds east of it belong to Iraq, and all landing grounds to the west of it to Egypt. This meant that if an aeroplane were forced to come down with some mechanical defect that was incapable of repair by the crew, and the place at which it forced-landed was, for example, west of *L.G.* R, then the Royal Air Force Headquarters at Cairo would be responsible for despatching a relief aeroplane to go and help the lame duck; and similar arrangements from Baghdad applied to forced landings east of *L.G.* R. This zonal division did not always apply absolutely rigidly, and by the nature of the circumstances there was a certain amount of give and take between the two Air Commands in Egypt and Iraq. This piece of organization, however, did ensure that an aeroplane which signalled for help was never left out in the Blue through a misunderstanding as to the person who was supposed to be looking after it.

At the end of 1922 and the beginning of 1923 other car convoys went out from each end and re-marked the track, straightening it out and improving it in places, and reploughing the furrow. The plough track is now complete along the whole route. The winter rains were apt to obliterate the track in places, so periodical re-marking was necessary. One of the Air Mail pilots' tasks was to report on the visibility of the track when they flew over it. Aeroplanes again co-operated with the cars and made many of the subsequent improvements possible. The officer in charge of the car convoy would himself go into the air at intervals and review his handiwork. These car parties had many hardships to endure, and sometimes manual labour such as would daunt a navvy. Cars would become bogged in soft ground and take a whole day to pull out. Amazing improvizations were used and seemingly unrepairable vehicles somehow made to work. A colossal fund of human energy was sunk in the construction and maintenance of the track; all of this is implicit in the track as it exists to-day, the frail thread through the wilderness that binds the pilot to civilization and to the needs of life itself.

I mentioned earlier that it became necessary to instal special desert refuelling points on the track because the aircraft were frequently unable against an adverse wind to fly from Ramadi to Amman, or vice versa, without taking in some petrol *en route*. The early aeroplanes that flew across the route before the installation of these refuelling points, were forced to strap on as many as twelve 4-gallon tins of petrol underneath their wings, so that they looked something like kangaroos transporting their young. This accretion of weight and air resistance had an adverse effect on their performance, and they could only climb up into the air quite slowly. Very soon after the opening of the route, this method of carrying petrol tins externally was felt to be intolerable. A petrol dump was therefore sited at *L.G.* V, where there is a large mud flat. *L.G.* V is about 360 miles east of Amman and 112 miles west of Ramadi. So if an eastbound aircraft by the time it reached *L.G.* V judged itself unable to reach Ramadi on the petrol that remained in its tanks, it could land at *L.G.* V and take in enough petrol to complete the journey. As petrol was alleged frequently to be robbed from the dump, probably by the Bedou, who had little use for the petrol but a great desire for the comparatively worthless tins which contained it, a sunk, thief-proof tank with a pump was installed. This sunk tank held 600 gallons of petrol, and could only be opened by a special key that the pilot took in his aeroplane, which effectively put a stop to the petrol pilfering.

After the dump had been provided at *L.G.* V, and after considerable deliberation, a similar dump was installed at *L.G.* D in the basalt country. This landing ground is 390 miles west of Ramadi and 79 miles east of Amman, and offered similar facilities to westbound aircraft. Troubles with the dump were also experienced at *L.G.* D. It consisted of a steel box set in concrete. The Bedou were apt to fire their rifles through the keyhole. Consequently another sunk tank with a pump, similar to the one at *L.G.* V, but holding 1,000 gallons of petrol, was fitted up. Against an exceptionally adverse wind it was occasionally necessary on the westbound trip to land and take in petrol at both refuelling points. The tank at *L.G.* V was refuelled by air from Ramadi. An aeroplane was able to fly the 112 miles to *L.G.* V, carrying a number of petrol tins in the hull; and in addition it was normally able to dispose of the contents of one of its own tanks and still have enough left to get back to Ramadi. The tank at *L.G.* D was refuelled by motor transport from Amman.

When the Nairn Transport Company started running the motor mail in the summer of 1923, their cars ran from Damascus and joined the Air Mail Track between El Jid and Rutbah, at *L.G.* IX. Their wheel-marks rove a track which was easy and clear for the pilot to follow. Even then, after the autumn rains, and in the strange elusive lighting of the desert, which has been described as "full of things that are not there," it was by no means impossible to lose touch with the track, especially in the low cloud and rain of the winter months.

In a flight across the Mail Route east of Amman, unless the weather is perfect, the track is the beginning and the end; the pilot's present, his past and his future.

CHAPTER II

THE ROUTE IN BEING

The Air Mail Track between Transjordan and Iraq covers nearly two-thirds of the whole route from Cairo to Baghdad; 600 miles out of the 866, although the 60 odd miles of track, or road as it is called, linking up Ramadi and Baghdad can hardly be counted because the aeroplanes normally steered a compass course instead of following it. It was simply a question of jumping from one river to another.

The Air Mail Route between Amman and Cairo, on the other hand, passes over relatively civilized country, and there is not the same scarcity of landmarks or other amenities as there is in the eastern section. The Jud Hills form the backbone of Palestine; and in order to go down into Egypt you have to cross them somewhere. They are very rugged and there are few places where an aeroplane, if it is forced to come down, can make a safe landing. The idea, therefore, was to cross them as nearly as possible at right angles in order to reduce the time of flying over bad country as much as possible. The original route from Amman was to steer slightly south of west over the deep Jordan Valley and pass over Jericho, where a landing ground existed. It was not a very good one, but it would suffice in an emergency. The pilot then steered for Jerusalem, the towers of which he could see perched up on the hills unless the weather were very bad. A small landing ground was also available there, which has since been superseded by the landing ground at Kulundia, 6 miles north of Jerusalem The course then changed to a little north of west for the town of

Ramleh, lying in the plain between the Jud Hills and the Mediterranean Sea. Ramleh was made famous by the Crusaders, and the aerodrome there was made by the Germans during the war of 1914–18. The surface soil of the plains of Palestine becomes sticky and soft after rain, of which there is plenty during the winter, and consequently aerodromes are apt to become unfit for use. A fresh site was later selected for Ramleh aerodrome adjacent to the old one but covering a low hill which slopes down from the hangars. The part of the aerodrome on the hill drains sufficiently to remain permanently serviceable during the winter; but the pilot cannot afford to land down the hill even against a moderate wind. He had far better land with the wind and rely on the upward slope to pull him up. Pilots who have landed with the wind on the level, and have not been able to pull up, will appreciate that the slope of the hill has to be quite pronounced for it to be preferable to land down wind. I believe that no really successful wheel brakes have yet been evolved for aeroplanes. One of the difficulties is that they tend to tip up on their noses if you apply a brake when they are running along. If anybody wants to appreciate what the absence of brakes means to the pilot, let him take a car, accelerate it up to 40 miles an hour, put it into neutral gear, and then see how long it takes to stop.[1] If there is not much wind to land against, aeroplanes run a long way on smooth desert aerodromes after they have touched the ground; moderately long grass has a fair braking effect; a slight upward slope is the best if it can be found. That is why the best sort of aerodrome is one that is slightly convex, and allows you to land up hill towards the centre from all directions. Ramleh aerodrome is like this with one half missing.

When the pilot leaves Ramleh all he has got to do is to follow the coast-line. The railway that was made during the British advance into Palestine during the War, runs fairly near the coast and can be followed in low clouds and rain. After flying down the coast of Palestine for about 60 miles, over alternating sand dunes and palm or orange groves, the dark green of which shows up in striking contrast, the pilot will sight the railway junction at Rafa. To his right is the open sea, bordered by its line of midget breakers, and here and there in the distance a coloured sail will show up in the distance and enhance the rich blueness of the Mediterranean. To the left are the brown and purple and green fields, looking somewhat of the quality of pastel, rising up step by step to the slate-coloured skyline of the Jud Hills. Beyond Rafa the character of the country changes. The coast-line still continues its graceful swerve to the west; the sea, the breakers and the foreshore move past with hardly a variation, but the land dries up into an endless maze of dunes, pale yellow and arid in the shimmering light, stretching away into the twisted hills and wadis of Sinai.

Rafa marks the borders of Palestine and Egypt. Not far into Egypt is the Wadi el Arish, with a little town beside the wadi, the red roofs of which make a pleasing spot of colour in the universal yellow of the sand. A few miles up the wadi is a good landing ground which is marked with a circle. You can nearly always spot these landing grounds by the tailskid marks of aircraft, which make a pattern of loops and twists like a muddled ball of string laid out on the ground. Some marks are more distinct than others, which show that aeroplanes have been down there recently.

The coast-line then becomes variegated with whitish-looking salt flats, which look something like the mud flats east of Transjordan except that their colour is quite different. The sea is apt to encroach on them, and if you land on one—when they are dry the landing is good—you have to be careful that the sea has not been over it recently. It is not so easy to tell whether they are wet or dry by their colour as with a mud flat. They used to remind me strongly of the look of an overflow from a dye-works. After passing over the landing grounds at Moseifig and Romani, which are situated on these sort of flats, you eventually see the long straight line of the Suez Canal, and perhaps the smoke of a P. & 0. liner on its way home to England. To the south the blue of the Great Bitter Lake and Lake Timsa appears, set against the grey heights above Suez. On the western horizon the dark misty green of the Nile Delta sets a limit to the spacious table of sand; and as you turn south-west you draw nearer and nearer to it until the details become distinct, and white houses and roads show up clear cut against the myriad fields and dykes that look like a vast board on which you might play some game.

You pass over the battlefield of Tel el Kebir lying in a corner of the desert that thrusts itself into the cultivation. You then cross the strip of green that borders the railway from Port Said to Cairo and the sweet-water canal from Ismailia, where you can just see in the distance the airship mooring mast that stands up like a black spike against the waters of Timsa. Now you have only to follow the eastern edge of the cultivation, which ends quite abruptly in the sand, and in due time you will see the white plaster houses of Heliopolis, which appear like white boxes in rows.

Heliopolis is a suburb about 6 miles north-east of the city of Cairo, and performs the same sort of function that Golders Green does for London. Here is the aerodrome that is your journey's end. From there you can take a tram, or, if you dare risk it, an Egyptian taxi, and in twenty minutes you will be spinning in the hub of Egypt.

In order to assist in grasping the scale of the Air Mail Route, I will superimpose an imaginary flight from Penzance to the Shetland Islands, via Plymouth, Exeter, Bristol, Worcester, Harrogate, Durham, Edinburgh, Inverness and the Orkneys. This should help to give an idea of the distances involved. Imagine

Penzance is Baghdad. Ramadi would correspond to Plymouth. As we approach the great mud at *L.G.* V, which is 112 miles from Ramadi, we should be 12 miles beyond Exeter. When we pass out of the hills where lie the wells of El Jid, we should be a few miles beyond Worcester. By the time we had crossed the Jud Hills into Palestine we should have arrived at Inverness. Kantara on the Suez Canal would represent the northern shores of the Orkneys, and finally the end of the flight at Heliopolis would have just taken us to the Shetlands.

To take other examples, the distance between Cairo and Baghdad is, within a hundred miles or so, the same as the distances from London to Stockholm, London to Warsaw, London to Vienna, London to Rome or London to Madrid.

We may now turn to the history of the actual flying over the Air Mail Route. The section that lies between Cairo and Amman was the battle-ground over which the British and the Turkish and German aeroplanes fought during the War. Aeroplanes had flown as far east as the Azrak district in co-operation with Colonel Lawrence's Arab forces Egypt and Palestine were therefore well known to flying men. On the Iraq side aeroplanes constantly flew out to Ramadi and up the Euphrates. But nothing except the eagles and vultures had crossed the great plateau of El Jid. Sir Arnold Wilson was a passenger in the first flight from Baghdad to Cairo via Damascus. The party set out in February, 1919, in two D.H. aeroplanes. They flew from Baghdad up the Euphrates to Abu Kemal, thence across the desert to Palmyra, the city of Queen Zenobia, to Damascus. After a considerable number of adventures they reached Ramleh and completed the journey to Cairo. Sir Arnold says that they were careful not to say anything about these adventures, which were far from amusing, lest it should be considered advisable that he should return by a more conventional route. He went back to Baghdad six weeks later with two D.H.9a aeroplanes via Aleppo, and Deir ez Zor on the Euphrates.

The second crossing was made in May, 1919, when a young Royal Air Force pilot flew Sir Arnold Wilson from Ramadi to Damascus by himself, the accompanying D.H.9a having given up the ghost half an hour after leaving Baghdad. These flights were real adventures.

The Air Mail Route between Cairo and Baghdad was opened on June 23rd, 1921, on which day the three aeroplanes accompanying the first Desert Route survey party reached Baghdad from Amman. On June 30th Wing Commander (now Group Captain) Fellowes flew from Baghdad to Cairo in one day, his actual flying time being eleven hours, an average speed over the ground of 79 miles an hour. On July 11th Air Vice-Marshal Sir Geoffrey Salmond flew from Cairo to

AEROPLANE HANGERS AT HINAIDI

THE FLOOD AT HINAIDI LOOKING EAST ALONG THE BUND

Baghdad in one day. After considerable negotiation with the Postmaster-General, civil mails were carried almost from the first. By sea mail a letter from London to Baghdad travels via the Suez Canal, Red Sea, Karachi, the Persian Gulf and Basrah, and takes approximately a month, thus making Iraq, from the point of view of communications, considerably further away than India. The Air Mail altered all this and telescoped the twenty-eight days into nine or even less.

On July 28th, 1921, the first consignment of official air mail left Baghdad for London, arriving on August 9th. On August 4th the first bag of official-marked mails consigned "London-Iraq, by air, Cairo-Baghdad," left London and was delivered in Baghdad on August 17th. On October 8th the service Air Mail was thrown open to the public at a special fee of 1*s*. per ounce in addition to the ordinary postal charges. On December 13th the special air fee was reduced to 6*d*. per ounce. As time went on the regularity, and as more experience was gained, the reliability of the service was increased, the amount of mail carried in the first sixteen months multiplied tenfold, and the Air Mail was timed as far as possible to fit in with European sailings. The special air fee was finally reduced to 3*d*. per ounce.

During 1921 and early 1922 the D.H.9as of No. 47 Squadron at Heiwan in Egypt and similar aeroplanes of No. 30 Squadron at Baghdad West shared the Mail duties. At this time the aerodrome of Baghdad was situated on the west side of the Tigris, and was called Baghdad West. Later on the Squadrons were shifted over to the great cantonment of Hinaidi on the other side of the river and 6 miles out of the town. Hinaidi contains a big camp where the Royal Air Force and some Army units lived. Within the high mud bank or "bund" that surrounds it is the flat mud aerodrome, one of the largest in the world. The bund is very necessary to prevent flooding if the river bursts its banks, as it did in 1926. You could then stand on the bund and see the flood extending to the northern horizon; and an army of men had to work day and night repairing the bund with sand-bags to prevent it giving way under the water pressure. Hinaidi lies in the angle formed by the confluence of the Tigris and Diyala, and the water burst out from the former and joined the latter right round the other side of the cantonment. Before the flood abated it rose sufficiently to cause the gravest anxiety. It gives a fair idea of the size of the cantonment if I say that it took about two hours to ride round the bund at an easy trot.

To return to the flying over the Air Mail Route; No. 216 Squadron at Heliopolis in Egypt assisted Nos. 47 and 30 Squadrons to work the mail. This Squadron was equipped with twin-engined D.H.10 aeroplanes. As in those days there were no desert refuelling points, the D.H.9as, as I explained previously, had to strap extra petrol tins on to see them through. When the D.H.10 was declared obsolete, No. 216 Squadron was re-equipped with Vickers Vi the type of aeroplane on which the late Sir John Alcock flew the Atlantic and the late Sir Ross Smith flew to Australia; and the Vimys then operated on the route.

Towards the end of 1921, No. 70 Squadron formed in Egypt, and after it No. 45 Squadron, both of which units had fine war records and had been temporarily disbanded. In November, 1921, No. 70 Squadron flew to Hinaidi across the track, and in March, 1922, No. 45 Squadron followed. These squadrons were equipped with Vickers Vernons, which were really Vimys with saloon hulls capable of carrying a number of passengers. During 1922 Nos. 30 and 47 Squadrons gave up the regular service on D.H.9as, which was maintained by Nos. 5 and 70 Squadrons between them, assisted by No. 216 Squadron at Heliopolis.

Soon after the Air Mail started it became customary to take a short cut from Rafa to Jerusalem, instead of using the longer route via Ramleh, which was only resorted to if the weather were bad. The direct route to Jerusalem meant flying rather longer over the hill country, but quite a considerable saving of time altogether; so it became adopted. In summer time the air becomes heated up and rarefied; it therefore does not support the aeroplane so well, the climbing power of which consequently falls off. In addition to this, in the ordinary course of events, the air becomes more rarefied as you go higher and higher, and aeroplanes when they rise into the air climb more slowly as they go up. Otherwise of course, given the petrol, they would be able to go on climbing forever and half our pilots would never be seen or heard of again. The most important effect of the rarefied atmosphere is on the motor itself, which needs to suck in air to mix with the petrol and explode it inside the cylinders. The less air it can get, the less petrol can it make use of, because the mixture of petrol and air has to be in a given proportion; so that air rarefied, due either to heat or height, means a serious falling off in engine power. On the Mail Route you unfortunately get both, and the aeroplanes that were originally used had not sufficiently powerful motors to give them adequate climbing power under all conditions that might be encountered when the weather was hot. That is why it was often necessary to wait until the cool of dawn to take off the ground with a heavy load, when the maximum engine power was needed. Once the aeroplane could be successfully coaxed up into the higher and cooler air, the engines could be eased down because less effort was required.

The Vickers Vernons belonging to Nos. and 70 Squadrons were fitted with twin Rolls-Royce Eagle VIII engines giving 375 horse-power each. Good as these engines were, they did not give the Vernon with its heavy saloon hull a sufficiently good performance when fully loaded in hot weather When the air heats up it becomes not only thin but turbulent. That is because the hot thin air becomes light and tends to fly upwards. Something has to take its place and so colder air from above rushes down to fill the gap. These currents of air are called convection currents. The downward or upward speed of the air may reach as much as a hundred feet per minute. It will be obvious that if an aeroplane passes into one of these and its rate of climb under full engine power at the particular height at which it is flying is less than a hundred feet per minute, then it will slowly drop. If a range of hills interposes itself, the aeroplane has nothing for it but to turn round and go away if it can; on the other hand, it was not impossible to fly into a gorge and be trapped by a down current. In taking off the high aerodrome at Amman, which incidentally looked over a gorge, difficulties of the sort that I have described were sometimes experienced.

Amman aerodrome, besides being high, is situated amongst hills which come quite close to the aerodrome on two sides, and which formed a considerable obstacle to the heavily loaded Mail aeroplanes. Aeroplanes on local work would be less heavily loaded and therefore easily able to surmount the hills. The result of all this was that a search was made in the surrounding country for another landing ground for the use of the Mail aeroplanes which would be kinder to them. In the end the landing ground of Ziza was chosen, 12 miles south of Amman Ziza itself is an insignificant village, but it possesses a station on the Hedjaz railway which was built to convey pilgrims from Damascus to the holy cities of Medina and Mecca The railway station consists of two or three buildings like dolls' houses. The ground rises up from the railway in a gentle slope to the east. At the top of this rise you can see the landing ground spread before you on a slight downhill gradient. Beyond is the line of the Jebel Mugher, across which runs the Air Mail track from Amman. The advantages of Ziza were that the landing ground was about 300 feet lower than that of Amman, and the sides of the basin formed by the surrounding hills were more open. Nevertheless a Vickers Vernon with full load in hot weather was practically incapable of rising from Ziza after 11 a.m. It may be observed here that the temperature at Ziza was never anything like so high as in Iraq. Whereas at Hinaidi on a hot afternoon, in July or August the temperature would rise in the shade to between 115 and 120 degrees, at Ziza it probably would not

ZIZA STATION ON THE HEDJAZ RAILWAY

exceed 100 degrees. On the other hand, this temperature was quite sufficient to take the 'body" out of the air.

In order that the Air Mail pilots might pick up the Air Mail Track that ran from Amman to Azrak via the fort at Kasr Kharana, a plough track was made from Ziza which cut into the Amman track at the foot of the Jebel Mugher. There is no distinctive landmark by Ziza landing ground, and it was often difficult to pick it up when approaching from either the east or west. My experience was that it looked completely different every time I went there. The line of the Hedjaz railway showed up but faintly, in common with most eastern railways, the track of which is laid more or less straight on the ground without the conspicuous ballast that characterizes an English railway.

Ziza was not a very pleasant neighbourhood during the earlier times of the Air Mail. No station-master lived there. Legend had it that the station staff were at the bottom of the well that yawned at the back of the station buildings. Having no fence round it, it might easily have performed the same offices for an unwary pilot. The Wahabis once came up there on a raid, and were repelled by armoured cars and aeroplanes, leaving a considerable number of their dead in the neighbourhood of the landing ground. When the Mail aeroplanes were coming through, a party with petrol and oil used to come down by road from Amman; and a rough road it was too.

It was most desirable to equip the Mail aircraft with more powerful engines as soon as they became available. The 450 horse-power Napier Lion engine was therefore installed in the Vickers Vernon to give it a higher performance; and No. 70 Squadron's Rolls Vernons were converted to Lion Vernons. It happened almost inevitably that No. 70 Squadron with its higher performance aircraft took over the Mail entirely from about September, 1923, until September, 1924. Meanwhile, in the summer of 1924, No.45 Squadron began to get its Lions, and in September, 1924, took over the Mail and ran it until February, 1926. All this time No. 216 Squadron was assisting from the Egypt end with Vimys.

During the summer of 1924 an altogether new route between Rafa and Ziza was explored. This was the culmination of the effort that had been going on for some time to find the safest way to cross the Judæan Hills. Instead of flying from Rafa to Jerusalem and then over Jericho to Ziza, aeroplanes struck east over Beersheba and then across the Dead Sea, after which they turned north-east and made for Ziza. On this route it was possible to find better intermediate landing grounds than Jerusalem and Jericho; and though the total length of the two routes was practically the same, the existence of the improved landing grounds, considering the precipitous nature of the country, made the passage of the Judæan Hills far less unpleasant. A landing ground was made on the sandy spit that projects from the eastern shore of the Dead Sea, called El Lisan, which means "The Tongue." Although the landing ground at El Lisan was 1,180 feet below the level of the Mediterranean, the width of the cleft in which the Dead Sea lay made it practicable to climb out by flying north and south over the water until the requisite height was obtained to fly east or west. Another landing ground was made at a place called Tel-a-rad, half-way between El Lisan and Beersheba. At Beersheba itself there was quite a good landing ground that was used during the War. The El Lisan-Beersheba route was called the "Southern Route" and was much preferred to the older route.

During 1926 another alteration took place in No. 70 Squadron's aircraft, which were changed to Vickers Victorias. The Victoria, while having the same engines as the Vernon, was a larger and more modern aeroplane; and its generous wingspread enabled it to cruise along through the rarefied air more easily than the Vernon. It moreover carried nearly double the "useful load."[2] No. 70 Squadron ran the Mail for the remainder of 1926 with Victorias, which were also given to No. 216 Squadron in place of their Vimys towards the end of the year.

The Royal Air Force had inaugurated the Cairo-Baghdad Air Mail and had run it for five and a half years. It must be remembered that when the service started comparatively little was known about long-distance flying in a hot climate. The design of aircraft had not been adapted to some of the special difficulties encountered, which only time and experience could bring to light. The men in the air and those who were responsible for the ground organization had to do the work and learn the job at the same time. One of the reasons for the creation of the route was that it would serve as an excellent means of investigating the suitability of various classes of material to flying in hot climates.

Another aspect of the situation that has to be taken into account is the fact that the service was run as a "service air mail" and not primarily as an "air mail service." This meant that no specialized machinery was set up with the express purpose of making the service efficient at the expense of other activities of the Royal Air Force, which were legion. Although the squadrons that were working the Mail certainly gave up the major part of their energy to the work, there were many other calls on them. This had the beneficial effect of keeping their outlook broad, and preventing them from becoming unprepared for the many varieties of work that might fall to their lot. In spite, then, of the fact that the Air Mail was run on the lines of what may be defined as an important side-show, such a high standard of efficiency was attained that it was possible at the end of 1926 to hand over the route to Imperial Airways, surveyed, constructed, pioneered, and made reasonably safe for a non-military organization to develop.

The history of the construction of the route from its actual inception in June, 1921, and of the flying organization slowly but surely fashioned to meet its peculiar hazards and difficulties, was something of which we, who flew over it in the latter days, were very justly proud.

Before proceeding, to describe the working of the route in a little more detail, I should like to say some thing about the types of aeroplane employed. The first of these was the D.H.9a, an exceedingly effective type of aeroplane for general flying in the desert. It was fitted with a 400 horse-power Liberty engine, cruised at about 80 miles an hour, but could only carry two people, the pilot and one other. It was very suitable for carrying mails, but could not of course carry passengers in any numbers The D.H.10, its larger brother, with two Liberty engines, was a fast and useful aeroplane, could carry two people besides the pilot, and had more room inside its fuselage or hull. It operated, however, for a short time only, and gave way to the Vickers Vimys and Vernons which had greater carrying capacity but were slower, their average cruising speed being 65 miles an hour.

The Vickers Vimy was made famous by its trans-Atlantic flight and its flight to Australia. It did remarkably good work on the route. It usually carried three people in addition to the pilot, or else two and the mail-bags. The Vickers Vernon had practically the same wings as the Vimy, but it was fitted with a saloon hull, capable of accommodating twelve people. On the mail route, however, a considerable amount of desert equipment, water and rations had to be taken, and so the number of people carried in addition to the pilot had to be limited to six. These would consist of the second pilot who sat beside the first pilot, and could relieve him at the wheel owing to the fact that he had a duplicated set of controls, a crew of two, and three passengers with a limited amount of kit. These passengers were principally officers going on and returning from leave to Egypt or England. If the mails were being carried one or two of the passengers would have to be omitted, according to the weight of the mail-bags. A Vickers Vernon, as it took off the ground with full petrol to last for nearly seven hours in the air, weighed just about 6 tons, supported by a wing area equivalent to the floor space of a village hall 70 feet long by 20 feet wide, and propelled by its two Napier Lion engines giving at maximum revolutions somewhere near a thousand horse-power, or the power that the average Atlantic type of locomotive gives.

An interesting point arises about the fuel consumption in long-distance flying. The petrol in a Vernon for full endurance weighed over 1¼ tons. Now suppose you only wanted to stay up in the air for three hours instead of seven, you would fill up with petrol for three hours only, and then have nearly 1,600 pounds extra carrying capacity to spare, and you could carry six or seven more people. It will be clear from this what an enormous difference the amount of fuel makes to carrying capacity. If the pilot only wanted to take enough petrol to fly from Baghdad to Ramadi, about 6 miles, he could carry four times the "useful load" that he could take with him on the Air Mail Route, provided that he could persuade it to fit inside his hull. For instance, when somebody rode up on a bicycle, leant it up against the aeroplane and got in, I said, "What are you going to do with that?" "Oh!" he said, cheerfully, "I thought you could manage to take it." And I did.

The Vickers Vernon, although it had no great turn of speed, was an extremely comfortable aeroplane for desert flying. It was like a sort of caravan; and if you landed for the night in the desert you could sleep in it, although I preferred to sleep outside under the wings. If it came on to pour with rain you had a little house to go into; if a swarm of locusts bore down on you or camel-flies started to pester you, the thing was to get inside and shut the gauze windows. And so your aeroplane bore you up in the heights during the daytime, and sheltered you by night. During flight it was possible for one pilot to fly and the other to go back into the hull, stretch his legs and have a meal, but the second pilot was usually young and inexperienced and it was inadvisable for the first pilot to be away for long. It all depended on the weather and the country over which the aeroplane was passing. If the weather was fine and the visibility good, there might be considerable periods when there was little to do but hold the aeroplane on a straight course and watch certain instruments to see that the engines were behaving as they should. On the other hand, things might be quite different and the aeroplane might need the guidance of an experienced eye and brain and hand the whole time. But the comforting feeling that it was possible to take short rests from flying reduced the fatigue greatly compared with that in an aeroplane like a D.H.9a, where the pilot was glued to his controls from the time his wheels left the ground until they touched it again The narratives that I give later of my flying over the Mail Route refer chiefly to the Vickers Vernon, which I have described above.

The Vickers Victoria, which superseded the Vernon, was even more comfortable, because it was larger. Indeed, it was a veritable palace on wings. It was possible to rig up a light table inside the hull and take meals in flight. Although its speed was no greater than that of the Vernon, it could climb better because of its larger wings which made it more lightly loaded. It embodied, too, the experience gained on the Vernons, and was in many ways better adapted to the work it had to perform.

It is not unnatural, however, that the pilot, with an innate conservatism, should remain faithful to the type of aeroplane that he has flown for a long time; and however many improved types I had flown, I should always entertain a sneaking affection for the Vickers Vernon.

As soon as aircraft began flying over the Air Mail Route, the idea was to run a fortnightly mail service, that is to say aircraft would leave each end of the route once a fortnight in alternate weeks, so that in one week the westbound Mail would be flying across, and in the following week the eastbound Mail. It was customary to send aircraft in pairs. They could then look after each other if one of them experienced trouble of any sort; and if one were delayed the other could bring on the Mail without losing any appreciable time. The detailed arrangements for operating the aircraft varied slightly from time to time; and I will take the procedure in the summer of 1925 as a specimen to show how the aeroplanes were worked.

The Iraq Vernons normally left Hinaidi for Heliopolis every alternate Thursday, remained at Heliopolis for the inside of a week and then returned. The exception to this was that every fourth mail was done by the Heliopolis Vimys, which flew over to Hinaidi and returned the following week. During the fourth mail, while the Vimys were flying to Iraq and back, the Iraq Vernons remained in Egypt, and did not return in this case for three weeks. This arrangement involved the Iraq Vernons doing three mails to the Vimys' one; and for the Iraq Vernons, the Mail on which they stayed over in Egypt for three weeks instead of one, came round once in two months.

Supposing, for example, that July 1st was a Thursday, then Vernons Nos. 1 and 2 would fly from Hinaidi to Heliopolis. On July 8th they would return. On July 15th Vernons Nos. 3 and 4 would fly from Hinaidi to Heliopolis, and return on July 22nd. Only July 2 Vernons Nos. 5 and 6 would fly from Hinaidi to Heliopolis, but would not return till August 19th. Meanwhile Vimys Nos.

VALKYRIE READY FOR THE MAIL

1 and 2 would have flown from Heliopolis to Hinaidi on August 5th and have returned to Heliopolis on August 12th. The whole cycle was thus completed, and started all over again.

Each Vernon had its first pilot, who was the captain of the aircraft and responsible for the perfect condition of his "ship" and her safe pilotage in the air. He had, as I have said, a second pilot under him who was hoping on some great day in the future to blossom into a first pilot, a first and second engine-fitter and a first and second rigger, in addition to which there was a wireless operator. This made up the Vernon's crew. On the Mail it was only possible to take one of the fitters and the wireless operator, if wireless were being carried on that particular aeroplane. A second pilot was normally taken unless one of the passengers was himself a pilot, when he might be allowed to occupy the second pilot's seat to enable an extra passenger to be carried.

The length of the flight from Baghdad to Cairo is between 860 and 870 miles, and the average flying time, excluding halts on the ground, was for Vernons just over twelve hours. As the prevailing set of the wind is westerly, the eastbound trip was usually performed rather quicker than the westbound trip. But so great was the variation of the winds encountered that the flight was accomplished with a favourable wind in a little over nine hours, whereas with an adverse wind it could take as much as sixteen hours. Although an aeroplane may cruise at a steady speed of 65 miles an hour through the air, its speed over the ground is directly affected by the strength of the wind. For instance, an adverse wind of 15 miles an hour would bring the speed over the ground down to 50 miles an hour, while a wind astern of the same strength would raise the ground speed to 80 miles an hour. In the former case the aeroplane would take two hours to fly a hundred miles, whereas in the latter case it would only take one hour and fifteen minutes. The importance of a correct allowance for wind on the Mail Route was great; for on this factor depended the amount of petrol necessary to reach any point. When it is realized that the wind was apt to vary considerably in different parts of the route, it will be appreciated that the pilot had to be careful in his calculations to allow for an adequate margin of petrol in case the wind turned badly against him. It is also obvious that an aeroplane with a higher cruising speed, say 100 to 110 miles an hour, is not nearly so much affected by adverse winds, and this is one of the chief reasons why a high cruising speed is such an advantage.

Going westward the Mail aircraft used to leave Hinaidi on Thursday afternoons, fly to Ramadi and fill right up with petrol. It was not possible in the normal course of events to fly right through from Hinaidi to Ziza without refuelling. If the aircraft had left Hinaidi at dawn and had then stopped at Ramadi to fill up with petrol, in summer time the air would have warmed up and it would have been difficult to take off. Ramadi is only 170 feet above sea level, but the landing ground is not large enough to permit of a long run. The Mail used to leave Ramadi at the crack of dawn on Fridays, or even just before it was light, and hoped to reach Ziza about eight hours later. By the time that the aircraft approached the desert refuelling point at *L.G.* D, 86 miles short of Ziza, the decision had to be taken whether they had enough petrol to carry them through to Ziza. If they both had wireless one would ask the other if it proposed to land or not. The amount of petrol they had left would depend on how long they had taken, which itself depended on the strength and direction of the wind. In exceptional circumstances a landing was made at *L.G.* V on the westbound journey, and a small amount of petrol taken. The rule used to be that if the aeroplane took as much as two hours to reach *L.G.* V from Ramadi, which meant that it was only making 6 miles an hour ground speed, then a landing was made and a few gallons of petrol taken to ensure being able to reach *L.G.* D if such a strong adverse wind held all the way. This landing was only necessary on rare occasions. It was, moreover, undesirable to land in the desert unless it was absolutely unavoidable, because there was always a chance of a puncture with camel-thorn, which meant putting on the spare wheel that was carried, with a consequent delay.

The Mail aircraft were met at Ziza by the party from Amman with petrol and oil. With the help of the crews the aeroplanes were filled up and given a rapid look over to see that everything was trim. Some times one or two minor adjustments were necessary. If anything had broken in flight the aeroplane would send a wireless message to Amman and the necessary spare part would be waiting for it on the landing ground at Ziza. The flight on to Heliopolis was a further 330 miles and an allowance of five hours' petrol was taken. The fuel used for the Napier Lion engine was a mixture of petrol and benzol in the proportion of 80 to 20. The petrol was supplied in 4-gallon tins and the benzol in 4-gallon drums. The fuel for five hours consisted of 300 gallons; and as for every 5-gallon drum of benzol, five 4-gallon tins of petrol were needed, filling up one aeroplane involved manhandling sixty tins of petrol, weighing approximately 30 pounds each, twelve drums of benzol, weighing about 40 pounds per drum, and, say, two 5-gallon drums of lubricating oil. If the weather was warm it was an arduous business. The Vernon had two large petrol tanks on the top planes, which meant one man squatting on the plane and filling, while another man stood on the bottom plane where there was a walkway by the hull, and passed up the tins or drums from a third man who stood on the ground. There was a third tank at the bottom of the hull which could be filled by a man standing on the bottom plane only. To refuel two aeroplanes in this way and give them a rapid inspection normally took two hours.

On the westbound trip this two hours could be counted as one only, because you were catching up the sun, and Cairo time is one hour ahead of Baghdad time. Incidentally it is two hours behind Greenwich time. If there were four or five hours of daylight left when the aeroplanes were ready again for flight at Ziza, it was customary to push on over the Judæan Hills. This was left to the senior pilot's discretion. If it was decided not to push on, the aeroplanes were taxied down as near to the railway station as possible, and securely picketed down by the wing tips and the tail portion of the hull; for if a sudden dust storm were to get up in the night it might carry all before it. Whenever aeroplanes were left out like this, the controls were also fastened up in the pilot's cockpit so that the hinged surfaces such as ailerons and elevators should not thrash about in the wind and strain themselves. Meanwhile the pilots, passengers and crews made themselves as comfortable as they could in the little station at Ziza. There were two upper rooms, one for sleeping and the other for reading, playing musical instruments, comparing exaggerated stories of the adventures of the day, and feeding. In the bedroom there were some iron bedsteads and mattresses. If there were not enough to go round those who had beds gave up the mattresses to those who elected to sleep on the floor. In summer, when the nights were pleasant and warm, it was preferable to sleep outside. Every one was pretty tired, but there was usually some bore who would go on talking late into the night when all the rest wanted to get to sleep! However, a well-aimed flying boot was often an effective remedy.

In the long days of summer time when the wind was favourable the trip from Ramadi to Helliopolis was now and then completed in one day, but more usually the run over Palestine was made on the Saturday morning, the aircraft arriving at Heliopolis at 10 or 11 a.m. The mail train for Port Said did not leave Cairo until Sunday evening, so there was still a margin for delay. But it was the consistent aim of the Air Mail pilots to carry through the flight as rapidly and tidily as was consistent with safety. If one did happen to complete the flight in one day, and fly over the four great rivers of history, the Tigris, the Euphrates, the Jordan and the Nile, between dawn and twilight, it brought home in a forcible way the astounding military achievements of the ancients. The means by which they supplied and maintained enormous armies in this sort of geographical vacuum, and kept any semblance of military organization, fills the mind with wonder.

Going eastward, the aircraft used to leave Heliopolis on Thursday mornings, at 5 a.m. in summer and 7 a.m. in winter, fly to Ziza and then refuel. If the weather was hot and they were not ready to leave the ground again by 11 a.m., they usually stayed there and waited for the cool air of Friday's dawn, because, as I explained previously, the pilot might get air-locked on that elevated basin of rolling upland if be tried to take off when the air was too warm. If it were possible to leave Ziza on Thursday, the aircraft would push east as far as they could before dusk, and with a favourable wind might possibly get right through. More often they would reach a point on the wide upland between the basalt country and El Jid, somewhere perhaps between *L.G.* J and *L.G.* P, and camp there for the night. If, however, the start were delayed until dawn on the Friday, the aircraft would arrive at Hinaidi sometime in the afternoon. When they approached *L.G.* V the same decision had to be taken whether it was necessary to land and fill up with some petrol to see them through to Ramadi. In any case it was nearly always imperative to refuel at Ramadi itself on the way in.

It was very pleasant arriving home after a trip across the Mail Route. Sitting in a comfortable chair, in winter time in front of the Mess fire, and in summer on the verandah or on the precious patch of green that was in Iraq proudly called a lawn, you could indulge that soothing relaxed feeling that comes after sitting for hours in a slightly constrained position, with your eyes on the track and the deep thunder of the engines in your ears. I always think that it is when you have come down to earth that you enjoy flying most.

1. Since writing the above, I have heard that wheel brakes have been developed in the U.S.A., and are being used successfully.

2. That portion of the load not concerned with the operation of the aeroplane. For instance, a passenger or a mail bag is part of the useful load, whereas a member of the crew or the petrol in the tanks is not.

CHAPTER III

WIND AND WEATHER

I have said that the normal number of aeroplanes that went on the Mail was two. One of these aeroplanes would be carrying the mail-bags, and one or two passengers, according to the weight of the mail. The other one would be carrying three passengers, which would make a total of four or five passengers in all. If there were more officers who had been granted leave and Air Mail passages, a third aeroplane might be put on. On the special flight across the Mail Route to fetch over the Secretaries of State in the spring of 1925, four Vernons actually went. When aeroplanes cruise in company it is a usual to fly in an open "V" formation, the leader being at the apex of the "V." When flying across the Mail Route, however, it was essential that each pilot should watch the track, so that it should never be a case of the blind leading the blind. If the aeroplanes had been in a "V" it would have been difficult for the outside members to see the track; so the usual arrangement was to go in it pairs, each pair being "staggered," that is, one aeroplane rather in front of the other. If there were three aeroplanes, two might go in front and one follow behind; if there were four, the two pairs would keep close enough to be comfortably in sight of one another.

The load that it is carrying makes a perceptible difference to the speed of the aeroplane, and if one aeroplane was carrying a good deal more than another, as it very often was, it was not always easy for the pilots to fly comfortably at the same speed. During the difficult parts of the track, it was necessary to keep station as well as could be managed; but when nearing the destination, or flying over country with good landmarks,—for instance, along the coast between Palestine and the Suez Canal aeroplane with the Mail on board might go ahead if its companion could not easily keep up and also had wireless. The general principle was that an aeroplane without wireless should never go by itself, on the other hand, it might be allowed in certain circumstances to draw ahead provided that another aeroplane with wireless was following fairly closely, so that should it come down, it would be bound to be picked up by its companion.

Without an efficient wireless service, to put it bluntly, the operation of the Mail Route would have been an impossibility. The Headquarters at each end was kept in touch by wireless with the movements of the Mail aircraft the whole time they were in the air. There was a big map on which the positions of the aeroplanes were marked up at frequent intervals by means of flags. If you cared to, you could watch the flags moving along. These maps were also kept at the Squadrons whose aeroplanes were out on the track; and there was quite a fascination in watching the flags walking along if one was expecting a letter from home. If you were bringing over the eastbound Mail yourself, you anxiously looked at the mail bags and wondered what they contained for you. Iraq is still sufficiently far from England for the advent of the Mail to be an excitement.

The pilot normally gives his wireless operator a message to send when he passes over each landing ground. Suppose there are two Vernons flying east on the Mail, and they are passing over *L.G.* VI. Each of them has a wireless call sign into which the wireless operator turns the number of the aircraft when he sends the message. If I were in the Vernon working wireless, I might send, for example, "To all Air Mail Stations (which means Heliopolis, Abu Suweir, Ramleh, Amman, Ramadi and Baghdad), Vernons No. 7134 and No. 7135, O.K. passing *L.G.* VI at 13.30 hours G.M.T. Landing to refuel at *L.G.* V. Two cars seen going west miles west of *L.G.* VI at 13.25 hours. One car about a mile behind stopped but does not appear to be in trouble." Thus the authorities in Egypt and Iraq were supplied with information about everything that was happening along the route. The aeroplane that was working the wireless always flew behind, in order not only to be able to see the track, but also the other aeroplane or aeroplanes. The wireless aerial was unwound out of the hull, and it had a lead weight on the end so that it trailed under the aeroplane. Before landing the pilot had to be careful to see that the wireless operator had reeled in the aerial; and when he sent his last message on sighting his destination he would include the words "winding in," to show that he was shutting down his wireless. This procedure, of course, also applied to any landing made in the desert. At Ramadi there was a wireless station in a little building where the people on the Air Mail used to spend the night on the way. The building was in a barbed-wire serai, or enclosure, which included a petrol store for the Mail aeroplanes. This building came to be called "Ye olde Windinge Inne" because the wireless operators had to wind in their aerials when landing at Ramadi.

Each aeroplane that carried wireless was equipped with a ground mast which was telescopic and was stowed inside the hull. If the aeroplane landed in the desert for any length of time the mast would be rigged up, and the aerial carried from it to another small pole fixed up on the hull. The electric current for the wireless was supplied by a small hand generator which had to be ground like a barrel organ. In flight this was not necessary, because a wireless generator was fitted on a strut with an air fan, which was driven round by the wind made by the aeroplane going through the air. When the ground mast was up, the operator did not keep watch the whole time, but sent a message to say that he would listen in for messages for ten minutes before every hour. The possession of wireless made the whole difference to a party out in the desert, and kept it in touch with civilization.

Besides being able to signal to each other by wireless, the pilots could keep in touch by means of coloured lights fired from a pistol, called a Very pistol, after the name of the inventor. Very lights look like the Roman candles that form part of the celebrations of November 5. A red Very light meant that the aeroplane was forced to land. Each aeroplane also carried, as part of its desert equipment, a set of white American cloth strips with weights sewn into the ends. These strips were about 8 feet long by 2 feet wide, and were used to lay out on the ground in various patterns to convey messages to an aeroplane flying above. For instance if two strips were laid out in the form of a "T" it meant that the aeroplane flying above was requested to land. The "T" was laid out so that if you looked at it the right way up you were facing the wind direction, which gave you the direction in which to land. The strips were laid so that if the pilot touched his wheels on them he would be landing on the most favourable piece of ground, and he would have a clear run on the windward side of the transverse arm of the "T." A cross meant that the ground was unfit to land on. The following signal, _|‾ P meant, "Can repair aircraft with spares on board-petrol required." These ground strip signals could be seen comfortably from a thousand feet.

The Air Mail pilots were provided with an excellent handbook which they always carried with them. It contained Dr. Ball's maps of the route, and a summary of all that was known about it. There were also instructions as to what it was advisable or necessary to do in almost every conceivable circumstance.

On the other hand, it was usually the unexpected that happened, and no Mail pilot was fit to be trusted on the route unless he possessed that vital grain of common sense, imagination, or initiative, call it what you will, for which no regulations or advice, however admirably framed, can be an effective substitute. And it was in this spirit that the Air Mail handbook was written.

Among other things the handbook contained a Time and Distance Table, to enable the pilot to calculate the speed he was making over the ground. The distances from landing ground to landing ground were given, and all the pilot had to do was to take the time with his watch and read the answer in the book in miles an hour.

If anything went seriously wrong with an engine, the pilot would make an effort to reach the next landing ground. If he could not do so and the aeroplane were losing height due to the failing power of his lame engine, he would have to make the best of it and land where he thought he could see the least unfavourable-looking piece of ground. Luckily over large stretches of the route the ground is one huge aerodrome. If he had time the pilot run would get off a wireless message giving his position and the reason for which he was coming down. The operator would then wind in the aerial as fast as he could. The next thing to do was to find the direction of the wind. On a flight over a civilized country there is very often some smoke visible, and the pilot always watches the whole time for signs such as this which give him an indication of the wind direction. The movement of cloud shadows over the ground, if there are clouds in the sky, is another help in gauging the wind; but the shadows only give the wind direction at the height at which the clouds are floating. This is normally different from the direction of the surface wind, which is what the pilot is interested in from the point of view of landing. It used to be taken as a rough guide that the wind between 2,000 and 3,000 feet differed from the surface wind by about 20 degrees in a clockwise direction. In order to observe the wind direction more definitely, a number of smoke candles were carried. As the aeroplane was gliding me down to land, one of these would be lit by a member of the crew and dropped over the landing ground. The candle emitted a dense grey smoke for a minute or two, and gave the wind direction quite clearly. These candles can also be lit on the ground, if one aeroplane is down on a landing ground and another one comes and wishes also to land. A Very light fired on to the ground from a low height is a possible substitute for a smoke candle, but the smoke is much fainter and more evanescent. It is advisable to land as quickly as possible after dropping a candle, and to touch ground before the smoke is finished, because the wind in the desert has a nasty habit of blowing from all angles of the compass in the space of a few minutes in certain types of weather,

One had to be extremely careful, when lighting fires or firing Very lights in the desert, not to set the thin dry grass which covered certain parts on fire. Such a fire might go on for days and travel along over many miles. A pilot who had thus started a fire to leeward of his aeroplane, if it happened to be stopped on the ground, would be in an unenviable position if the wind were to change and turn the spreading horseshoe of low crackling flames in the direction of his aeroplane before he could start it up and fly away. It is interesting to note that the Latin historian who tells us about the advance of the Roman army of the Emperor Julian the Apostate up the Diyala in the fourth century A.D., says that the Persians who were opposing him delayed his advance for several days by starting one of these desert fires.

When the pilot has settled the direction of the wind he has still one more important thing to remember. The aneroid barometer that is fixed on his instrument board only tells him the height he is above sea level or the point he started from, depending on how he has set his instrument. The ground he is landing on in the desert may register perhaps 2,000 feet on his aneroid. Unless either he knows the height of the ground by experience, or else it is a landing ground the height of which is given in the Mail handbook, he has to be careful in making his approach. Ground that looks quite flat from the air may resolve itself into hills that suddenly rear themselves up in front of the aeroplane; and it needs considerable experience to take in the contours of unknown ground in the few seconds that are available.

Another point is that if the landing ground is at some height above sea level the air is thinner and the aeroplane lands rather faster. The ideal is to arrange matters so that the aeroplane touches the ground at the minimum air speed at which the pilot can effectively control it; on the other hand, the pilot may want to manœuvre his craft during the approach to land, and to do this he must have a certain margin of speed. In hot weather and on high landing grounds the margin of speed for manœuvre has to be increased somewhat. If the pilot brings his craft down too slowly under these conditions, when he comes to "flatten it out" to make a gentle contact with terra firma, it may, in flying language, "drop out of his hands" and arrive with an unpleasant bump, which jangles the nerves of the passengers and the structure of the aeroplane. To take a crude comparison, a bicycle requires a certain amount of forward speed for safe control; and if you try to ride it too slowly you fall off. An aeroplane suffers from the same limitation. But you cannot bring an aeroplane down to land too fast, because if you do, when you flatten it out, instead of settling comfortably on to the ground, it goes on floating and floating like a feather in a wind; and the essential thing is to persuade it to stop in the shortest space possible. To appreciate rightly the conditions of the moment and to suit the gliding speed of the aeroplane to them, is an art at which the pilot can never become too adept. He goes on learning it all his flying days; and if anything will teach it to him, it is landing in the relatively uncharted wastes of the desert.

When I was talking about mud flats I said that their smoothness and the glare of the sunlight off them made the pilot apt to misjudge his height when flattening his aeroplane out to land. The best way out of the difficulty is to arrange the approach so that contact with the ground is made quite near and if possible parallel to one edge of the mud flat. In this way the pilot is given a guide to his height above the ground by the rough border of basalt boulders. It is also possible to drop a smoke candle some where in the centre of the mud flat, and to land by the side of the smokes The disadvantage is that, unless the wind is fairly strong and steady, the smoke is apt to go up nearly straight for a little, flatten out, go up again, and flatten out again. The smoke thus "steps up" and would be quite misleading. The pilot therefore would have to watch the smoke carefully; and if there were signs of its blowing unevenly, he would ignore the smoke except for its general direction, and land near the edge of the mud flat. The seaplane pilot who has to alight on water with a glassy surface is up against the same difficulty; and he tries when possible to do it near a buoy or something floating to give him a sense of the level of the water.

I have made a number of passing references to the weather along the Mail Route which runs from Egypt through Palestine to Iraq. The climate in all three countries is different. Going from one end to the other you start at a height of under 200 feet above sea level, pass over a plateau nearly 3,000 feet high, and go down again to the height you started from. You would naturally expect the climate in the high parts to be as a whole, cooler, and this is so. In Palestine and Transjordan, at any rate in summer, it is cooler than at either end. Egypt is slightly nearer the tropics than Iraq, and it might be expected to be warmer for that reason. What actually happens is that Iraq, being further from the sea, suffers from greater extremes, and is considerably hotter than Egypt in summer and colder in winter.

In Iraq there are on an average four really hot months, from June to September. Many people prefer to sleep out on the roofs of their bungalows during this

THE LANDING-GROUND AT RAMADI

KING FAISAL OF IRAQ AT RAMADI
(ON THE RIGHT)

season. Not many of the nights are unbearably hot, and the temperature usually falls in the early morning to between 70 and 80 degrees. During most of the hot weather there is a steady north-west wind blowing; and although this wind feels burning in the middle hours of the day, it makes the warmth much easier to tolerate. Occasionally the wind turns round to the south—there is a south wind that comes in September called the "Date Ripener"—or drops altogether; and then it is that one tends to feel fagged out. Now and then there is a dust storm in the summer, and every one goes indoors, unless he has the misfortune to be out in the desert, shuts up all the windows, and waits till it is over. Even with a large electric fan going, it feels moderately uncomfortable. But with fans, ice and modern conveniences, the heat amounts to nothing more than a certain degree of bodily discomfort. As you go north towards the hills, though the summer days are very hot, the nights are perceptibly cooler. It is nearly always pleasant sleeping out on a roof at a place like Mosul, and you may find it comfortable to have one or even two blankets over you. The same sort of night temperatures hold on the higher parts of the Mail Route. The summer nights are usually perfect for sleeping out at El Jid, for example. In the autumn and spring the weather for considerable periods is ideal. You feel neither too hot nor too cold; and there is a soft, balmy feeling in the air which makes it feel pleasant to be alive. At Baghdad you may get rain between November and March. The first rain, after the brazen cloudless skies that follow each other with mechanical regularity for weeks together, is an absolute blessing. The rain is fairly regular in its habits; comes for a bit, and then stops definitely. It is not, as in England, a visitor who is half in and half out of your house the whole time. The trouble with the rain in Iraq is, as I have mentioned, that it quickly turns the ground into a sticky mess, and everybody has to walk about in gum boots.

Snow falls in the hills of Northern Mesopotamia in the winter; occasionally it comes down as far south as the Mail Route, but more usually the cold is not severe, except on a winter night with a strong wind. Then if you are sleeping out on the Mail Route, you are glad to roll yourself up in your sleeping-bag with every blanket you can lay hands on. If the worst comes to the worst, you can sleep in your Sidcot flying suit, only this is rather stuffy. If you had flown over the eastern part of the Mail Route only in the heat of summer when everything was dry and arid, and you then flew over it again when it was cold or rainy, you would not think you were in the same country. You might look at some place where you had simply ached for the sight of water, and there it would be a dark purple flood. It is indeed a country of violent contrast.

If you leave Baghdad when it is just warming up in May, you may find it quite cold at Ziza. I have finished up the Mail with my pyjamas on underneath my uniform, because I had nothing else extra that I could find to keep me warm when flying over the Judæan Hills. In Palestine the hills draw to themselves masses of cumulus cloud in the winter months, and frequently in autumn and spring too. These clouds form quite a serious bar to flying across the hills, because they often come down and rest on top of them. Egypt too is a more cloudy place than Iraq, and you often get fleecy white clouds in summer just like England, which you practically never do in Iraq. There is little mist or fog in Iraq, except occasionally in the early mornings over the rivers. Over the Nile delta, however, quite heavy mists form and blow over at dawn, so that you can hardly see an inch on the aerodrome at Heliopolis. They normally clear away during the morning.

The glare off the mud plain of Iraq is trying to the eyes; it seems to bounce up off the scorched ground and hit you. Most people find it comforting to wear dark tinted glasses. If you go out in the middle of the day when there is a hot wind blowing, your eyeballs feel as if a hot iron were near them; and this is why dark glasses are all the more protection. When flying you do not feel the glare in the same way, although personally I found that I saw better if I wore lightly tinted goggles. If one were sitting in the shade on a hot day, one felt as if one would like to assume a state of nature if decency allowed, and a bath towel and tie-pin was an excellent rig in private. But in the sun it was protection that was needed. The Bedou know this well and don their thick woollen abbas or cloaks, some of which have a hood which they can pull up over their heads if necessary. In summer the pilots usually flew in a flannel shirt open at the neck, over which a spine pad was worn. This was a strip of thick material, sometimes lined with red to blank off injurious sun rays, which buttoned on to the back of the shirt. On the head was worn a flying topee, which looked like an ordinary sun helmet except that the brim was cut down so as to avoid being blown off in the wind. The pilot was, however, so well screened in a Vernon that an ordinary service topee could be worn back to front with comfort. The brim then made an efficient shield for the eyes from the glare of the upper sky. In winter the pilots wore the same clothes as they would when flying in England.

What strikes the pilot most of all when he first flies over Egypt and Iraq is the transparence of the atmosphere compared with what he has been accustomed to in England. There are far more days when the visibility is good; and on these days the distinctness of far-away objects is uncanny. From 6,000 feet it is no uncommon occurrence to make out the bend of a river that you know is at least 80 miles away. Features of the country like distant hills look unnaturally small because it is impossible to realize how far away they are. When flying over the aerodrome at Hinaidi the pilot can see in the west the snow-line of the Pusht-i-kuh, 80 miles or so away; and feels that he can pick out individual snow slopes with the sun shining on them. Pusht-i-kuh is the Persian for "Back of the hill." On a day in spring when there is no dust in the air and no heat haze, the air is as bright as crystal. But when the weather becomes hotter the lines of the landscape distort themselves. Very often out on the Mail Route in the middle of a hot afternoon the whole desert appears as if it were tilted up. Viewed from the ground the horizon shifts about in a queer manner. The commonest kind of mirage is a strip of blue sky transplanted into the middle distance, looking like a blue lake. Distant palm trees or hills detach themselves and hang a little way above the apparent horizon connected to the ground by thin pendent stalks. It is said that occasionally a whole village that is below the horizon can come into view due to the refraction of light; but I never saw such a phenomenon. The general impression, however, that you have when the light starts playing tricks, is that you feel uncertain of yourself. When it is a question of finding your way in an aeroplane the task is not thereby made any easier.

If you go out into the desert in summer, it is sure not to be long before you see a dust devil. The dust is drawn upwards by an ascending spiral of air, and builds itself into a column of grey smoke rising into the sky. Sometimes a number of these dust devils can be seen together moving along like silent spectres. They always haunt the landing ground at Ziza. Anywhere in the world you can see tiny whirlwinds that whisk up the dust with a sharp sigh. In Ireland I believe they call them Sheelan na gig. If you are standing near your aeroplane in the desert and a large dust devil passes through you the aeroplane rocks in the swift vortex of air. When flying, unless you want a rough passage for a minute or two, it is well to give them a wide berth. They are quite capable of reaching up to 3,000 feet and more. But their bark is worse than their bite.

There are not many kinds of weather that will force an aeroplane on to the ground nowadays. Aeroplanes can fly in almost any wind; the difficulty is handling them on the ground before they go up and after they have landed. A sudden storm once blew up at *L.G.* V and caught a Vernon that was picketed down. The aeroplane wrenched its screw pickets out of the ground and travelled backwards for about 80 yards. Luckily very little damage was done; but the tailskid suffered through being forced to plough through the ground in the reverse direction to that in which it was meant to go. Dust storms, as I have said, are not prevalent on the Mail Route; and there is next to no fog. The main trouble is low clouds and rain. It is possible to see the way in quite a heavy downpour of rain. But if the clouds come down on to the hills or ground, then it may be impossible to see. When flying in country with good landmarks it is sometimes feasible to make a detour and so avoid rain if it is not too extensive. For instance, if the weather were hopeless over the Dead Sea, the pilot might be able to work his way through by skirting the north end of the sea via Jerusalem. But on the route between Ziza and Ramadi it was not possible to leave the track; so if the clouds came right down the only thing was to land by the track if the ground was good, or else to turn back, fly along the track and land at the landing ground before. A halt had then to be called until the weather again became possible for the aeroplane to proceed. Such halts for weather were seldom necessary.

The hot-weather up and down currents or "dunts," as they were called in flying jargon, were not a factor seriously to be reckoned with unless the aeroplane were being taken off a high aerodrome when fully loaded, or when it was necessary to pass over some high hills. Under these circumstances the aeroplane might be nearly at its "ceiling," that is to say, it had practically no margin of power for further climb. When taking off at Ziza, even before the air had become very warm, it was with Vernons sometimes quite difficult to rise for the first few hundred feet. The pilot usually cruised about in the hope of finding an up current. These have been known to be located by watching the flight of large birds such as kites. If they were seen soaring upwards without moving their wings, the pilot might be certain that they were, with the instinct that these birds must surely have, making use of an up current. One of the Air Mail pilots invented a useful instrument called a "dunt indicator," by which you could tell fairly sensitively whether the aeroplane was rising or falling. It was extremely simple, consisting of an empty 2-gallon petrol tin fixed behind the pilot's instrument board. The cap was sealed on, but through it was drilled a tiny hole. The tin was connected by a small pipe to one side of a pressure gauge visible to the pilot. The other side of the pressure gauge was open to the atmosphere in the pilot's cockpit. When the aeroplane climbed and passed into slightly rarer air, the air inside the tin, being at a higher pressure, although it gradually escaped through the leak hole in the tin, showed a pressure on the gauge. Conversely, when the aeroplane sank, and the air outside the tin rose in pressure, the air inside the tin was at a lower pressure and showed a reading on the gauge in the opposite direction.

The pilot would fly about until he saw the needle of the gauge swing over to register the fact that he was rising; he would then endeavour to stay in the up "dunt" that he had found, and so gain height. If he passed out of it, he would circle and come back to the place in the hope of finding the same condition prevailing.

It was also observed that the wind, when it struck the top of a ridge of rising ground, tended to follow the contour and to flow down the reverse slope. It became apparent that if the pilot approached a hill when he had nearly exhausted his power of climb, in an up-wind direction, he was likely to be sucked down as he neared the crest. On the other hand, if he approached in a down-wind direction, he would find the air flowing upwards towards the crest and so surmount it quite easily. An appreciation of this fact was a great help in flying about among the hills.

At certain places on the Mail Route the vertical air currents were strongly marked. The eastern edge of the basalt country was one. The pilot would be flying along and suddenly the aneroid would register a rise of about 500 feet in a few seconds. This was all to the good; but when the movement took place in the reverse direction it was disconcerting, and meant that the engines had to be opened out to regain height. In certain types of weather the up currents appeared to occur at more or less regular intervals of perhaps 5 miles. It felt like passing over enormous waves. Before each rise the aeroplane would be rocked violently from side to side. It was always the aim of the pilot to maintain the requisite height, once he had attained it, with the minimum of engine power. With increased experience pilots became acutely sensitive to the onset of the rising and falling periods; and while gaining as much height as possible in an up current, they were able, by manipulation of the aeroplane, to mitigate considerably the effect of a down current. It was noticeable that when an old hand had been at the wheel and had set the throttles just to maintain height, if he handed the aeroplane over to a novice, it would immediately start to sink, and the throttles would have to be pushed further open. The importance of keeping the throttles back as much as possible lay in the fact that the lower you could keep the engine revolutions within reason, the less wear would be entailed on the engines and the better would they run.

A knowledge beforehand of the wind and weather that was likely to be encountered along the track was of the greatest value to the pilot. This information was supplied by the meteorological service to the pilot in two ways. Before he left Baghdad, Ramadi, Ziza or Heliopolis, he was handed a weather forecast, showing what sort of weather was ahead and the strength of the winds at various heights. Secondly, when flying along in the air he was able to ask for a report by wireless. The wind used to vary in strength and direction at various heights, and a knowledge of this would enable the pilot to select a height, if he could reach it, where the wind was blowing most strongly in his favour, or in cases when it was against him at all heights, where it was least unfavourable. The pilot could also be told by wireless if an aerodrome were temporarily unfit to land on owing to its having become too soft with the rain. The advantage of Ramadi was that however much it rained its gravel surface would always remain fit for aeroplanes to take off or land, but Hinaidi might easily become too soft after a heavy fall of rain. In this case the eastbound Mail might have to be stopped at Ramadi until Hinaidi dried up. If the meteorological service was important by day it was doubly so by night. Bad visibility at night is a greater hindrance than by day. As time went on a considerable amount of night flying was carried out over the Mail Route. It became customary to finish the journey by night if the pilot on the eastbound journey had reached *L.G.* III by dusk, and his engines were going well. Even on a moderately dark night it is possible to see considerably more from the air than is generally supposed. Near the ground all is dark, but as the pilot rises up into the higher atmosphere, he shakes off the Stygian gloom of the earth and passes into a grey-blue half light. The earth lies beneath like a dark bowl, above is the translucent blue dome spangled with star dust, which becomes paler towards the black lip of the horizon. Water shows up the clearest, and it is possible to follow a river with comparative ease.

The Mail aeroplanes were all capable of carrying night flying gear. Aircraft flying at night carry navigation lights: a red light on the port wing tip, a green light on the starboard wing tip, and a white light on the tail. The pilot's instruments are either painted with luminous paint, or he can switch on little bulbs, which, though shaded from his eyes, just give him enough light to see his instruments. He is also provided with a portable Aldis lamp, which is like a small searchlight, with which he can signal, in addition to white lights above and below, fixed to the aeroplane.

In order to show the pilot where and in what direction to land, a series of flares are laid out on the aerodrome in the shape of an "L," with the long arm parallel to the direction of the wind. The pilot brings his aeroplane down and lands it along the "L," finishing up his run after landing somewhere between the two flares that mark the ends of the transverse arm of the "L." At least that is what he aims at doing. The most elementary form of flare is a bucket filled with some petrol and oil and perhaps some old rags which act as a wick. The modern flare, though not quite so simple as this, works on the same principle. When landing, the pilot does not look at the ground, which he could not see to any extent if he did look, but uses the perspective of the flares forming the long arm of the "L" to give him the level of the ground. The disadvantage of flares in Iraq was that on a still night the smoke from them formed a pall which used to hang about 50 feet above the ground, and make it rather difficult for the pilot to see just as he was going to land.

The aeroplanes were also equipped with two flares, one under each wing tip, which could be ignited electrically by the pilot, who pressed a button on his instrument board. These "Holt" flares were like fireworks and gave a dazzlingly bright light for about three minutes. They were intended principally to enable the pilot to carry out a forced landing at night if he had to land without ground flares They possessed one disadvantage, and that was if there was any ground mist at all, or even a thin dust cloud, the bright light of the flare reflected off it and gave a false level. Nevertheless "Holt" flares were very popular for night landing, even when ground flares were laid out, because if the air were clear they lit up the ground brilliantly.

A third method of night landing was to use the beam of a searchlight mounted on a lorry. The beam was shone along the ground into wind, and the aeroplane came down over, or by the side of the lorry, and landed along or on the edge of the beam. The beam gave the pilot an excellent level, but the unfortunate people working the searchlight endured a plague of insects, such as would have made Pharaoh envious.

Rockets, which rose to about 1,500 feet, were frequently used to guide the pilot borne. It was possible on a clear night to see these rockets when you were over 40 miles from the aerodrome. The only difficulty was at great distances to distinguish them from some low star.

The secret of finding your way at night is to keep the retina of the eye in a sufficiently sensitive condition to appreciate the delicate gradations of shadow that form the chiaroscuro of a night landscape. In order to do this it was necessary to cut down lighting to a minimum, and to switch on cockpit lights only when it was unavoidable, for instance to read a map, write a message, or to verify the reading of some instrument. Even the flames of the engine exhausts of a Vernon, unless the pilot kept his eyes away from them, were enough to dull the edge of his vision. It was surprising how the night vision of pilots improved with practice. A pilot who possessed good night vision was said to have developed "pink eyes."

During the warm-weather nights in Iraq it usually felt much hotter up in the air than on the ground. This was because the ground cooled down by radiation as soon as the sun's heat was removed. But a layer of intensely hot air hung from about 1,000 to 4,000 feet above the ground, and flying up into it was sometimes like the feeling you get when you stand in front of a furnace door and it is suddenly opened. In spite of this the conditions at night over the Mail Route were a good deal more pleasant than by day, and the air settled into a steadier state. It would be useful to be able to fly over half the track in the dark; for in many cases it would mean that the journey from Cairo to Baghdad could be finished in one day, when otherwise this would have been impossible. With the modern high-performance aeroplanes that cover the ground much faster than the Vernons used to do, this argument does not carry so much weight; but still it is always annoying to the pilot to think that he must land when darkness falls. On the other hand, if he is capable of flying on through the night he has a splendid unhampered feeling; and he just goes on till the journey is over. When finishing the Mail trip at night on Vernons, it was possible to land at Ramadi, have some supper while the aeroplanes were being refuelled, and then complete the rest of the journey to Baghdad afterwards.

If night flying is to be practised regularly over the Air Mail Route it will probably be necessary to instal automatic lighthouses every hundred miles or so, in order to assist the pilot in his navigation. These could be arranged so that in jumping from one to another the pilot would never be more than a few miles from the track. The only difficulty with such lighthouses is that the Bedou might treat them as Aunt Sallies, and practise their rifles on them. I think, however, that it is safe to say that as time goes on means will be found to make pilotage in the air at night as safe and practicable as it is on the sea. The superior speed of aircraft over that of other forms of transport will then come into its own.

CHAPTER IV

EQUIPMENT AND ORGANIZATION

When the Air Mail Route was first opened grave fears were felt in some quarters as to the fate of the crew of any aeroplane that might be compelled to make a forced landing in the desert. It was hoped, however, that the regular passage of aircraft over the desert would have a tranquillizing rather than a disturbing effect on the desert and border tribes. This hope has been more than justified. The tribes have on the whole been nothing but friendly, sometimes embarrassingly so.

The wandering Bedou that you meet on the Air Mail Route are quite a different type to the Arab townsmen of Baghdad, who have picked up a veneer of Western civilization. It has been the delight of many writers to describe the temperament of the Bedouin; and there is no need to enlarge upon it here, one only has to remember that the man of the desert appears to have the greatest contempt for the townsman. He sees no necessity to pay taxes for roads and policemen; he thinks them frankly a nuisance, when he can trek over the open desert with his rifle slung across his back. He likes to be able to indulge in an occasional raid, when he is short of camels. You can tell from the air pretty well if the Bedou are out for trouble. If they have flocks and camels with them they are just enjoying a walk; but if there are not more animals than men, they are probably on business. However, they are friendly to the Inglezi, whom they would like to regard as a benevolent neutral in their squabbles.

The townsmen are amazingly casual. For instance, the sort of thing they are capable of doing is to hail a doubtful-looking taxi in the streets of Baghdad and tell it to drive them to Aleppo or Damascus. It starts off with practically no water, drops its spare wheel by inadvertence a few miles beyond Ramadi, and runs its bearings out near *L.G.* V, where the occupants are lucky if they are found by a Nairn car or possibly an aeroplane.

The Bedou most likely to be met with on the Air Mail Route are those belonging to the Amarat section of the great Anizah tribe. The Anizah is probably the largest of the nomad tribes. The sheikh of the Amarat was a splendid old man called Fahad Beg ibn (son of) Hadhal. He was extremely friendly to the British, and, having once been picked up wounded, in the desert and conveyed to hospital in Baghdad by air, he was always grateful. He became an ardent motorist, and bought a Ford car. His chauffeur was a Baghdad taxi-driver. After he had had it for about a year he noticed that it was not going so well as it used to, and it is said that he asked his driver why he did not give it anything to eat when he was giving it water to drink. His previous means of transport, the camel, although it could go for some time without food, could not do so indefinitely. Fahad Beg died not so long ago. His section of the Anizah, while wandering almost anywhere along the Mail Route, normally do their shopping in Ramadi, or in the holy cities of Kerbela and Nejef, further south. The three remaining big sections of the Anizah gravitate in the other direction towards Syria; but they may be met with.

There is another tribe which is settled along the Euphrates with its headquarters at Ramadi, where lives its sheikh, Ali ibn Sulaiman ibn Bekr. This tribe is called the Dulaim. While on the whole pursuing agriculture it possesses nomad elements which wander up and down between Rutbah and Ramadi. The nomads of the Dulaim who are most likely to be found on the Air Mail Route belong to the Albu Mahal group. Their sheikh is a young man called Aftan ibn Sharqi, who is a bit of a character. I met a sheikh near *L.G.* VI who answered to his description, and he was politeness itself.

It is not impossible to run into nomad sections of other tribes wandering from north to south in search of grazing for their camels. In the Transjordan districts Arabs of the Beni Sukr tribe are sure to be met with. They live at the western end of the track in the same sort of way as the Dulaim do at the eastern end. In addition to this, the track between *L.G.* M and Azrak runs quite close to the frontiers of the Nejd, which lies to the south of it. The Nejd, the kingdom of the Wahabis, or Akwan (brethren) as they are sometimes called, is ruled by Ibn Saud, the biggest Arab personality of to-day.

If you land on the route anywhere near to a Bedouin encampment, it will not be long before you see the little black figures rapidly shuffling over the desert to have a look at the "tiara," as they call your aeroplane. Some will squat down and stare into vacancy, but others may be extremely inquisitive. They like to pull you about, pick up your arm to examine your wrist-watch, or even

ARABS OF THE BENI SUKR TRIBE AT ZIZA

try to look into your mouth if they should catch sight of a gold stopping! All this is just to show you how much they like you, and they thoroughly enjoy a joke. If you are so unwise as to hold your cigarette case out to them they will take cigarettes, case and all, as an Englishman would march off with your box of matches. It was therefore less expensive to take a cigarette out and give it to them. The Bedou seem to be on the whole quite lax Mahomedans; for they do not object to smoking. But eating pork would be going too far; and for this reason they are a little shy of accepting meat. If you offer them food, they like you to eat some with them.

The Bedou are not above pilfering, and the pilot has to keep a sharp look-out for odd things left lying about or they will silently disappear beneath the capacious abbas of the tribesmen. On the other hand, these Arabs are the acme of hospitality, and will always press you to have a meal with them. If the pilot is making a temporary halt on the Mail, he is unlikely to be able to accept such an invitation. The "meal" would possibly last for the remainder of the day. It is no good when replete to refuse further offers of food; for your host will merely think what he has provided does not suit your taste, and will order another and more delicious animal to be killed and cooked. This all takes time; and though calculated to cement the good relations between pilots of the Air Mail and their Arab hosts, it is a luxury that has to be foregone unless one can afford to make a special trip by car to renew an old acquaintance. If the pilot does by any chance stay the night in camp with a friendly sheikh, he must not be surprised at a sheep on either side of him for bedfellows. I am told that they are more effective in winter than the downiest merino blanket.

In the event of the Bedou becoming troublesome in a minor way while visiting a forced-landed aeroplane, the thing for the pilot to do is to try and get hold of one of their responsible men, a sheikh if possible. He will be sure to know what the British "raj" means, and will restrain his too inquisitive or obstreperous followers. For instance, there was once an aeroplane down at *L.G.* X. On the horizon appeared about five hundred Bedou, trekking towards Rutbah Wells. A party of fifty or so came over to the aeroplane, and one of them tried to force his way past a sergeant who was guarding the rations in the hull. The sergeant said "Boo" to him, so he went to his camel and produced an enormous two-handed sword which he brought along. After executing a number of imaginary passes in the air, he drew his fingers across his throat. At this moment the pilot of the aeroplane came to the rescue and found the leader of the party. He explained to him that ten more tiaras were on their way, and

SLIDING A PATIENT INTO A VERNON AMBULANCE

POLICE POST AND WIRELESS STATION NEAR RUTBAH WELLS

that it would be advisable for him to behave himself and to see that his men did the same. The Arab quite understood and the incident closed.

It is rather an odd feeling, however, to find yourself a long way from anywhere with half a dozen Englishmen face to face with perhaps a hundred Bedou armed to the teeth, be they never so friendly. It is essential to treat them with complete confidence and to keep all guns well out of sight. All gestures should be of the most amicable kind; and the most effective way of getting on good terms is to make a joke of some sort which the Bedou can appreciate. It does not require any great ingenuity to do this. Friendly as the Bedou on the whole are, they cannot be of much material help. It is very different having a forced landing in the desert from having one in a civilized country, where telephones are available and the village policeman arrives and mounts guard till a relief party can come out by car. It was therefore necessary on the Air Mail aircraft to carry a complete desert equipment; for the omission of anything essential might mean twenty-four hours' delay.

The desert equipment carried in Vernons used to weigh about 300 pounds. A supply of aeroplane spares was carried, such as fabric and dope for mending up tears in the wings caused by stones flying up and hitting them, or other accidental damage. The engines had to have their spares, such as sparking plugs, magnetos and valves, besides odds and ends like clips for piping, washers of various kinds and some electric cable. In addition, items of general equipment were carried, such as a jack for lifting the aeroplane up to change a wheel when the tyre was punctured, a foot pump, petrol and oil funnels, screw pickets and rope to picket the aeroplane down, canvas covers for the pilot's cockpit and the propellers, to protect them from the weather—the wooden propellers used to warp if left long in a hot sun—and last, but not least, a supply of chewing gum! Wonderful stuff this was. With the help of insulation tape it would stop up water leaks, which occurred rather frequently with the water-cooled engines. The engine-fitter carried a tool kit and the wireless operator had with him a small supply of essential spares. The signalling apparatus that I have referred to formed part of the aeroplane's equipment. There were the white ground-strips, the Very pistol with red, white and green cartridges, some smoke candles and some message bags in case it was required to drop any messages.

Three days' rations for each person were carried; and the pilot usually took what was known as a "desert box" containing comforts, a few luxuries in food—tomato ketchup was good for making bully beef slip down easily—and probably some whisky or brandy, or gin if the pilot had spent his early days in the Navy. There were two First Aid outfits hung in wallets inside the aeroplane, with some compressed bandages, ampoules of iodine, and a picric acid dressing for burns. Most pilots also took some aspirin, chlorodyne, and permanganate of potash crystals. The latter could be used in case of a poisonous bite, if a small incision were made with a razor blade and a crystal pressed in. But the only attack that the pilot need fear was that of a chance scorpion; for snakes are very rare on the Mail Route.

The Vernons were capable of performing almost any kind of duties if put to it. They were fitted up to carry stretchers on brackets inside the hull. The patient could be slid in through a door in the nose of the aeroplane; and on receipt of a wireless message severe cases could be transported by air from lonely outstations to hospital in Baghdad in a few hours. If the patient needed an urgent operation, it might easily mean the saving of his life.

One of the most important items for desert flying was the drinking water, which was carried in 5-gallon oil drums. Ten gallons was taken in winter and fifteen in summer in a Vernon. In summer the water in the drums got pretty hot and was exceedingly unpleasant to drink. It was possible to cool the water by emptying it into chattis, porous earthenware jars, and by putting them in the shadow of the planes immediately after landing. If there was any wind blowing, the water cooled down in them quite quickly. Another way of cooling the water was to have a chargol, or waterproof bag, which could be filled with water and hung out in the draught of air made by the aeroplane in flight. These were often used by the smaller aeroplanes, which carried one chargol tied below each wing tip.

The pilots had also in their "desert boxes" sets of knives, forks and spoons, enamel plates and cups, saucepans and frying-pans, and I can answer for it that there were some first-class meals produced in the desert. It made a great difference to the trip if the pilot was one who cared for the bodily comfort of his passengers and crew. When out in the desert, the meal of the day was the evening meal when the flying was done, and the aeroplanes safely parked. Then it was that the camp fire was lit and the stew bubbled and the bacon or sausages fizzed in the frying-pan; and every one felt thoroughly happy and contented.

The passengers were normally allowed 35 pounds of kit in the summer and 55 pounds in the winter when the air was thicker and the aeroplanes could support more. It is needless to say that the pilot had to calculate his load very carefully before starting off; the aircraft were allowed a certain maximum load, depending on the time of year; and this load had on no account to be exceeded. All the passengers' luggage was carefully weighed at Heliopolis or Hinaidi, to make sure that they had not brought too much. The punishment for bringing too much was that you had to leave it behind, which was unpleasant in that the unfortunate passenger might not see it again for some time. It would have to come over when an aeroplane happened to be returning without its full load, a not very frequent occurrence

Enough spares were carried to repair any ordinary engine breakdown. On rare occasions something would go wrong which it was impossible to repair in the desert. As time went on these major fractures occurred less and less frequently. When they did happen the only thing to do was to wireless for assistance and sit down and wait until a new engine was flown out from Heliopolis or Hinaidi, depending on whether the aeroplane was down west or east of *L.G.* R. In the case of Vernons the spare engine was mounted on the lower plane, between the starboard engine and the hull, and a sheerlegs, tackle and portable trolley were carried in the hull itself. The weight of these was considerable, and aeroplanes carrying them could not carry their full petrol. An aeroplane loaded with a spare engine, sheerlegs and tackle, could carry four instead of seven hours' petrol.

In practice, if the distance to the forced-landed aeroplane was great, the load was divided between two relief aeroplanes, one carrying the new engine and the other the gear. The Vernon with the spare engine would land, beside the Vernon needing it. The sheerlegs was set up in front of the broken engine, which was swung out of its bearers by means of cables passed round it, and lowered on to a cradle of petrol tins. The portable trolley was assembled and connected up to the runners of T-iron on which the spare engine was mounted. This engine could then be slid backwards off the lower plane on to the trolley, which was wheeled round to the sheerlegs. It was then picked up off the trolley, swung into the engine bearers from which the broken engine had been removed, bolted down and coupled up. Meanwhile the broken engine was mounted on the trolley and taken to the relief aeroplane. The trolley was coupled to the runners again and the engine was slid up on to the lower plane and made secure there. The trolley had then to be dismantled and packed away inside the hull, the sheerlegs had also to be stowed away, and the new engine fitted with its propeller and run up on the ground to see if everything was in order.

An engine has been changed in the desert and a Vernon ready for the air again in four hours from the time of arrival of the relief aeroplane. The average time was half as much again. The operation, considering the number of men available, pilots, crew and passengers all doing their bit—and in hot weather it was an exhausting bit—left them dirty and tired, but with raised spirits at the idea of continuing the journey so rudely interrupted. If the heat was great it became necessary to suspend operations in the middle of the day. In summer, if you left a spanner out in the sun, it would probably be too hot to hold after a little; and in winter it was necessary to keep a fire going so that the fitters could go to it every now and then to warm their hands which had become numb through touching cold metal. Whatever conditions they had to work in, the airmen fitters, and riggers if there were any, were consistently cheerful. You never heard a grouse, and often humorous remarks, which set you laughing.

If an aeroplane that was carrying the Mail broke down like this, the mail-bags had to be transferred to the accompanying aeroplane. The bags and packets were all carefully checked and weighed at either end of the Mail Route before being handed over to the pilot, who held a list of them in duplicate. The Mail would frequently consist of half a dozen post-office bags and a number of small packets, some of these being service or Government despatches, which had to be carefully safeguarded. As there was no special place to put them in the aeroplane, it was a little difficult to see that none of them got mislaid. The weight of Mail carried at the time of which I am speaking, 1924 to 1926, averaged 200 to 350 pounds. At Christmas time it reached as much as 700 pounds.

Seeing the Mail off at Hinaidi on Thursday afternoons used to be something of an event. The prevailing wind was from the north-west, and so the aeroplanes were normally taxied out to the far side of the aerodrome from the hangars, facing the wind. The passengers and Mail were conveyed to them by tenders. A considerable crowd would assemble, consisting of people seeing their friends off to England on leave, or sometimes for good. Behind them was the grey bund. Private cars would be parked close by. If the time for leaving was 3.30 p.m., the aeroplanes would be in position by three o'clock and would stop their engines. From that time the crowd would be collecting. All around was a buzz of excitement. "Has the Mail come yet?" every one asked. At 3.15 a little trail of dust might appear in the distance in front of the hangars. Out of the dust a tender would emerge coming over the aerodrome with the Mail. Soon the bags were being tumbled out and the pilot walking round checking them. The Lion engines were started up and their low sobbing rumble drowned the conversation and good-byes. Then the word would pass round for all to embark. Perhaps a momentary panic would arise because some passenger could not be found. All the while he was on board. At last the time came. A sound like a peal of thunder; a dense cloud of dust; and then above it the wings of the aeroplanes mounting upwards on their long journey.

The Mail aeroplanes all had names, which invested them with personalities. Valkyrie, Venus, Vesuvius, Vagabond, Aurora, Ancaeus, Argo, conjure up stirring memories. Their work is done. Other faster and more modern aircraft have succeeded them. But it was the work of the past that made the present possible. There was a time when the mails used to travel from Baghdad to Damascus on the backs of racing camels. Compared with the centuries during which that method of transport remained unchanged, the coming of air transport seems to have occupied no appreciable interval of time. But the 1,300 horse-power air liner as we see it in 1929, more wonderful in its construction than those monuments of the past that watch over the desert, was not conjured up by the rubbing of a lamp.

In laying stress on the difficulties encountered by the Royal Air Force during the earlier days of the Air Mail, I have only described what must inevitably happen in any new and arduous undertaking before experience is gained and suitable remedies are applied. One by one these difficulties were overcome, until by the time that the Service was ready to hand over the route to a civil organization an extraordinary degree of efficiency had been attained. The Air Mail was running with perfect regularity, and the forced landings, which were not infrequent during the earlier days, had become a thing of the past, which veteran pilots were able, as it were, to recount as events of their youth!

The civil air service, which is to run from Cairo to Karachi, was inaugurated in December, 1926, when the Secretary of State for Air, Sir Samuel Hoare, accompanied by Lady Maud Hoare and Air Vice-Marshal Sir Geoffrey Salmond, flew from London to Delhi. To run this service a fleet of five air liners was built by the De Havilland Aircraft Company. The type of aircraft, the D.H.66, or "Hercules" as it is called, is suited in every way to the work it has to perform, and has given excellent results. It is fitted with three air-cooled Bristol "Jupiter" radial engines giving 425 horse-power each. The aeroplane can actually climb when using two of them only. This means that when cruising the engines can be run well throttled down and made to give the requisite power under very favourable conditions. The aeroplane, moreover, has an ample reserve of power for flight when the air is thin or it has to take off a high aerodrome in

A DE HAVILLAND HERCULES AEROPLANE AT HELIOPOLIS (AS USED BY IMPERIAL AIRWAYS)

hot weather. It seats twelve people including two crew, and possesses a range without refuelling of 525 miles.

Each passenger is allowed a weight of 22 pounds for himself and free luggage. A passenger weighing eleven stone can therefore take 70 pounds of luggage free. The ticket includes meals en route, and excess luggage is carried at half rates. The Hercules has a top speed of 130 m.p.h., and can cruise comfortably in warm-weather conditions at 95 m.p.h.

During the preliminary organization of the route to India via the Persian Gulf, a hitch occurred, and the Persian Government failed to ratify a provisional agreement allowing Imperial Airways aircraft to fly over Persian territory, with the result that instead of a fortnightly service between Cairo and Karachi, a fortnightly service between Cairo and Basrah was actually put into operation. The first normal service was operated from Basrah to Cairo on January 7th, 1927, and in the reverse direction the following Wednesday. The service was run at fortnightly intervals until April, 1927, when, the whole fleet of five Hercules aircraft having been delivered, a regular weekly service was started which has run up to the present time.

It was desirable in organizing a route of this sort to have stages, not too long, say 250 to 300 miles, and as nearly as possible of equal length. In the Cairo-Basrah section the stages became Cairo (Heliopolis)—Gaza (in Palestine)—Ziza—Rutbah Wells—Baghdad (West aerodrome)—Basrah (Shaibah). The total distance from Cairo to Karachi is 2,500 miles, and it was considered that in order eventually to maintain a regular service between these places a fleet of five aircraft would be required. The idea was that, except for a period when each aeroplane was undergoing its annual overhaul, they should all be kept in service operating in relays, like stage-coaches; and that they should follow each other all the way round the route, which would subject them all to the same conditions and allow them to return periodically to the main workshops at Cairo.

Near Rutbah Wells, beside the Air Mail Track between *L.G.* 8 and *L.G.* IX a combined police post, wireless station and rest house has been built, and a landing ground cleared in front of it for the use of Imperial Airways. The grey stone building, with an avenue leading up to it from the landing ground, is strangely impressive, and seems to dominate the uplands overlooking the Wadi Hauran.

In addition to many distinguished passengers, the Hercules aeroplanes have been called upon to carry urgent medical supplies and serums, sick and injured people, and very young children. Among the freight, bullion, precious stones, scientific apparatus, machinery parts, samples of ladies' dresses, and newspapers have frequently been consigned, while on the last aeroplane to reach Baghdad before Christmas, 1927, the letter mail from home to Iraq totalled over half a ton.

The Hercules air liners, "City of Delhi," "City of Cairo," "City of Jerusalem," and "City of Baghdad" have been christened by the rulers of the countries through which the civil air route is to run. The Persian difficulty having been overcome, it is hoped as a result to put into execution this spring (1929) the original proposal of running the service to India. This will be a great step forward to the ultimate connection to Australia.

In the last century a poet

> "Saw the heavens fill with commerce, argosies of magic sails."

In this century we see his vision coming true. Air transport is bringing about by peaceful means an increased sympathy between component parts of an empire such as Alexander dreamt of, but could not build by force. The merchandise of Cathay will be borne westwards, not to the sound of camel bells, but on the wings of the wind by a magic that neither the divinations of the priests of Horus nor all the science of Alexandria of the Ptolemies could compass.

The spirit of Puck, the fairy of Shakespeare, who announced that he would put a girdle round the earth in forty minutes, is abroad to-day.

CHAPTER V

NAMES AND FANCIES

The country of the Air Mail Route between the Euphrates and Jordan became to me a wonderland; the more I got to know its hills and wadis and lonely uplands, the more did I feel like a child roaming through a land of fable. To the pilot hurrying along the track on his urgent mission the regions on either side were forbidden kingdoms, the frontiers of which he could not cross. This country never seems the same, every time you go across it looks at you differently. It possesses numberless moods, and changes its expression almost like a human face. Sometimes it beams with wide-open eyes; sometimes it looks mournful; sometimes listless, and at rare intervals it stares with a long-drawn scowl. It is most exhilarating to fly when the dry wind hums over its amber face, and when the wings of the aeroplane lift to the unseen rollers passing by or breaking round in transparent spray.

Of all the features of the desert that are visible not many have names that we know. The Bedou have their names doubtless, but they are not written down yet. So I came to invent my own names for some, which are wholly unpractical and do not even possess the virtue of being short. I have marked them on my sketch maps because they pleased me. Other places took names, as all such places in this world will, from events that happened there. Along the track from time to time some small adventure happened to a pilot; once or twice an aeroplane came to grief altogether; and, after its engines and all other removable parts had been taken away, was left in the desert. These spots were given names in which that of the pilot, or more usually his nickname, was incorporated.

These are some of the names that I remember. As you fly from Baghdad to Ramadi you strike the Euphrates at Fellujah, where there is a landing ground marked in the desert not far from the town, which hugs a loop in the winding river. On one side of the landing ground there is a spot called "Titch's Tumble" after an exciting episode that occurred in the darkness of a hot night in July, 1925.

Between *L.G.* II and *L.G.* III there is a low range of hills through which the track passes; these hills I called "The Hills of Lost Thoughts." They lie about 50 miles west of the landing ground at Ramadi, and when you are coming in from the west it is usually at about this point that you first sight the long pale blue line of Lake Habbaniyah. Some people call the place "Two and a half" because of the two landing grounds between which it lies. The hills always presented to me a curious vagueness of outline; and in their form and contours there seemed to be no visible plan, such as is nearly always apparent in nature's architecture. They looked as if they had been dumped down there by mistake. The sloping plain between the "Hills of Lost Thoughts" and Ramadi, I called the "Land of Nearly" because, after a long day's flying, it was here that you could ease your engines down with the comforting thought that you were nearly home.

A few miles east of Rutbah lies *L.G.* 8 on a stony plain overlooking the Wadi Hauran to the west of it. To the south and east of the landing ground are ranges of limestone hills, flat-topped except where some freak of erosion has caused them to split and assume queer broken outlines. This plain I christened the "Plain of Unfulfilled Desire." It feels empty and wistful, although many a time will you see the Bedou moving along the horizon with their camels and flocks, looking for all the world like a carved frieze under the pediment of heaven. Amongst the hills to the east of the plain two stand out prominently, side by side. One of them is conical in shape; and the other flat-topped, making an irregular quadrilateral. They are marked on the map as Twaidat el Chaleb; I called them "Cain and Abel."

Then if you turn round and look towards the west you can see far over the Wadi Hauran a line of blue hills. On the other side of them is El Jid. Legend has it that there was once a king of this country who ruled from Rutbah to El Jid. Perhaps it was he who dug out the deep wells in the limestone at these places. On the barren hillsides there are still to be seen the remains of walls of houses and mine shafts. These hills I called the "Kingdom of What Wasn't." In the middle of the "Kingdom" the Air Track bends sharply south-west from west. Other tracks continue along valleys like the fingers of an outstretched hand, which have been hollowed out by the system of water-courses that drain into the Wadi Hauran. Tracks branch off to Damascus and Aleppo, and although an arrow with the word "air" has been ploughed to guide the pilot safely round the

CAIN AND ABEL

corner, the other tracks have more than once been followed by mistake. This was, however, in the earlier days, when the track was not so clear. In the western part of the "Kingdom" the track runs parallel with the line of the Wadi Hauran. It is a strange thing that a change of wind is very frequently met with at this point. If the pilot has had a bad headwind over the "Plain of Unfulfilled Desire" it is as likely as not to turn round and help him as he leaves the forgotten king's dominions; and therefore, because I once lost a very favourable wind there, I called the track from *L.G.* X to *L.G.* XI, "Fickle Furlong."

Across the track in "Fickle Furlong" runs an insignificant wadi, a tributary of the Hauran. One day the king of "What Wasn't" claimed an aeroplane and captured it in this wadi. The place is called "Wu's Wallop" Even a section of armoured cars with machine guns could not persuade him to give it back to the Royal Air Force, so there it had to stay. It is said that if you go there at the time of the new moon you may, if you are lucky, see his phantom sentries who guard its remains. But do not go down into the wadi; you can see quite well from the rising ground behind it, and you will be safer. When the pilot passes through the gates of the "Kingdom" at El Jid, he flies across what I called the "Upland of the Winds." It is 40 leagues broad, and stretches southward into the heart of Arabia. In winter the wind sometimes shrieks across it like a demented spirit, while in summer time when the air is hot and thin the wind blows uneasily first from one direction and then from another. The plain seldom sleeps under a truce of the winds, which come out to battle for causes that are hidden in the heart of nature. At times one of the winds gets the uppermost hand and you can feel it in hot pursuit of its beaten rivals; and then the others gather up their broken forces and carry on the sullen quarrel. I have seen a west wind lash up the clouds till they spurt columns of rain, and I have seen it, almost at one blast, send them scurrying away and tumbling as fast as they can below the horizon. If you happen to be marooned on the upland there is not a stick or stone behind which you can shelter, the wind just goes on blowing and you cannot get away from it. Anyone who has had experience will vouch for it that wind is harder to endure cheerfully for any length of time than almost any of the other companions that force their company on sojourners in the desert.

Not far from the highest point of the Air Track across the "Upland of the Winds," to be more precise between *L.G.* O and *L.G.* P, an aeroplane came down by the track never to rise again. Its skeleton long remained as a landmark, and it was called "Grummet's Grange." By now, but for a few metal parts, it has probably fallen to dust; but those who know its story will remember the name of "Argo," which the pilot called his aeroplane, and the wings as proud and white as the sails which carried the argonauts of old in search of the golden fleece. Towards the western side of the "Upland of the Winds" you will see, if you look to the southward, about 30 miles away, a hill standing up by itself. It must be a considerable height because you can see it so far away. It has two peaks connected by a yoke. This hill I called "Jacob's Pillow." As the pilot flies westward across the "Upland of the Winds" he will see on the horizon, soon after "Jacob's Pillow" has come into view, the ugly tops of the ridges of the basalt country. My name for the basalt country was the "Land of Conjecture." I will not refer to it any more at the moment because I have a little story to tell about it later on. Having passed through the dark hills and over the twin mud flats at *L.G.* D, the pilot emerges on to the "Plain of Sorrows." This is the wilderness that fills in the space between the "Land of Conjecture" and the Pools of Azrak. I named it thus because of the feeling of depression from which I suffered after flying through the basalt. In the rains the Azrak pools overflow and convert large parts of the "Plain of Sorrows" into a swamp, which gave much trouble to the motor transport convoys from Amman trying to take petrol out to the tank at *L.G.* D.

You finally arrive at Ziza landing ground and look towards the Judæan Hills over which you must pass on the next stage of the journey to Cairo. To the south-west the ridges of the hills culminate in a point which is higher than anything near it. To the right of it is a gap and then another distinct but

JACOB'S PILLOW

lower eminence. This gap is what you make for when you leave Ziza for the Mediterranean, and it is the cleft in the hills made by the Wadi Seil el Mojeb. The higher hill to the left I called "Jehovah's Rest," and the lower peak to the right "Vision of Israel." Beyond them is the Dead Sea.

And now for my story of the "Land of Conjecture." It is about a lost village, which is called "Esmeralda" in my dreams. The experience happened to my friend Fitz H—— when he was flying over the Mail Track with Flight-Lieutenant G——. They were flying along through the basalt hills, between *L.G.* F and *L.G.* H. They lost the track and got rather south of it. Fitz did not get worried, for G—— is an old hand. Now the basalt hills are so desolate that it is always thought that nothing inhabits them. Their beginning and end are lost in conjecture. That is why I called them the "Land of Conjecture."

G—— was tracing his way through the unknown valleys of the "Land of Conjecture," where nature broods in the silence of a hundred thousand years, and where perhaps the ghosts of peoples of times gone by come out when the golden moon finds her way about among the dark hills. Fitz suddenly looked down and saw in a valley a green spot, and on the bright green was a village: the village "Esmeralda." But in a second it was gone.

When they landed in Iraq he told the story to various friends, who did not believe him; so he thought that he must have dreamt it. Then he asked G——, who said that he had also seen the lost village.

I wonder if I shall ever find it. If we could fly high enough we might. But no one dares intentionally to leave the track in the "Land of Conjecture," which is a maze for the unwary. I should love to come upon it. Perhaps there are people there who have lived apart for years uncountable. Who knows that there are not a King and Queen of Esmeralda, and a beautiful Princess? They may be white people with fair skins and hazel eyes, with a language of their own; and they may know the things that are privy to the "Land of Conjecture."

The great eruptions of the past may have buried them away. Perhaps a magician struck the basalt rock so that a stream of crystal water poured out and nourished the people. I like to fancy that at dusk the little bright-eyed gazelle run about on the green grass; and that myriads of peeping flowers with faint thrilling scents come up in springtime. I believe, the folk of Esmeralda must be fairies.

When flying over the "Land of Conjecture" I have looked long to the south, yet never have I seen the faintest sign of Esmeralda. Perhaps I was not in the right mood. In the desert, however, one feels as if anything might happen quite naturally. What would be a miracle in your own world would pass without comment in such places as the "Land of Conjecture."

CHAPTER VI

FROM THE PILOT'S POINT OF VIEW

So far, I have discussed the Air Mail Route with the idea of explaining its origin, sketching its development, and giving a hint of its future. The chapters that follow deal with the route from rather a different point of view: that of a pilot flying over it, inquiring neither why he is flying across, nor how the route came to be there, but intent simply on marshalling his aeroplane safely, and as rapidly as possible, to its destination, so that he may deliver up his precious burden of mails, or the yet more precious one of human beings.

During the two years that I was stationed in Iraq, from October, 1924 to September, 1926, I wrote down my flying experiences, which relate mostly to the Air Mail Route. I hope that the picture that I have endeavoured to paint in the foregoing chapters will enable the following narratives, written down casually, and often rather incoherently, in the winter evenings and hot summer afternoons, to be sympathetically understood.

FIRST FLIGHT TO IRAQ (OCTOBER, 1924)

Heliopolis to Ziza. The first stage of the Mail Route to Baghdad. We started off in the bright sunny morning, two Vernons; ourselves and Flight-Lieutenant Dalzell on "Aurora" J 7141. We kept along the eastern rim of the cultivation, passed over Tel el Kebir, and to the west of No. 4 F.T.S.[1] at Abu Suweir, where we saw an aeroplane flying in the distance. Saundby told me that we should eventually have to climb to about 6,ooo feet to get over the Judæan Hills; but as we were heavily loaded we climbed fairly slowly in spite of the fact that, being early in the morning, it was cool. We sent messages back by W/T[2] as we passed every place. When, the Mail is going, these are picked up by Heliopolis, Abu Suweir, Ramleh, Amman, Ramadi and Hinaidi. Abu Suweir sent us their weather report by W/T and we asked for one from Ramleh, which we got back in about half an hour. I sat in front with Saundby; he took the Vernon off, but I flew the whole of the rest of the way. After flying in a N.E. direction we passed over the Suez Canal. There was light cumulus at about 2,000 feet, which we managed to get above. Then we came along the coast and the sun began to get warm. On the left the blue Mediterranean with little white breakers; on the right the desert.

We worked up the coast till we came to El Arish, which is near the border of Egypt and Palestine. After this we turned a little more east and opened out the engines a bit to prepare for the hills. On the left we passed Gaza. It was getting pretty bumpy, and there was a considerable amount of cumulus, broken and in places rising to great heights, 8,000 to 10,000 feet, with enormous ragged tops leaping off and detaching themselves from their bases. We dodged the clouds where we could. Palestine looks quite different from Egypt. It looked a dull grey brown colour, cut up by tracks and in a few parts there seemed to be grey brown cultivation. Everything looked rather seared. The villages were few and far between: they looked geometrically arranged, hard cut in the strong light, but of a dull colour, with flat mud roofs, full of little black dots, men and camels. As we flew along, the country almost imperceptibly rose up under us, and became hilly. It looked less and less possible to land if one had engine failure. To the east the hills rose up to a long blue line. There were sharp gorges between them, and it looked as if there were hardly any flat places. The tops of the hills were mostly round, and they looked rough and scaly in texture, like enormous limpet shells all bunched together. Then under the clouds and on the far edge of the hills I saw dimly two towers. It was a city—Jerusalem. It looked most impressive from the air—on the hill-tops. On the right, a few miles to the south, was Bethlehem on another hill-top, all terraced, and with dull green shrubs interspersed with rectangular houses. I do not know whether it was association or not, but the sight of these places gave me a queer thrill, coming upon them, suddenly, in those gaunt hills. And I realized the meaning of the words "down to Jericho."

The hills fell away in steep terraces to the Jordan Valley, and we passed over the Dead Sea, which looked—and this surprised me—a soft hushed blue. It had little white ribbons of foam on it, traced out in patterns. The grey cliffs dropped sheer down to it. Jordan twists and wriggles down its flat valley, which holds apart the menacing cliffs which look as if they might move together and crush any living thing as would a vice. I looked back and saw Jerusalem with the sun on it; the rocks had become ethereal and the city seemed to hang in the air, under the clouds, with the rocks festooned below it and looking pale against the warm blue of the Dead Sea. Finally we saw a kind of mud plateau rising away into the distance, and on this was Ziza, which consists merely of a landing ground and a little station on the Hedjaz railway. We found R.A.F. desert tenders ready with petrol, and after I had landed we filled up. I had lunch of a sardine or two and biscuits and lemon. This was the place where the Wahabis were recently shot up by the armoured cars; about six hundred of them were killed, as they were chased for 80 miles in one day. Many more must have perished in the desert for lack of water. They had committed atrocities and nobody had any sympathy with them. I found some small pale mauve desert lilies growing in the dry mud of the desert. Having taken in petrol at Ziza, we took off in the comparative heat.

Ziza to El Jid. Ziza is 2,000 feet high, and this makes climbing out in the afternoon an extremely arduous process. Saundby took the aeroplane off, and we had to fly round for about quarter of an hour amongst the hills before we could climb over the easterly ridge. It was curious watching the "dunt" indicator. If you approach a hill down wind in the normal way you get an "up dunt." You must never approach it up wind or you may be bounced on to it. We then picked up the track and flew eastward. The track from Ziza branches into the track to Amman some way east of these places. We passed an old Roman fort on the right. Then we followed on over the landing grounds C to R. We passed by volcanic hills with flat tops, looking dirty and black, with red mud flats between them, but the main part of the in the desert was mile upon mile of yellow or pink-grey mud with faint grey-green mottlings on it. From time to time one would catch glimpses of hills sticking up out of the desert like dark cones. The most striking feature of the desert was perhaps the light-coloured, oval-shaped mud flats, sometimes 1 or 2 miles across. The sun got lower and lower, and the whole desert took on a ruddy hue. The atmosphere was so clear that the little fluffy strato-cumulus looked as if it were fastened on to the blue sky. Just before the sun went down we landed at El Jid, after dropping a smoke candle to show us the direction of the wind. We taxied "Valkyrie" and "Aurora" to the circle; Harris ran up his flag, and in the deep silence of the desert, we made our evening meal. It seemed like another world; perhaps like what one may experience in waking up after death: a feeling of utter aloofness, and yet of peace. Then we lay down under the wings of the aircraft and slept.

*El Jid to L.G.*V. On again in the morning. As the sun came up over the rim of that quiet mysterious world, and lit the little stones of the desert, we made tea, and drank it with relish. The wind had now turned against us and as it blew from the east we made less headway. Soon we saw little trails of dust on the track—I thought at first they were fires burning—and these proved to be motor-cars dashing across the desert at perhaps 2-mile intervals. The Damascus Mail reaches sometimes, I believe, 70 m.p.h. Near the Rutbah Wells we passed Fahad Beg and his crowd strung over the desert. They looked like little ants; men, camels, and goat-hide shelters. We had a W/T message to say that one of No. 45's Vernons was refuelling at *L.G.* V, and when we arrived, sure enough there it was. There is a sunk petrol installation, and from this we took in some petrol. On this landing ground there was a lot of camel-thorn, and, as we afterwards found to our cost, it made havoc of our tyres.

*L.G.*V *to Ramadi.* The desert was now sloping down to Ramadi, and we appeared to gain height. The sun was hot and it got very bumpy. We passed over one of the two bituminous lakes which lie between *L.G.* II and *L.G.* I, and as we passed over you could smell the bitumen very strongly. Ramadi lies to the north of a big lake which looks soft blue in the desert. When we landed at Ramadi I noticed the sharp difference in temperature, and the air felt like a hot iron. Two of our tyres were quite flat. We took in about 70 gallons of petrol. There is a little depot and wireless station there especially for the Air Mail. As we landed, and again, when we took off, I noticed all the old trenches that were made during the war.

Ramadi to Hinaidi. Harris flew the last bit of the way, as he thought that it might be his last flight on "Valkyrie." We sent a W/T message out to No. 45 to keep tiffin for us, as we should be late. We flew over the winding Euphrates, and I noticed how different was the cultivation from that in Egypt. It looked so poor and pale and dusty. Then, in the far distance, I had my first view of Baghdad on the edge of the Tigris. Baghdad is so much the colour of the desert that it is difficult to pick out a long way away. I had curiously raised feelings as the goal of our journey came in sight, of which I had heard and thought so much, and yet of which I had been able to form so little idea. I understood what was meant by the "scorching plains of Iraq." They did look hot and sun-baked. Beyond Baghdad lay the huge cantonment of Hinaidi, where we duly landed, and found plenty of people waiting for us. I thought it seemed at least fitting that I arrive at my new squadron by air. I felt hot and tired and dusty.

I had had so many new experiences that my mind could hardly accommodate itself, and I felt as one in a dream. The grey dust of the desert, the grey walls of the buildings, the sky almost colourless with heat—although it was quite cool compared to midsummer—and the grey green dust colour of the shrubs, and the thick heavy odour of dust, gave me a feeling of having entered a new world where values were different and where I should experience new things passing imagination.

FLIGHT TO RAMADI (NOVEMBER, 1924)

Hinaidi to Ramadi. I flew over with Saundby to Ramadi, I sitting on the right. We took over Mr. Matheson of W. & B.[3] to inspect the building at Ramadi. We also took over his Sikh overseer. It was a lovely November day. The sky was full of alto-cumulus inter-mixed with curving stratus. There were some clear windows of blue. The alto-cumulus was whitely translucent in parts; in parts soft melting grey, interwoven with little dark wedges of stratus. Far away over the blue to the south were banks of dim cumulus. It was very clear, and it was almost the feeling of seeing for ever. The flat spaces of the desert give you a sort of feeling that they go on for ever. The lake to the south of Ramadi was exceptionally beautiful. It was covered with patterns; I suppose different qualities of water, or water of varying kinds of surface. The alto-cumulus was reflected in parts as from a mirror; and the mirror looked as if parts of the silvering had come off. Part of the water was dull, part bright. The whole impression was that of mother-o'-pearl; the soft blue, pale vivid green, pale violets and greys mingling in a gentle sheen. We ran a long way landing, as there was no wind. I did rather an awkward turn coming in, but pulled off quite a decent landing, except that I nearly ran over the circle, which is a dangerous thing for the tailskid. As we were landing a native was running across the aerodrome slap in front of our starboard bow. I suppose he had the wind up. There were also other natives wandering about on the aerodrome.

Ramadi to Hinaidi. And so home! We stayed to lunch with the Administrative Inspector and his wife. They gave us a good lunch in their pleasant country house. It is foursquare with an open courtyard.

MY FIRST MAIL TRIP: HINAIDI—HELIOPOLIS—HINAIDI (NOVEMBER, 1924)

Hinaidi to Ramadi. I was accompanied by Saundby on "Morpheus" J 7138. I had intended that the three of us should take off in formation, and taxied out into position as a triangle. Laing could not start in time, so Saundby and I had to take off alone. Saundby was conveying Squadron-Leader Geoffrey Bowler to be married in Egypt, and had decorated "Morpheus" with ribbon bows and flowers tied to the windscreen. It was a bit misty passing Fellujah, but cleared up as we approached Lake Habbaniyah. I made a slight bounce in landing at Ramadi. It is a bit difficult with a heavy load.

Ramadi to L.G. D. We made a splendid trip. We had stayed at Ramadi for the night. Supper had been interrupted by a black scorpion running out from underneath a plate. We got up in the cold dawn. Just after sunrise I taxied out, and was in position when Saundby, who was following me, did in a tyre. I waited, and when he came on, I took off. Then I saw he was held up again, so, after circling round, I pushed off. He had another tyre gone, but followed me and eventually caught me up on the big plain after *L.G.* V. The sunrise had an unearthly beauty. The sun rose up over the grey solitude, and suddenly flooded it with amber radiance. One or two tiny flecks of cloud glared like lamps above the sun, heralding the day. I passed over the Bitumen Pools, and on over the little hills between *L.G.* II and *L.G.* III. The mud flat by *L.G.* V showed like a thin blue line on the horizon, and as I approached I saw it was all wet, and reflected the high alto-cumulus. A Nairn car had evidently driven on to it in the night at full speed and was disconsolately bogged about 70 yards from the edge.

I passed on over the plain and the sun came up and shone into the cockpit and warmed me a little. I had a drink of tea and some digestive biscuits which I had brought. Then we approached the hills near *L.G.* IX, and passed through the winding avenue, a pathway of flat orange sand between the flat-topped hills. It curves off sharply southwards, leaving the Aleppo track going north-west. Out again into the rising plain, past El Jid, on to the darker mottled mud desert, intersected by wadis, with cross-markings of vegetation like a tiger's skin. Far on the left one could see the double cones of the distant hill, and farther still two faint blue hills. Then in the distance loomed the broken line of the basalt country, and the sky darkened a little and looked grey and dull. We passed *L.G.* H and F amid the blackened hills, and saw the orange and almost indian and lacquer red gravel bottoms, and the pale mud flats.

Saundby asked me by W/T if I had enough petrol to reach Ziza. I said "Yes" at first, but then decided to land at D. I tried to get a smoke candle out, but three were duds. Saundby dropped one at last and landed first, running into the very camel-thorn against which he had expressly warned me! I landed afterwards and stopped short, more by luck than good management. I took in 50 gallons of petrol from the sunk-steel plate dump. There is a D.H.9a crash at D, where someone crashed on a D.H.9a and was buried just beside the wreck, which may remain as his pathetic monument for centuries to come. D is very like Farnborough in many ways. Saundby says it is a typical bit of Asian steppe. The contour of the hills, the shape and colour of the vegetation, sparse and poor, the long line of the pale mud flats remind one strongly of Long Valley. It was wonderfully quiet in the pale afternoon sunlight, which lit up people's faces and the struts and silver wings of the aeroplanes.

L.G. D *to Ziza.* On again after we had refuelled. We followed the track out of a winding wadi on to the plain again, across to Azrak (C). We passed south of C, across to Kasr Kharana, one of the eastern outposts of the mighty Roman empire, standing like a sentinel in the desert. We were now flying with the sun on our port bow, and it reflected off the smooth grey desert, as if the desert were polished. The markings on the desert looked like the grain of fancy polished wood. We flew across the ridge where the track goes on to Amman, and tried to find the plough track to Ziza, but it had apparently in this part been washed away by the rain. We circled round to see if we could see it, and Saundby, thinking we were lost, turned up and nosed towards us. We then turned down and landed at Ziza. Two Bristols from No. 14 Squadron were already flying overhead, and one nearly landed on top of me as I was taxying in. They took the Mail for Palestine. We stayed at Ziza the night in the funny little station buildings. We had the luck to see the Hedjaz train, which came in from Medina. Ziza to Heliopolis. We made a splendid run with a following wind. We climbed a bit over Ziza, which is itself about, 400 feet high, in order to get height for the crossing of the Judæan Hills. We went over the Dead Sea Peninsula and Beersheba. From Ziza you can see the gap in the crags which is opposite the peninsula. It looks rather like the gap at Butser Hill near Petersfield, except for the fact that it is on a much larger scale. We approached it over a broken ravine, flanked by flattish topped hills, working up to a climax, where, to the left of the ravine, a mighty crag tumbles sheer down through twisted and jagged ledges 3,000 feet into the rippling blue water. Flight-Lieutenant Roche said to me, "I always feel younger after this bit is over!"

Soon after we had passed the Dead Sea, Beersheba hove in sight. Saundby was flying on my left over the hills and slightly lower, and I thought what a striking colour his floating red streamers looked against the dark tumbled crags, 2,000 feet below. Then one saw the dim blue line of the Mediterranean stretching in a far-flung curve as far as the eye could reach. We passed down the coast, over the wadi at El Arish, which divides Egypt and Palestine; on our left the wind-swept sand of the desert which looks like waves rippling in on a calm evening, on our right the blue, blue sea with midget white breakers. On towards Romani and the Suez Canal, with big ships steaming up slowly and majestically, on the left Lake Timsa, and further south the Great Bitter Lake, unlocking the door to the Red Sea. Following the sweet-water canal to the slim strip of cultivation which cuts across the desert to the main Nile Delta and Tel el Kebir, we sailed on the wings of a following wind, through some detached cumulus, turning more south along the eastern edge of the cultivation as it narrows towards Cairo. I saw the line of whitish sand hills which lie north of Heliopolis, then glided down below the clouds, passed to the left of Bilbeis, and flew in to Heliopolis in good time. I just caught the end of "Vimy Ridge"[4] in landing, and made a slight bounce. I handed over the Mail and had "Valkyrie" put away after a magnificent run of 12 hrs. 10 mins. flying time.

At Heliopolis. I did an hour's test, preparatory to returning with the Mail. Everything was running satisfactorily. Saundby, who landed before me, said he stood twenty minutes in the sun to see me land (crash?). I judged in from 2,000 and made a perfect landing. However I ran over the road which divides the North and South Aerodromes. I hardly felt it. I worked on "Valkyrie" quite a good deal while she was at Heliopolis and polished her up. My little St. Christopher, sent to me by Dr. Williams, is screwed to the dashboard.

Heliopolis to Ziza. The engines ran splendidly, but we had quite a strong head wind. We were somewhat delayed in starting by a fog, which is apt to come up at this time of year. It was clear out to the north-east. As we passed to the left of No.4 F.T.S. at Abu Suweir there were low patches of white mist, strung out over the ground like delicate white tresses of hair. Near Moseifig I had a feed off ham and rolls and a swill out of my Thermos, while Roche flew. Then he fed. While I was eating I put my tinted goggles up and let in the sunlight and outer air. When you masticate in the air, with every movement of your jaws the engine roar swells and subsides like the roaring crash of breakers against rocks with hollow caves. I climbed steadily with engines doing 2,050 r.p.m. in preparation for those gaunt hills, which rise like a menacing barrier to the Arabian desert. We passed slowly over the aerodrome at Beersheba beating up against the wind, up the wadi which Saundby discovered, until the sandy peninsula in the Dead Sea came into view. Then over the great crag, the apparent summit of the "promised land," out across the tableland on its further side, over the broken ravine and on to the plain. We missed Ziza and found ourselves against the opposite hills before we realized it. We turned back and eventually found Ziza. Saundby had all the way been behind, as he had been delayed leaving Heliopolis by a dud magneto and tyre troubles. We were filling up as he landed. We were met by the Bristols as before and I embarked a cargo of six sucking pigs. I had a little trouble in starting my starboard engine owing to a dud starting magneto. Sergeant Cochrane ran a lead across from the other engine.

Ziza to L.G. F. I was a bit heavily loaded leaving Ziza and I hardly climbed at all. I turned after about 1,000 yards and lost height badly and seemed to be going to hit the deck again. I turned into wind, found an up dunt, and shot up about 300 feet. Saundby followed about fifteen minutes later. I made across the hills, past Kasr Kharana, south of C and the blue pools of Azrak, across the plain to D, over the D mud flats and into the basalt country. The sun was getting low and flooding the desert with a warm orange light, and the track was terribly difficult to see. Before F I lost it and circled. Meanwhile Saundby passed me. He wirelessed saying he thought we could just make H before sundown, but Roche advised landing at F, so I signalled I was going to do so. I did not land on the mud flat, as Roche said it might be wet, but just on the edge, where the "F" is ploughed. I landed all right, but nearly ran into a bad basalt boulder heap. Saundby followed, struck a bad boulder with his tailskid (which I had missed by a fluke) and smashed the skid. I taxied "Valkyrie" round and drew up by "Morpheus." The red sun had dipped below the horizon and I saw almost the most vivid colouring I have ever seen. To the west there was a line of rugged basalt hills, quite low, and vivid orchid purple. The sky was alight with pale flame greens and blues, but a hundred times brighter was a little ribbon of flame-red cloud, illumined by the departed sun. It was the most intense and palpitating colour, and I could hardly believe my eyes. Just by us was the great mud flat, and beyond it rose a flat-topped gaunt basalt hill, with gentle slopes, steepening towards the hard bare top.

We cooked our supper, during which my Primus stove, the one I bought for our expedition to the Wyre Forest, did yeoman service. The crews repaired the tailskid, working by little electric lamps long after the stars had come out and the moon was shining brightly. I had the cargo of pigs in their crates, six pigs, two in each of the three crates, unloaded and placed by the aeroplane. The inside of the hull stank of them and they had made a watery mess all over the floor.

The temperature was surprisingly warm, and I slept in my valise by the end of my wing. I slept fitfully but peacefully. I would wake sometimes and find the moon and stars had gone round. As the moon sank in the north-west a thin layer of cloud came up. The moon and stars, as you lie on your back and look at them, in the deep untroubled silence, have a character which is peculiarly fitting to the desert. They make you think of how God created the world, and how the world was before mankind wandered over its face and built cities. Before I went to sleep I saw a shooting star, which flashed with such amazing brilliance that I thought someone had fired a Very light. Early in the morning I saw a light flashing far away in the desert, and I thought it must be the headlamps of a car; but it disappeared and never came nearer. I got up at 05.20 hours and cooked up some water on my Primus. I saw a dusky figure approach (it was dark) and I thought it must be a Bedouin. I found it was Cooper who had also just got up.

L.G. F *to L.G.* V. I taxied out across the mud flat to take off, as we found by walking on it that it was quite hard. Saundby was not quite ready, so I pushed on. As soon as I got going I found that we had a following wind, and the weather report from Ramadi by W/T said it was strongest at 1,000 feet. We made a very good run. I flew the aeroplane as far as El Jid, and then had a second breakfast off tea out of my Thermos, ham, rolls and chocolate. As we were approaching the avenue through the hills at *L.G.* IX I could see afar off the two hills, one triangular and one flat-topped, through which the track passes at *L.G.* VII, and we more or less cut straight towards them. The visibility was wonderful and we could see for miles and miles. No sooner past the hills than Roche pointed out the faint pale streak on the dim horizon of the great mud flat at *L.G.* V. It must then have been nearly 50 miles off. We made straight towards it and were not deceived. Near *L.G.* VI I saw two cars in the desert drawn up a few hundred yards off the track. I wirelessed to Saundby that I was landing to re-fuel at *L.G.* V. I dropped a smoke candle and landed. The great thing was to find an avenue through the camel-thorn, which is so bad at *L.G.* V that no tyre is proof against it. I did a wiggle after touching the ground and managed to keep out of it. I taxied over to the tank and began filling up. Saundby appeared over head and we lit a smoke candle for him.

L.G. V *to Ramada.* I left before Saundby in order to push on with the Mail. As I was passing *L.G.* I after having left the Bitumen Pools on my right, I saw a D.H.9a and a Vernon in the desert with a sheerlegs. It was Flight Lieutenant Divers' D.H.9a in which he had been bringing Group Captain Brooke over to Iraq, and it was having its second new engine installed (the first one had been put in at Kantara). I rather flew into Ramadi, but made quite a good landing. I found the Overland Mail stuck there, owing to the Euphrates bridge at Fellujah having gone west in a flood. Saundby arrived soon after.

Ramadi to Hinaidi. The final stage of my 1,720 mile trip to Egypt and back. We went along very fast, followed about 10 miles behind by Saundby. There was a good wind with us and we arrived at Hinaidi at 15.05 hrs, local time. The last bit of the way after I had passed Baghdad West and the Tigris I put my nose down and opened out my engines a bit, and came in low over the Cantonment. I then turned round into wind at the far end of the aerodrome and made quite a decent landing. The total flying time of the trip was 24hrs. 57 mins., and during that time over hills and desert, from morn to pale evening, the engines ran with a steady murmur like the surge of the sea heard afar off. I felt an extraordinary affection well up in me for the craft which had borne me so faithfully and well over the gaunt hills and the vast silent spaces of the desert. Anyone who can look unmoved at an aeroplane after it has been a long run must indeed be insensitive to romance. An aeroplane home at last, with the oil dripping gently off her and the stains of travel evident about her, has something extraordinarily grand. She is the symbol of conquest, the earnest of fresh conquests to be. The wind has been singing through her canvas and taut wires; the white-hot flame driving the pistons of her engines; the sun has blazed on her through the long day; the moon looked on her through the lonely nights in the desert; and now she stands relaxed, yet majestic, with the breath of fire gone from her, resting after her great effort. She has served her master to the uttermost of her capacity, and she asks no more.

A RESCUE JOB (DECEMBER, 1924)

Hinaidi to Ramadi. I went out on a rescue job. Cudemore was down with a broken engine at *L.G.* X on the return Mail Trip. I took an engine out on my starboard wing, and the sheerlegs and engine trolley inside the hull. I was very anxious to go out on this trip to see how an engine was changed in the Blue. I was due to start at dawn, but it was foggy; and although it cleared at Hinaidi about eight o'clock, it was quite thick at Ramadi. It was pretty misty on the way out to Ramadi, and after passing the ruined tower at Aqqar Kuf I wandered a bit too much to the north, but saw the branch of the Tigris and kept south of it. Attwood was returning from Ramadi on J 6872, and said he saw me, but I never saw him. I then cut across to Fellujah and came out into rather clearer weather. I landed with rather a bounce at Ramadi. The engine on the wings makes the Vernon rather dud to fly, especially on turns. She tends to skid outward a great deal. I did not have any drift on, so I did not hurt the under carriage. Louis Paget was there waiting for me; he was to come on to *L.G.* V with me and give me petrol to carry on with, because I could take so little due to the weight of the engine and tackle.

Ramadi to L.G. V. I flew on after having a quick tiffin and a refuel at Ramadi, with Louis on "Vampire." He flew behind me on my port wing tip. The clouds were fairly low, and as the desert slowly rose up to *L.G.* V, which is about 1,200 feet high, I had to fly nearer and nearer the ground. It is an extraordinarily desolate open plain between *L.G.* IV and *L.G.* V, rising all the way, and we plugged slowly across it against a rather strong, cold north-west wind. From *L.G.* I to *L.G.* III the desert is much more red and orange, with broken lighter bits, looking like lumps of limestone. As you pass *L.G.* III it becomes flatter, darker and more mole colour with mottled grey-green vegetation (at this time of year) in curving lines, like an animal's skin Between L,G, II and *L.G.* III I could see the Euphrates stretching far up to the north-west, and the sun was catching buildings, perhaps 30 miles away. One patch of white I thought must be Hit. At last, away on the plain, I saw the dim line of the *L.G.* V mud flat. When past it I flew over the petrol dump and told Barrett to tell Goodenough to drop a smoke candle. The first one he tried was a dud, and as I was getting into position again, he dropped a second one which fell rather far away from the circle.

I made quite a fair landing and Louis landed after me. We parked for the night near the petrol dump. A few Bedou came up, but we managed to push them off. Nevertheless we arranged for two members of the crews to stay awake and walk up and down between the aeroplanes in three-hour shifts. We cooked our supper, in which my Primus again figured. Café-au-lait, stew of bully and some tinned beans I had bought, and bread and butter. We made a fire with oil and petrol in a tin and sat round it with the men talking, around us silence, darkness and the illimitable desert. I slept under the wings. Occasionally I woke up and listened to the soft tramp of the guard and watched them come round in the dim starlight once, twice, thrice—then a doze—and round again. Early in the morning dark clouds from the south-west veiled the stars and the wind began to moan a little, and the rain came:

for about three-quarters of an hour. I listened to the drip-drip on the planes. Sometimes it sounded like the distant rumble of an army marching. Just before the light the rain stopped. The dawn came ghostly white, then amber, warming to orange, then diminuendo to sullen orange grey, for the clouds were again in the ascendant. We got up, cooked our breakfast and prepared to trek again, Louis going home eastwards, I towards the west, where the clouds looked dark and threatening

L.G. V *to Point near L.G.* VI. I flew along westwards, and soon the clouds came down and it began to rain, and little flecks of rain came all over my windscreen. I came lower and lower in order to see the track, which is ordinarily very clear here: and lucky for me it was so. I thought I ought to be approaching *L.G.* VI and was wondering if I had missed it, when on the rising ground ahead I saw what I judged to be a solid wall of cloud festooned to the desert. I turned back, but was anxious to land so as not to have to retrace my steps all the way back to *L.G.* V. So I turned again to what I thought was into wind, and landed just across the track. I bounced rather badly; from that height with a heavy load you rather tend to drop out of the air, and it takes some little time to get into a proper glide. The ground was good. I carried away my aerial, as I did not give Goater time to wind in. We set up the ground W/T station, but could not get any messages through owing to the rain. Before I landed I had noticed the black specks of numerous goat-hide Arab tents on the plain.

Soon afterwards forty Bedou came up, little figures far away, getting larger and larger. It left off raining and just drizzled. I dared not take off because the clouds seemed still to be nearly down to the ground to westward.

These Arabs had not got rifles, but all had very serviceable-looking knives in their belts. They were wearing Shaffias round their heads. Some of these are very heavy, and the Arabs sometimes wrap their faces right up, for example, when it rains. The Shaffia appears to be held on by a sort of black cord fastened round the head. Then they have enormously thick and coarse Abbas, and sometimes a goatskin garment underneath, with the hair inwards. Some of them started to be a nuisance, poking the aeroplane about. We gave them cigarettes and matches, although most of them did not appear to know how to strike a match. But they pocketed a box and continually made signs for more! They would insist on smoking underneath the engines, and it was a terrible job to keep them off. But they seemed very friendly and grinned, showing large numbers of teeth. They moved about in a funny cat-like way. The real desert Bedouin is unlike the man you see in Baghdad.

By and by the Sheikh rode up, a handsome young fellow with an incipient beard, I should judge about twenty-five years of age.[5] The rest seemed to be in considerable awe of him and murmured, "Sheikh! Sheikh!" I went up to him, leaving Barrett to guard the door of the Vernon, and said in my best Arabic, "Salaam Aleikum," "Peace be on you". He replied without hesitating, "W'aleikum es Salaam," "And on you be peace". He had a sort of right-hand man with him. I found this man could read Arabic. He had a cigarette lighter, the sort with an orange cord. I had a sheet of paper with a certain number of sentences written in English and Arabic So I got this out and induced him to read to me, so that I could learn how to pronounce the words. Soon I was getting on famously and they understood me when I said "Mam-noon," "Thank you," to them

Meanwhile I was dishing out cigarettes and matches—I had a box of fifty "Gold Flake" in readiness and Barrett, my second pilot, had fifty "Players." I then thought I would draw pictures of things I wanted to know, and ask the Sheikh's Grand Vizir to tell me the names of them; so I drew the sun, moon, and stars, and he told me what they were in Arabic. I copied them down as nearly phonetically as I could. He also told me all the numbers, by means of finger signs, the names of his clothes, limbs, parts of the face, and some animals. I got down a list of about fifty words. They wanted to know where I had come from, so I said "Baghdad." They pronounced it something like "B'gerd'd." I then mentioned Fahad Beg and asked if he was by the Wadi Hauran (near El Jid), and they said he was. However, the political officer at Ramadi told me afterwards that he had information that F. B. was about four days away in the Blue from there. In Switzerland you measure journeys by hours. In the desert by days. It gives an idea of the space. Then I drew the Sheikh a picture of his horse and the Grand Vizir a portrait of himself, and they were very pleased.

Meanwhile I had to keep an eye on "Valkyrie" to see that the Arabs were not interfering with the aeroplane. I did the trick of burning a match under my fingers and they thought that was rather wizardly. I then produced bully beef and ate a little before offering it. They were a bit doubtful of this. Perhaps they thought it was bacon. But they said "Jamal," which means camel. So I drew a picture of a cow on a piece of paper, and when I put the horns in they suddenly understood and laughed. However, they did not eat much. Then I dished out ration biscuits, being careful to give the Sheikh two, whereas to the others I gave only one each. They ate these. There were several children, and they fairly gulped down biscuit. Two children had a rather nice dog, a little like a small

VALKYRIE AND VESUVIUS ON THE UPLAND OF THE WINDS

greyhound. They said "Saluki," but I do not suppose it was a pure-bred one. It had a little blanket coat. By this time the Arabs were fast friends with us. They wanted us to go and have a meal with them, but I politely refused, saying the "Tiara" (aeroplane) could not wait.

After staying just over three hours it cleared up sufficiently for us to get off. The Arabs were quite useful; they helped us to pull the propeller round. They were overjoyed when the engines started, and grinned all over. When we wanted to take off they all stood back in a most orderly manner.

Point near L.G. VI *to L.G.* X. I took off and as soon as I rose off the ground I saw the blue serrated hills over the brow of the rising ground. The sun came out, and everything looked more cheery. I flew along with the limestone hills dotting the plain on my left, round the curve of the hills to *L.G.* VII, from whence I could see another black storm gathering over *L.G.* 8. Far in the distance I could see the triangular and flat-topped hills through which the track passes on the way to 8, but as I approached them, they got fainter in the grey gloom. Then on came the rain; but I could see that it was clear to right and left. When I was feeling rather miserable, a bit of rainbow suddenly leaped up out of the desert on my right: God's promise! And I plunged on more cheerfully; soon after I passed between the two hills, which I call Cain and Abel, and emerged from the shower and saw the hills about the Wadi Hauran, which I shortly passed over.

I swung round the curve, left the car track which goes to Aleppo and turned south-west, telling Barrett to keep a sharp look-out for Cudemore's Vernon. After about quarter of an hour he touched me on the elbow, and sure enough there it was. As I approached I saw he had put out a "T" on which I landed, again, carrying away my aerial, which was very stupid. It was a bare upland plateau, and the wind was blowing sharp and cold with distant cumulo-nimbus in the west; and cold biting showers of rain swept across this barren upland. Nevertheless, we set to work to dismount the engine from "Valkyrie" and put it into "Vesuvius," Cudemore's Vernon; and by evening it was nearly done. We cooked our supper and sat round a petrol fire. Then I turned in under the planes of "Valkyrie." Soon the rain set in, and it rained steadily till about 5a.m. in the morning. I pulled my valise cover over my head and snuggled down to get what sleep I could, under these somewhat uncomfortable conditions. With the dawn the rain gradually abated. My night's sleep was coloured by the drip-drop of the rain and the moan of the desert wind in the planes and wires. My feet were in a puddle, and I kept wriggling round so as to try and shift my valise into the driest or least damp spot! Good old valise! I slept in you the night before Loos.

Corporal Goodenough brought me—no, it was Corporal Searle—brought me hot coffee in bed(!). I then got up and we finished Cudemore's engine, and started him up. The clouds gradually cleared, but the wind blew strongly from the north-west to help us home.

L.G. X *to L.G.* V. I had to wait about twenty-five minutes for Cudemore to start, for apparently after I started he discovered a broken clip on his water piping. When he took off, I cut straight across towards Cain and Abel by way of the Wadi Hauran. We had a rattling breeze abaft the beam and it was pretty bumpy. Between *L.G.* VI and V I saw two cars dashing along the track; I dived down and swooped past them. I approached *L.G.* V again, and was forced to get Barrett to fire a Very light on to the ground, because my smoke candles were dud. I landed and taxied to the tank. Cudemore passed over in "Vesuvius," but appeared to change his mind and came back and landed. We both filled up and I pushed off first.

L.G. V *to Ramadi.* We flew off across the mud flat and went rattling down the track making 86 mph ground speed. I let Barrett fly. After three-quarters of an hour or so the dim line of the Euphrates appeared on the horizon The wind was bitterly cold. We passed over the Bitumen Pools and sailed into Ramadi about 3 p.m. I made a fairly decent landing, though I rather flew in. I got Sergeant Pitt to get us tiffin. Cudemore arrived and we refuelled. He took off, but just as I was taxying out, my little copper overflow pipe from the starboard radiator broke in half, and I had to stop the engine while Goodenough jumped out to fix it up. Meanwhile Abbas, one of the boys at Ramadi, came running out across the aerodrome with a negative weather report from Hinaidi. So I decided to stay the night. Barrett and I went to a Christmas-party at the Administrative Inspector's house at Ramadi. Sergeant Pitt and his men were there; two Americans, a doctor and his wife, and Dr. Wakefield, a lady doctor and aunt of Wakefield, the Rugger player, who were motoring. We played charades with great vim, and some embarrassment to me.

Ramadi to Point near Police Post (Khan Nukhta). I set off in fairly good weather, but with sheets of grey stratus flung across the sky. As I approached Fellujah I had to glide right down to fly under a rain shower, and I saw the sinuous bends of the Euphrates, glimmering silver and gold in the rim beyond; and the distant grey waste of Aqqar Kuf on the far horizon. After about 5 miles I came through it; and as I was approaching the jeel by the police post my port engine started packing up. I tried her on each magneto with no avail. I turned, glided down into wind, picked a flat-looking spot which appeared to be dry and landed successfully. My first forced landing. We put up our ground W/T station and signalled to Hinaidi. The police corporal, Corporal Abbas, rode out from the post, and I got him to fetch a native policeman; both of them helped us and kept off the inquisitive Bedou who appeared. Two, a Sheikh and another, were allowed to squat down and look on. We took down the carburettors and emptied much mutty[6] and water from them. We had a terrible job with them, as my fitter had apparently left some essential spanners out of the kit. I heated a spanner up on my faithful Primus stove and we filed it out to fit. We started up and the engine ran up O.K. Nairn turned up with two cars—we were just by the track, although I did not realize it until after I had landed. The cars were mud-covered up to the roof, and they thought that one had broken a spring and the other had had its steering wrenched out of truth by the awful state of the track between there and Baghdad. However, they had a rough look at them and passed them as O K. Nairn had passed Louis and me at *L.G.* V on 23.12.24, on his way into Baghdad with these same two cars.

Point near Police Post to Hinaidi. And so home! The port engine ran O.K. for a few minutes and then started vibrating again. I hastily looked round for places on which to land, and they looked remarkably damp and intersected with irrigation ditches. So I decided to push on if it could possibly be done. I was on tenter-hooks the whole time, wondering how long the engine would keep going. But it took me in. I landed at the far side of Hinaidi, as it looked drier there, and made a good landing. When I had taxied in I found that the intake pipe to the port engine single carburettor was all lolling over on one side, having shaken loose with the vibration. Nevertheless, I had got back after a most interesting, if arduous trip. And "Valkyrie" was still whole and sound! There is a tremendous fascination about these trips into the "Blue," which it is easier to enjoy than to describe. I think it is the communion with nature absolutely unspoiled.

1. No.4 Flying Training School.

2. W/T means Wireless.

3. Works and Buildings.

4. Nickname for a ridge on the south side of the aerodrome.

5. I believe he was Aftan ibn Sharqi, Sheikh of the Albu Mahal section of the Dulaim tribe.

6. Slang name for Iraq mud.

CHAPTER VII

FLIGHTS BY NIGHT AND IN STORMS

THREE FLIGHTS TO RAMADI, RETURNING BY NIGHT (JANUARY, 1925)

I

Hinaidi to Ramadi. I was settling down in my quarters for a quiet Wednesday afternoon, when we suddenly had a message to say that the Air Vice-Marshal was probably down somewhere between *L.G.* R and Ramadi, and someone was to go to Ramadi at once, and proceed on at dawn. Within an hour and a half of receiving the message I was in the air heading for Ramadi. I had had to fill up and get my desert equipment on board, and get accumulators for my W/T and lighting arrangements. We made a good trip, and it was just getting dim when we landed. I could see Lake Habbaniyah from about 50 miles away, when I was flying over the police post at Khan Nukhta. I had to be careful, when coming in to Ramadi, to avoid the W/T mast, as the sun had dropped below the horizon in a blaze of orange-red light, cutting the rim of the desert sharply, and had left a rapidly thickening twilight. I had a good meal at Ramadi and a chat with Captain Loder, the police officer, who dropped in. We passed a D.H. 9a just by Fellujah. This turned out to be the A.V.M.'s aeroplane, and we received a W/T message while in the air that we could return to Hinaidi the following morning. So I wirelessed for permission to return that night, as there was a nearly full moon. At about 19.30 hrs the approval came through.

Ramadi to Hinaidi. My first cross-country at night. I got Sergeant Pitt to put out some improvised flares, and I wirelessed for flares at Hinaidi, and the lighthouse, which we had just got going; or if not, rockets. It was a beautiful night, and bright milky white moon light. "Valkyrie" looked a grey fleeting shadow close to the little serai at Ramadi. I got in and tested a Holt wing-tip flare, which burnt with a bright orange light, and the smoke hung in heavy brown wreaths against the blue night. I then tested the lights. When I had run up the engines, I was waving the chocks[1] away and suddenly felt a blow on the first finger of my right hand! I had touched the starboard propeller! How I did not lose my finger I simply cannot imagine. It was luck! The propeller must have just grazed it.

I took off up the hill. The visibility was not good low down, owing to the smoke hanging about from the flare I had tested. But I soon mounted above it into the moonlight and saw the winding shadowy rivers. I steered by Arcturus (I believe), the star low in the eastern horizon to which the three stars in Orion's Belt point. I got my W/T working and, when over Fellujah, I saw a faint pinpoint of light glow like a star above the horizon. The first rocket at Hinaidi! About 50 miles away yet. So I plunged on through the greyness more confidently, crossing from the Euphrates towards Khan Nukhta and Aqqar Kuf. In places I could faintly see the track like a thin shadowy line. Every ten minutes or so a rocket glowed in the sky, and seemed to hang stationary for a long time. About 20 miles away I saw the lights of Baghdad, and to the right the lights of Hinaidi. As I came on, I saw an Aldis lamp flash out from the flare line towards me. I fired a green Very light to ask permission to land, and almost immediately a green one was fired from the flares. I flew round and landed. I flattened out a bit too violently, and dropped very slightly, but nothing to worry about. It is lovely flying cross-country on a moonlight night, all black, grey, green and silver; the quiet stars, and the ghostly desert, and the rivers with the faint golden glimmer of the moon on them, shining on some distant reach. And the friendly rockets to guide you home, as some ship far out at sea sees a beacon light, and knows that friends are there.

II

Hinaidi to Ramadi. I flew over to Ramadi in order to do a night flight back on a dark night. It was bumpy and cold, with that inhospitable veiled brightness that is frequently characteristic of squally weather. Nevertheless the sun shone brightly enough. I watched the "dunt indicator" and it did some most astonishing rises and falls as the bumps gripped "Valkyrie" and rocked her passionately to and fro, caught her up, and let her fall viciously. I had a strong headwind. Just past Fellujah my port oil pressure suddenly fell from 60 pounds to 45 pounds; so I kept over the best possible ground and worked round the north of the Euphrates, contrary to my usual custom. I saw two Vernons on Ramadi; Louis Paget's and Banting's. Louis was on the Mail and held up with engine trouble, and Banting, who was to have come with me, had flown over in the morning to take a radiator stay to Louis. I also took over some new carburettor jets. I made an odd landing; I seemed to flatten out all right, but I hit the ground rather a crack and stayed there, hardly running at all. Owing to the strong gusty wind, I was left in ignorance whether I had too much speed or too little. Louis asked me whether my second pilot or I had landed! I went in, and Barrett, Louis and I had tea off poached eggs and potatoes.

Ramadi to Hinaidi. I waited till dark, and just after sunset clouds appeared like a dark shadow against the bright western glow, half covered it and then veiled the nascent stars, nearly over to the eastern horizon. With the coming of the clouds the wind had changed to south. I got Sergeant Pitt to haul up a hurricane lamp on one of the wireless masts, in case I had to land again with dud oil pressure. I had told Sturman to clean the port oil filter; and as it turned out that cured the trouble. Captain Loder turned up as usual, and Uncle Lees. It appeared that the former's driver, one Schultz, had cut his hand and got mild poisoning. I sent for him and suggested taking him back. He suddenly got well! He evidently did not relish the thought of a nocturnal passage. Corporal Searle said there was a "short" somewhere in the lighting system; however, the lights worked O.K. I think he loves to think there is something wrong at the last moment! I tested a Holt wing-tip flare; and by the time I ran up it was black dark. I taxied out, Barrett using the Aldis lamp to see by. I found Pitt had placed the pilot flare about 50 yards from the end flare; and it looked a very small gap to dive through. When I got off I could hardly see a thing, because the clouds made it so dark. I then turned east with a little south in it, to counteract the northerly drift, and pushed on into the seemingly impenetrable blackness.

I must confess to feeling a little frightened, it looked so hopeless ahead. Yet I knew it was not so, and my compass had been swung the day before, and it would surely guide me. Here and there, as I strained my eyes to see, I caught sight of lonely lights: probably the fires of wandering Bedou. For a moment or two I saw lights reflected in water, and. I knew I must be crossing the river. Then onwards and eastwards for about twenty minutes, when in the eastern night sky I caught a faint glimmer, like a pale bar in the obscurity surely the lights of Baghdad. Then I saw on my right the lights of the village before Fellujah, and then those of Fellujah itself, which were less conspicuous. I made out that I was about 6 miles north of Fellujah, which was just about right. I wirelessed "J 7134 O.K. passing Fellujah." Gradually, but oh so gradually, the lights of Baghdad got brighter and more definite; and then appeared the lights of Hinaidi, and every now and then a friendly rocket cut the sky, hung and twinkled ere it faded, and left the darkness blacker than ever. I peered down, shading my eye with my hand from the livid glare of the flaming exhaust to see if I could make out whether I was flying over the cultivation; I thought I was, so I worked round a little south-wards to try and get over the open ground. Then I saw the yellow twinkle of the flares; and just as I was passing Baghdad and watching the lights spangling the Tigris, a rocket shot up just in front of me, so it looked, leaving a little trail of golden dust. It looked wonderful, a bright messenger indeed. I flew round while Barrett got to work with the Aldis lamp and asked if there were any other aircraft up. "No," was the reply, so I circled out over the desert to land. It was very dark looking back towards Ramadi, although just before I reached Baghdad I had emerged from the cloud canopy, and saw Orion's Belt and Arcturus. I made a beautiful landing just close to No. 1 Flare, much to my gratification. I found that Banting had not started.

III

Hinaidi to Ramadi. I had arranged a night flying practice in combination with 70 Squadron and No. 4 Armoured Car Company. Three of 70's aircraft were to fly over to Ramadi in the afternoon, and fly back after dark. Maitland and Banting were to fly over to Ramadi after dark and return. Banting, whom I accompanied as second pilot, was to land at Ramadi; and Maitland was to take Wing Commander Wynn as second pilot and return without landing. No. 4 A.C. Company was to send three armoured cars and find a decent landing ground near Fellujah. Underhill and Embry, in "Morpheus," J 7138, flew over to Ramadi in the morning with some Works and Buildings officials, and on their way back dropped a copy of my orders for the show on the landing ground by the armoured cars. Summers then flew over with flares and landed at Fellujah in the afternoon and had the flares all ready.

Banting and I left punctually at 19.00 hrs. Clouds had blown up and we had had one or two spots of rain and the half-moon was shining mistily through high drifting alto-cumulus. But when we got into the air the weather improved, although there was a good deal of alto-cumulus and a thin lower layer of transparent stratus. As we passed Aqqar Kuf one Vernon of 70 Squadron passed just above us on our starboard bow. I could see her navigation lights a long way away. I winked ours, but got no answer. About half-way to Fellujah a second Vernon of 70 Squadron passed over us. Then we saw the flares burning near Fellujah and could not make out why they had been lit. It turned out afterwards that Quintus Studd, who was flying with Roche, dropped a Michelin flare[2] over Fellujah, and Summers thought it was us landing with a Holt flare on! So he hastily lighted the flares. As we passed by we signalled with our Aldis, but the communication was not very good owing to the W/T operator not training the lamp well. We pushed on through the soft warm night. It was very warm considering how cold it had been a day or two before. We kept as much as possible over the good ground to the north of the Euphrates.

Ramadi to Fellujah. We took off Ramadi and flew back towards Fellujah. As we passed along the river we came into view of the flares burning there. I asked Banting if he was game to land by the armoured cars, and he said he was. We spent some time signalling to them with the Aldis lamp, announcing that we wished to land, and then I fired a red light. Banting did rather a sharp turn coming in to land from the direction of the town of Fellujah, and I do not think he was properly off the turn when he came to flatten out. We hit with a pretty bad bounce and a certain amount of drift; but nothing broken! We taxied round and saw the dim outlines of the armoured cars. We spoke to Summers, who said he would come on directly we had left. We turned round and took off again into the obscurity.

Fellujali to Hinaidi. We had brought Connolly back with us from Ramadi. We had a nice comfortable flight back. I dozed for a little bit, as I was rather tired; and tucked my head away on my hand, resting on the left-hand side of the cockpit. We saw the lights of Baghdad almost immediately we got any height above Fellujah. Banting made a nice landing at Hinaidi, and we found Horrex waiting for us at the flares.

MY SECOND MAIL TRIP (FEBRUARY, 1925)

A final test before the Mail Trip. Everything was in fine order. It was a wonderfully clear day, and we climbed up through the sunlight to 5,000 feet. It felt quite strange being so high over Hinaidi! The ruin of Aqqar Kuf looked quite close; and I actually thought I could see Lake Habbaniyah, 50 miles away. At least, where it should be, there was a distinct softening of the horizon. The

Pusht-i-Kuh looked glorious, the snow-capped ridges glimmering faintly in the sunlight. I saw much more of it than I had ever seen before; and specially up to the north-east I saw faint blue rugged mountains standing up out of the plain. This may have been the southern hills of the Jebel Hamrin.

Hinaidi to Ramadi. The first stage of the Mail Trip. It was a gorgeous warm afternoon. Two No. 216 Squadron Vimys piloted by Mahon and Cox came with me. They were to take half the Mail each. My crew insisted on taxying out to the starting position with me, except Sturman. I photographed them in front of the aeroplane when we were waiting out on the aerodrome. I got off to time; but Mahon had trouble and taxied out late. I circled round once or twice until both the Vimys had got off. Then I set out for Ramadi. At Aqqar Kuf Mahon turned back, although I did not see this and went on signalling both Vimys O.K. I overshot a bit coming in to Ramadi, and for one terrible moment thought I would overrun and end up in the rough stuff. As it was I made quite a good landing in towards the serai, but swung on the ground intentionally, first one way and then the other, to shorten my run.

Ramadi to Point 5 miles west of L.G. J. We got up at Ramadi at 4.30 a.m. local time and had breakfast at 5a.m. It was still dark. When I went to the door I heard the soft hiss of rain. What more uncomfortable and depressing prospect than to get up in the dark with 530 miles in front of you, and to find dark clouds obscuring the stars, and the drip-drip of rain? Enough to daunt the stoutest heart! It was only on my arrival at Ramadi the previous evening that I discovered Mahon had turned back. Embry and Underhill then came on in Morpheus bringing Mahon's mail, which they handed to me. Just as the winter dusk was falling, a faint whir was heard and Mahon's Vimy appeared mistily out of a sky turning to soft shades of violet grey. Embry and Underhill took off with flares and flew back to Hinaidi in the dark.

It did not freeze in the night, but we had let our water out of the radiators, just in case. The Vimys got started up and left before I did, at 7.30 a.m. local time. My port engine turned stubborn. I tried my Heath Robinson shock absorber starting device,[3] but it pulled the pickets out of the ground. I finally left at 8 a.m. local time. I was heavily loaded with three passengers and the confidential Mail, so had to fly round low. It had just stopped raining, but the visibility was bad, and the whole of the eastern sky was hung with dripping clouds. Gleams of sunlight were in the west. I flew round and picked up what I thought was the track, and followed it. My compass showed S.W., instead of W., as it should have done; but considering it had been put in "Valkyrie"[4] the previous day and I had not had time to have it swung, I was doubtful of it. After about twenty minutes I expected the Bitumen Pools to appear, but they did not. I had an idea that Lake Habbaniyah was too close on my left; but the track I was following was a well-worn car track and I never thought there could be two leading from Ramadi, for I had never noticed a junction in previous flights. Then I turned back along the track and flew for about ten minutes. It looked all right, however, and I again turned. I was really getting very worried by this time and was obsessed by uneasiness, because I was wasting valuable time and petrol. Phillips, an old Mail pilot of 70 Squadron, who had been over the track a number of times, sent me a note: "Are we on the right track?" I decided to fly on till I struck some feature I knew was definitely strange; and I soon found one: two large brown patches on either side of this track, which I had mistaken in the distance and in the bad light for the Bitumen Pools. Then I turned and flew all the way back to Ramadi, which lay in front of a bank of gloom. I found where I had gone wrong, about 2 miles from Ramadi. There were two tracks branching. Amazing that I had never noticed this! It was 9.00 a.m. local time. An hour's petrol wasted through a stupid mistake. If only I had had my well-tested compass, which had broken its springs, I should have trusted it and turned back earlier.

Then I set out on the right track and soon came into bright sunlight. I found I had a following wind, and was making 90 m.p.h. ground speed. I passed *L.G.* V in an hour and eighteen minutes. I heard that the two Vimys had passed *L.G.* IX an hour and a half ahead of me. I passed *L.G.* IX at 11.12 local time, and turned round the corner into the "Kingdom of What Wasn't," and along "Fickle Furlong." The wind at this time had turned against me and I was now making under 60 m.p.h. ground speed. Between *L.G.* N and *L.G.* M I had a W/T message to say that the weather at Ziza and Amman was negative, that the detachment was unable to reach Ziza and a convoy would be at *L.G.* D with petrol. I should have to land at *L.G.* D in any case as I had wasted petrol by getting lost. About this time I saw low down a little speck going ahead, which turned out to be one Vimy. What had happened to the other? As we went on I gradually overhauled it. The weather was getting very dirty again, and the northern sky was swept with storms, with great ladders of inky rain, driving across the "Upland of the Winds." It was terrifically squally and bumpy, and my shoulders were beginning to ache from battling with the controls. The Vimy was flying very erratically, up and down and from side to side; and owing to the necessity of keeping near the track in order not to lose sight of it, I could not pass outside, neither could I pass inside, neither could

I cross over, as one cannot see over the left-hand side, if one is sitting on the right. I climbed over the top of him. I was wondering all the time whether it was Mahon or Cox.

At *L.G.* L I was leading, and a little after we had passed J, Phillips sent forward a note: "Vimy down." In case he had the other half of the Mail I turned back at once, and scanned the bare desert, darkened with the storm. I nearly missed him as he was about one and a half miles south of the track However, I flew over to him and he lit a smoke candle, into the smoke of which I landed, with a bad bounce, just six hours after I had left Ramadi. As I flew over him I saw his port propeller still revolving, and wondered why his starboard one had stopped. When I landed and taxied to him, "Valkyrie" rocked in the squall, which made the control wheel rip over from side to side as the gusts struck the ailerons, and nearly wrenched it out of my hands. I then found the truth. Cox came over to me with a face the length of the Mail Trip, and told me the gears of his port engine had completely stripped and the gear casting had bulged out the radiator, which was all that was holding it from falling completely off. I quickly took over the rest of the Mail, gave him a bottle of whisky, and took 30 gallons of his petrol, as we had such a headwind I was doubtful even of making *L.G.* D, which was 79 miles away. I started off at 4.00 p.m. local time, and sent a long message asking for a new engine for Cox.

Point 5 miles west of L.G. J *to L.G.* D. "Valkyrie" had been so shocked at the Vimy's gear stripping that almost at the moment Phillips noticed the Vimy go down he saw my front port engine bay long landing wire snap off at the top and lie down over the port engine. When I landed by Cox I found out what had happened to the two Vimys. Cox had landed at O with valve trouble, and Mahon had landed with him. This is how I caught them up. Mahon only waited for Cox to get his engines running again and then pushed on, and got so far ahead that of course he never saw him go down, after I had caught up and passed Cox. This was why I saw only one Vimy instead of two. As a matter of fact Phillips told me afterwards that he had actually seen two tracks of dust at O when we were about passing P. This must have been the two Vimys taking off. I was sitting in front with a much better view and never saw them. Between H and G, just after I had entered the Basalt country, "The Land of Conjecture," I sent a message asking for a spare landing wire or failing this some cable, to be ready at Ziza when I arrived.

When I left Cox, I was doubtful if I should ever get through to D that day, as the whole northern sky was ink, and even where we were heavy drops of rain were beginning to hit the planes as the desert wind moaned and howled through the wires. The southern sky was bright, with the unnatural brightness of a stormy day. But at any moment might not the storm spread southwards and envelop the landscape with a black pall? And if I were caught in the "Land of Conjecture" in weather like this I should never see the track. Looking in the direction I had to go, I saw the track appearing to run along the southern fringe of the blackness; and as it turned out, I was able to fly just in the clear weather, with the storm on my right hung like a dark and tragic tapestry in the troubled heavens. I wound my way through the gaunt basalt bills, following the track up and round wadis, along the whale-backs of dark hills, in and out like a maze. If one were lost in the "Land of Conjecture" it would be like a nightmare. One looks and is sure that the track runs down a certain wadi, or round a certain hill, and looking again, one sees a dozen wadis the same The features of the land repeat themselves again and again with maddening persistence, and trick the eye and mind. There is something weirdly uncanny about this and country, the kingdom of lava, ordered and patterned by the eruptions of the times of long ago.

After we had passed over the kidney-shaped mud flat at F I asked Barrett to get out our afternoon tea biscuits and the tea-filled Thermos, for it was more or less tea-time. And as we went along over the blackened hills we consumed afternoon tea. On the outside of the box there was a picture of two ladies of the eighties or nineties with waists and mutton-chop sleeves having tea in a drawing-room! It seemed so incongruous eating these dainty biscuits in such a situation. At about 5.00 p.m. local time we passed into the western purlieus of the "Land of Conjecture" and wound across the undulating boulder-strewn plain towards D. As I approached D I saw a Vimy on the ground and a group of cars. This was Mahon, who had landed some time before. I circled round and landed, being very careful to avoid the famous camel-thorn. Flight Lieutenant Moore, in charge of the armoured car detachment that had come to meet us, was most energetic and considerate. I slept underneath a bivouac rigged on to the side of a desert tender. Once or twice I woke up in the night and looked out, and the moon was shining brightly, and the Vimy and the Vernon were there, as in a dream, in the milk-white light. I heard the footfalls of the armed sentry echoing through my dreams. When we woke next morning, low clouds were again blowing up from the west, and it looked like rain. We heard that Ziza was fit, so pushed on.

L.G. D *to Ziza*. I went on ahead of Mahon. I broke out of the wadi N.W. of D out on to the "Plain of Sorrows," and although the sky was brimful of broken rainy cumulus cloud, with, it must be admitted, patches of doubtful sunshine, almost immediately I saw the blue pool at Azrak. I went along the track south of it, came to the place where the short cut made by the armoured cars goes on, but decided not to follow it, as it did not look very distinct. The recent rains had in many places almost obliterated the track if seen in certain lights. As long as the light was more or less towards you, the track reflected it and showed up. If you were flying with the light behind you, the track became evanescent and merged in the desert. I turned up northwards to the pool, the finest duck-shooting area in this part of the world, and passed the second short-circuiting loop, as this also looked indistinct.

The ground here is covered with tracks made by armoured cars and shooting parties, and is most confusing. I hoped to find the track as it left the landing ground next to the marsh at C. I not only failed to see the ploughed C, but also where the track left. I turned round and saw the Vimy in the far distance flying west. I decided to risk abandoning the track and I flew west by compass, hoping to see Kasr Kharana. Moore had told me that the patch of ground north of Kasr Kharana was excellent to land on, but that Kasr Kharana itself was a gruesome place, as the Bedou were always putting dead bodies in it. I pushed along over the undulating hills, with a plain on my left, and could see the Jebel Mugher in the far distance underneath an awning of clouds. I was considerably worried, as I knew I was risking a certain amount in leaving the track. Then came a flash of sunshine which all of a sudden picked out Kasr Kharana from the dark hills, and gave me my direction. I passed it and toiled slowly up against the wind, over the Jebel Mugher where the track goes over it and drops down, away to Amman. There is a ruin on top of the hills here and a square reservoir in a sort of basin on the eastern slope. I found the plough track running S.W. which took me to Ziza, where I landed at 9.40 a.m.

Ziza to Heizopolis. We filled up at Ziza. I filled my tanks bung full, as it seemed probable that there would be a colossal headwind, and that the customary five hours' allowance would be insufficient. I was also a bit doubtful of my petrol pumps being able to empty the bottom tank entirely The clouds looked appallingly low over the Judæan Hills, and I was doubtful if we should ever get through at all. However, two Bristols from No. 14 Squadron had flown over from Ramleh. We decided to fly to the hills and have a look, and turn back if it was impossible. I was terribly heavily loaded, now having all the Mail, three passengers and full petrol. I took off into the strong wind marvellously and "Valkyrie" put forth her strength to good purpose.

THE PLAIN OF MOAB
ZIZA STATION IN MIDDLE DISTANCE. JUDÆAN HILLS ON SKYLINE

When we were at Ziza, I had walked up to the aeroplanes from the little station with Flight Lieutenant Russell, the M.O.[5] who was one of my passengers; and we had remarked that if one looked north the country might be Salisbury Plain. There was a very faint green crop of grass all over Ziza. You hardly noticed it if you looked straight down at the ground, but looked at in perspective, it altered the tone and colour of the whole landscape. Looking north-west, I remarked that it might be a piece of Devonshire.

The clouds were so thick that I could not from Ziza see the gap in the hills which lies on the Southern Route where the ravine breaks into the Dead Sea. I went by compass and sped over the hills, not climbing very much as I was so heavy. Here the clouds appeared to be 3,500 to 4,000 feet, giving not too much air room over the hill tops. I came to an escarpment which obviously fell away into a mighty gorge. I thought at the bottom I should see the Dead Sea. The sun shone on the far wall of the gorge, making it look faint in the shadowy light. I saw the great rocks towering pitilessly up, layer upon layer; the naked fissures and strata making them look like a giant's causeway. And when I looked over, behold, no water. This shook me. Then, away on my right I just caught a glimpse, low down in an opening of the hills, of that unmistakable hushed blue, indescribably soft and dreamlike, of the Dead Sea. So I turned towards it with the gorge sinking away into its deeps on my left. The north wind must have blown me far too much south. I got all my directions mixed up, and felt sure I must be flying north to reach the Dead Sea, when in reality I was flying

WADI SEIL EL MOJEB (RIVER ARNON)
LOOKING TOWARDS THE DEAD SEA

west; and the worst of it was, that my error would keep me half an hour longer than I need have been over these terrible hills.

As I flew towards the water the gorge side rose steadily, and there was less and less room between the ridge and the clouds, wisps of which began to float past my wings. The clouds wreathed and floated like vast ethereal draperies round the gaunt bodies of the hills, and the wind thundered through the echoing heavens, and rushed in and out of the chasms. The hills which seemed to surround and grip me on all sides seemed like some vast phantasm I hardly felt they could be real At last I came to the end of the ridge, which narrowed to a knife-edge, more or less made by the gorge on my left, and the ravine I should have struck had my compass course been calculated rightly in the first place. I opened the engines full out, and "Valkyrie" did her utmost. But it was almost too much for her, with her maximum load. I felt her sink, sucked down by the awful down current which curled over the end of the ridge. The engines were straining, and "Valkyrie" was tossed about like a midge, a plaything of the forces of nature. I gripped the controls convulsively as the gusts struck and buffeted her. The engines kept racing, as the propellers failed to grip the turbulent air. If even one dropped revolutions I must surely be into the rocks. I was only about 300 feet above them. On the right towered up the "Vision of Israel," a gaunt silhouette whose top was lost in racing cloud. On the left was "Jehovah's Rest," where perhaps God rested the seventh day when He had made the world. I seemed to be making hardly any headway at all, and the strain was awful. Once over the gnarled head of the ridge I looked down into the great jagged pit. Step upon step of twisted rock, down, down, down, as it seemed for ever. To go down into that pit would be to go down into hell itself. I looked round hopelessly for some place to land on, if an engine failed; and there was none. Clouds came down, and I had to keep throttling down to dive below them. And whenever a cloud blurred my vision, I wondered if it hid a rock.

How long I struggled over that pit I do not know. It may have been ten minutes. It seemed time ever-lasting. I sweated in a sort of desperate agony. And the Vimy staggered on behind, following my trail. "Valkyrie," child of the storm, came out at last over the Dead Sea, and I looked down and saw the little fringe of white foam beating on the rocks, 3,000 feet below, and flew along to the left of the peninsula. At last I could go down there with a reasonable chance of landing. There was a strong headwind blowing from the Mediterranean, and I had still to cross the ridge of hills to the west of the Dead Sea. I seemed to hang poised over them for an age. I steered a compass course for Beersheba, and when I saw it, it was some way on my left. I had had a message asking for my position, and I gave it. I was relieved to see Beersheba aerodrome. It was very cloudy, and I had to keep gliding down to get out of the clouds. I could now see the long line of the sea and made for the coast. Mahon had fallen behind; we last saw him over Beersheba. I sent a message back that we would like tea on the "conning bridge" at 4.00 p.m. The weather was now clearing, and the cumulus lifted till its base was about 4,000 feet. It was misty looking into the sun, and as I flew along the coast past Moseifig and towards Kantara I climbed to 5,000 feet to get out of the bumps. Even then I had not risen above the tops of the cumulus to cloud, and I could see very little.

The Vimy now came up, and as we approached Kantara, Mahon must have opened his throttle wide, as he shot ahead and left us. We flew down the fresh water canal, and along the strip of cultivation towards Tel el Kebir, and then down the last lap. Looking ahead, it was so hazy that one could hardly see anything. I went by the cultivation on my right. About opposite Bilbeis we

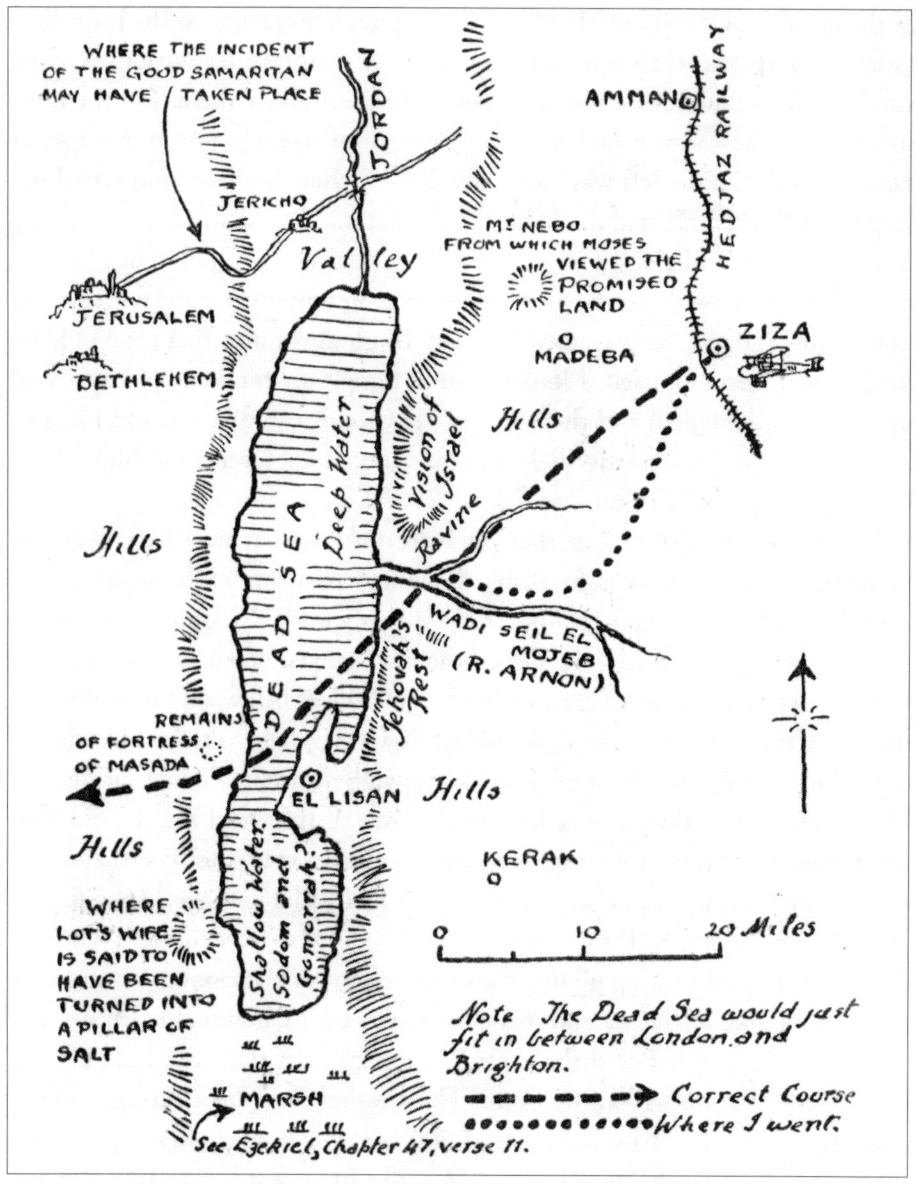

SKETCH MAP TO ILLUSTRATE FLIGHT OVER THE DEAD SEA

passed a D.H.9a flying lower and in the opposite direction. I was getting a bit cold. Finally Heliopolis came in sight, and I wirelessed our arrival and glided down. The sun was getting quite low. I did a little side slip coming in past the Reception Flight Sheds; but even then I finished up rather far down the aerodrome. I made quite a decent landing.

While I was in Heliopolis I went in to Middle East Headquarters and saw Air Commodore Clark Hall in his office. He showed me some photos of Masada, an ancient Roman fortress on the western cliffs of the Dead Sea. Crawford, a friend of his and an archaeologist, had written and asked him if he could get air photos of it, as they proposed to excavate a Roman site in Yorkshire this spring. It had similar characteristics to Masada, and they thought these would be helpful.

Heliopolis to Moseifig. We set out with three Vernons. Myself, Uncle Lees on Vagabond (7135) and Louis Paget on Vesuvius (7137). I had the Mail. I was flying the red Royal Mail Pennant instead of my Squadron Flag. I did not take my full run by mistake. I taxied out and came to a marking on the south aerodrome, which I thought was the end marking, because I was approaching it diagonally. It was in reality only one of the side markings. This made me very low over the big hangars at the opposite end of the aerodrome. Immediately we struck a sharp rain shower. All round the sun was shining through the rain. As I flew northwards out of it I saw, looking towards Heliopolis, an almost complete rainbow, standing out against the misty rain sheets. It hung poised in the sky and was singularly pure in colour. We had quite a good trip up to the Suez Canal, and the sun was shining through clouds. As we approached Moseifig I could see dirty weather ahead, and the rising hills were covered by a dark lowering fall of rain. Uncle and Louis were behind me, and I decided to land and discuss matters. I was also worried about my petrol. My starboard wing tank was leaking badly, and must have leaked some petrol away during the time "Valkyrie" was in the shed at Heliopolis. The trouble is that one does not detect the absence of the first 20 or 30 gallons in the glass gauge. I fired a red light and landed. Louis soon landed, and Uncle stayed up for a bit and sent off a W/T message, and then landed. Part of the reason why I landed was that we could get no weather report from Ramleh or Amman.

Moseifig to Salt Flat 10 miles E. of Moseifig. After a little we pushed on again, but as we approached Kilo 143 we ran into the heavy rain, and I came down lower and lower and followed the little winding railway. The rain beat into the cockpit and it became more and more difficult to see, so I decided to turn back. Uncle sent me a message suggesting that we should try and make El Arish, but I never got it. We were all three flying very low, circling about in the rain, and it was very unpleasant. Louis kept flying about over the top of me, which I hated. The elastic of my goggles must have loosened with the wet; for, as I glided down to have a look at one salt flat, with the idea of landing on it, they practically blew off and I had to hold them on with one hand. I flew low over this flat, but did not like the look of it, so flew westwards, and got out of the rain again. I finally landed successfully on another salt flat a little way further back. Louis landed after me, and Uncle flew about sending wireless. We lit a smoke candle and he landed. I found I had landed down wind. The wind was continually shifting. The salt flat was pretty soft and our wheels sank in. Uncle was afraid of it, because he said if there were much rain we might get stuck there. We still had no weather report from Ramleh. The storm still hung over the north-eastern sky and shrouded the far hills in gloom. Towards the Mediterranean the sky was cloudy, but the sun had broken through the clouds and only made the rain clouds look more menacing.

I put up my ground W/T station and soon we heard that the three Vimys, Cox and his two relief aeroplanes, had crossed the Dead Sea and were coming down the coast. We had some lunch. I heard a faint rumbling over the dunes, which we thought must be the sea. I strolled up over the scrub-covered dunes with Wing Commander Corbett Wilson, one of our passengers, to have a look. Every time we topped a rise we thought we should get a view and many times were we deceived. At last we saw the faint blue water and beyond the pale gold line of the spit of land which runs out like an enormous chevron.

Salt Flat to Ziza. After a halt of two hours we pushed on. Just as we took off this salt flat I saw three specks in the sky: the three Vimys flying west. One was much higher than the other two. We flew along over El Arish. The weather looked a little better to the north-east, but still stormy. Over Rafa we struck a bad hailstorm, and the hail beat down and was terribly painful. We were almost immediately driven inside the cockpit, trying to shelter our cheeks and foreheads from its pitiless onslaught. I could hardly see my instruments as my goggles were frosted over with rime. After ten minutes or so we emerged. Away on our left over the Dead Sea and Beersheba was black ink, and I had half a mind to make for Ramleh. I had taken 20 gallons of petrol each from Uncle and Louis on the salt flat; even then I was not over-sure of my supply. However, at this juncture Uncle sent me a message suggesting the northern route via Jerusalem, as the weather looked better there; and I decided to risk it. I sent a W/T message that three Vernons were making for Ziza via the northern route and struck a compass course for Jerusalem.

We climbed steadily, and rose up over the foothills, leaving Gaza on our left. No need again to describe the gaunt hills which have so bitten into my imagination. At 5,500 feet I was sailing through the lower tiers of stormy

THREE VERNONS ON THE SALT FLAT NEAR MOSEIFIG

cumulus cloud, and "Valkyrie" rolled and breasted the air rollers as they burst into invisible spray around her shivering planes. I had a good height, which comforted me. Soon I saw the twin towers on the hills which signalled Jerusalem, and I found I had steered well and truly. I took a photo of the hills and one of Bethlehem on my right. I was struck by the red roofs of some of the houses, which made sharp patches of colour in the general greyness like tiny red flowers in a grey land. Then onwards toward Jericho. Here Louis disappeared off to the right and was enveloped in the rolling clouds. I saw the road from Jerusalem to Jericho, and the hills looked particularly hopeless from the landing point of view. There seemed literally not one flat spot. Ouf! I breathed a sigh of relief when we came into the Jordan Valley. Uncle was flying steadily on my right. I saw the Jericho landing ground, and there seemed a fair piece of possible landing ground where Jordan flowed into the Dead Sea, looking like flat grey-blue sand. Over the Dead Sea itself the storm still brooded like a curse. Ahead of us the hills mounted up, terrace upon terrace to the flat tableland, which slopes gently down to Ziza.

We flew on, and scanned the tableland for the railway. Ziza is terribly difficult to pick up from the air, especially when the ground is broken up with cloud shadows, which are much more significant than the local features themselves. This piece of ground is like a chameleon, changing its colour and tone. It is quite different every time you see it. Now it was taking on a faint grey green, with a hint of spring. But it is a mirror of shadows and lights, and it is moulded by them into a country of deception. At last we saw the square grey-blue reservoir at Ziza, and I landed just after Uncle, who had pushed ahead of me. Louis came in about ten minutes later, having been led there by catching sight of us landing, out of the tail of his eye. We taxied our Vernons right down the road to the station and emptied the water out of the radiators. Soon the smoke of a train appeared in the hills, and it presently came down the long incline into the station. I got two photographs of it. I had a chat with the train inspector. He said he lived at Amman, but came from some village in Palestine.

At Ziza. When we woke up in the morning I looked out of the window and saw a thick mist. One could hardly see the three Vernons on the other side of the railway line. The evening before we had had supper in the little upper room in the station, and had sung songs to the lilt of Louis' mandoline, amid the indescribable debris of food. The pale guttering candles, the purple night outside, the not unmusical part singing, the weather-beaten faces of men in the full flood of youth seated and sprawling in every conceivable attitude, on the table, in chairs, in a row against the wall; the hissing stove against the wall, left a strong impression on my mind of friendship and good company born of trials and hardships endured together. It is curious how when men sprawl at ease after a long day's journey, and the candle-light glows on them, the lights and sharp weird shadows and the attitudes of the men fall into a rhythmical composition that thrills the eye; and if, added to this, there should be music and song, what more complete satisfaction could there be to a man's heart?

And next morning, through the mist glimmered fires in front of the Vernons, and the black petrol smoke stood up like pillars into the sunlit mist. It did not lift until about 9.30 a.m. We started up, taxied up the road again like great beasts going a-hunting. The mist had cleared and left low cloud, if cloud it was and not broken mist wreaths, drifting along at about 300 feet. Looking into the sun we could see little. I felt this would be a difficulty, as at Ziza one often flies at about 300 feet struggling with the down currents, and it might be hard to rise above the layer, for some time. If one were compelled to fly about in it, one might be partially blinded. I took off, and just as I was successfully surmounting the mist layer, which did not turn out to be so dense as I had expected, I noticed my starboard oil pressure had fallen right back, so I had, after firing a green light for Uncle's benefit, to land again This was nasty with such a heavy load. I accomplished it without misadventure The other two landed also. My fitter took the relief valve down, and after one or two runs up of the engine, the trouble was rectified.

Ziza to Point between L.G. M *and L.G.* O. To-day was Friday 13th, and I thought half-humorously what effect this would have on our journey. The sun was shining brightly and it bade fair to be good weather We had an uncomfortable weather report of rain from Ramadi. We sailed along over the Jebel Mugher without difficulty, past Kasr Kharana, south of Azrak. At this time the track was showing up exceptionally well as one looked towards the sun. From Azrak one could see the thin line of the mud flats at D, and half following the track, we made straight for it. I let Barrett fly and made one or two sketches of the "Land of Conjecture" from the "Plain of Sorrows". I noted the two characteristic mud flats on the "Plain of Sorrows" and the pied wadi going eastward from Azrak toward the hills at D. By the time we reached D we were over 5,000 feet.

This is the first time I had flown over the "Land of Conjecture" at a good height, and I was able to view it more in the broad. The track was extremely difficult to follow in places. The strain of gazing to keep its continuity is very fatiguing. You have it one moment; and dare you but take your eyes away to gaze at an instrument and then look back, it has eluded you. And again you watch this elusive ribbon, and you think it goes one way up a wadi; and you find that what you thought was the track is another one of the million writings on the face of the desert, or even some track that a wandering armoured car has made. You find it leads to nothing, and you hastily glance back and try to pick it up again a little further back, and trace it through again. It is like reading faint and faded writing in an old book, or a story when you are half asleep, and keep losing the sense thereof. I saw that there were two mud flats north of F. Then we three flew on, south of G, which I have never actually identified as it is not on the main track, till we came to H. I imagined that the track turned south along the mud flat, and as the track is never clear on the mud flat after rain, I turned to the right expecting to pick it up at the southern edge. No track. I must circle. In doing so Uncle and Louis got ahead, and I picked up the track going east across the mud flat. It turns south a little further on, then east again at the outer gate of the "Land of Conjecture," and at the turn is marked thus: ⊠ I followed along, and after a time Uncle and Louis turned round and fell in behind me again.

Between M and O, Barrett told me the other two were not in sight. I circled, and he saw one Vernon down and the other circling a little way back. Then the other landed. So I came down and landed too. Louis had one engine dud, but they said I had better push on with the Mail and they would follow in about half an hour. Actually they came on next day. We had passed over a considerable gathering of Arabs near M, and I had counted about fifty black tents, with one larger black tent in the middle which I judged to be the Sheikh's tent. Some of these men now came up with one or two camels. They were armed with rifles and plenty of ammunition, but were very well disposed.

Point between M *and* O *to L.G.* V. I now pushed on by myself, having sent off a W/T message about Uncle and Louis. The journey to *L.G.* V was uneventful. The sun was shining, but it was very bumpy. As we cut across the "Kingdom of What Wasn't" up the Wadi Hauran towards *L.G.* 8 I sent Barrett back into the hull to make sardine sandwiches. As I approached *L.G.* V I. saw far eastward the long-expected low bank of cloud. The afternoon was wearing on, but I did not want to risk going through without petrol. I threw out a smoke candle and landed. I had never opened the dump by myself before, having only watched others do it. Luckily I had brought the typed sheet of instructions with me.

Even then we struggled for three-quarters of an hour without avail. What if we failed to open it? Was I to stay there, or risk getting through, and possibly having to forced-land? Just as we were abandoning hope, we followed through the instructions once again; and the lid came off. Cheering for joy wasn't in it! Hastily we filled our tank.

L.G. V *to Ramadi*. It was getting late, but it was still fine, except for the grey bar hanging like a threat in the east. Slowly sank the sun as we flew homewards over the bare plain; redder and redder shone the light, and the whole desert turned crimson and orange. The sun was dropping behind the dark rim of the horizon, and as we passed *L.G.* III and approached the jebels between III and II the sight was amazing. A crimson glory lit the desert and the facets of the little hills till they glowed like fire against the dark curtain of clouds which seemed to steal across the fire-glowing mud to meet us. I kept looking back at that sun, and saw it reflected in my tail planes and hull, dyeing them with crimson pigment. The sun sank; the light faded; quickly, too quickly, the bank of cloud drew over us like a pall, and I had to come down to about 1,000 feet. We wirelessed to Ramadi for rockets and flares. How thankful I was that I had taken that extra petrol! I had no night flying gear buttoned on, however, which worried me. The track was getting harder and harder to see. What if I lost it and had to land in the dark without a Holt flare! A most unpleasant look-out! To push on was the only hope.

With the last light I picked out the Bitumen Pools like black shadows. Searle got the main cockpit light working, but was unable to get the compass light to work. No rockets were visible at Ramadi, for the very simple reason that they were shooting up into the low clouds. All I could do to keep direction was to keep the red streak of afterglow dead behind me. One saw this red streak under the fall of cloud, long and clear, far over the face of the darkening desert. Soon I looked back at the Bitumen Pools and they were turned to blood; pools of sheer blood in black basins. An unforgettable sight. Then I saw moving lights below. The head lights of the westward-bound Nairn convoy of three cars. Again, lights ahead! Were they the flares at Ramadi? Or some Bedouin encampment? Heaven grant they were the flares, or I was lost. All the time I was strained almost to the breaking point, wondering what the issue of it all would be. If only I could see Lake Habbaniyah! Then I thought I saw a faint line in the obscurity which might be the Euphrates. Soon I made out the "L" of the flares. So I had reached Ramadi! But how to land? It would be a tricky business without a Holt flare on such a difficult landing-ground.

I sent a message back to Corporal Searle to see if he could somehow ignite a Holt flare and drop it on the landing ground. This might give me some light. The answer was that he would try and work it at 100 feet. At the time I did not realize what he meant. After firing a green light and circling round for a little I set my teeth and put "Valkyrie" into her glide. I had to land down the hill towards the serai; and I must land short to avoid overrunning, yet I must get over the trenches. I judged the flares as well as I could, and just as they were coming together in perspective and I knew I was nearing the ground, there was a crack behind me and a sudden light. I gave one mighty yank back and landed, I know not how. There was practically no bounce, though I had some drift. No matter! "Valkyrie" was safe. And as I taxied in I looked back and saw Corporal Searle hanging out of one of the after windows on the starboard side *holding a burning Holt flare* in his hand on two short wires. He had hastily wound in, seized one of the W/T batteries, propped it up on the seat, made a circuit, ignited the flare, and, hanging out of the window as far as he could, regardless of what would happen if I hit the ground hard, and in imminent risk of falling out himself, was holding the burning flares by its two wires to give me light. It would have been difficult enough had the aeroplane been on the ground; as it was, in the hurry and darkness and the whizzing slipstream of the star-board propeller, it was an achievement. Loder was standing by No 1 flare and had been firing the futile rockets.

When I got out of the aeroplane Sergeant Pitt announced that there was a corpse in our bedroom! A N.A.A.F.I. manager had died in the Nairn and had been taken in. Before we could go to bed we had to get him out into the garage. We asked for permission to continue to Hinaidi, but were told it was totally unfit owing to the rain they had had. I was restless in my sleep early next morning, going through time and again that last half-hour's tension as we came in to Ramadi with the Mail. But we had landed with our Mail Pennant sturdily at the mast head.

Ramadi to Hinaidi. The next morning the eastward-bound Nairn convoy came in. They had a dead hyena strapped on the running board of one of the cars. They got a stretcher and took the corpse along with them to Baghdad. I could not get leave to start till noon. Even then they said I must be very careful about landing, as Hinaidi was a bog, and I must touch my wheels on the "T". I flew back on a fine morning with white fleecy clouds. When quite low I saw the tower at Aqqar Kuf as a tiny excrescence on the horizon from 60 miles away. I then tried to climb above the clouds, but found the cumulus tops rising up high enough to make it not worth my while; so when just past Fellujah I glided down to 1,500 feet and flew back under them. I flew over Hinaidi aerodrome low down, and saw most of the Squadron turned out to watch me land. A little group stood by a white cloth "T" and, as I came over, fired a light. I found I had to land half towards the sheds and half towards the gap on the near side (the side nearest the sheds) of the road running across the aerodrome parallel to our sheds. This was going to be very tricky, as it allowed practically no landing run. The road itself was in pools of water. I came down, using my engines, very gingerly, and just managed to drop over the road a few yards to the right of the "T". I only ran about 20 yards and made a perfect landing. Perhaps it was more by good luck than good management; still it was eminently satisfactory to be able to pull it off, as if I had over- or under-shot I should have been in the road between us and No. 1 Squadron, or in the bog!

1. Triangular chocks are placed in front of the wheels when the engines are being run up and tested, to prevent the aeroplane running forward.
2. Flares attached to a small parachute and used for reconnaissance.
3. An experimental apparatus for starting up the engines.
4. My Vernon.
5. Medical officer.

CHAPTER VIII

INTERLUDES AT SULAIMANIYA AND JERUSALEM

TO SULAIMANIYA AND BACK VIA KIRKUK AND KINGERBAN (FEBRUARY, 1925)

Hinaidi to Sulaimaniya. I went up to Sul as second pilot to Maitland. We were carrying 300 pounds of head ropes up to the Arab army. When we started off the weather did not look at all promising, and the sky was full of grey alto-cumulus and nimbus, and thin rain was falling fitfully. We sped off northwards into the grey sky and at 1,000 feet climbed into a layer of warm wet air. We flew up over Khan Beni Said, which Maitland told me was laid out like a typical old Persian town, between the Rivers Diyala and Tigris, following fairly closely to the left of the looping and winding River Diyala. Away on our left we could see the Tigris like a grey line in the "Blue." Insensibly the face of the desert turned darker and more broken as we entered the land of dull green cultivation. There seemed to be plantations of shrubs and palms in all sorts of queer geometrical shapes; and as we passed Baquba, the Diyala took a more easterly direction, and in the distance I could see the jeels[1] at Abu Jisra. At this point the Tigris and Diyala converge to form a neck a few miles wide before they part and open out like two mighty curling arms. We flew through the neck and saw rain storms ahead with slanting pillars of fine misty rain, blocking out the view like dim curtains. And through the obscurity towards the east I had a feeling that dim mountains were approaching.

We flew on till we picked up the Shatt el Adhaim at "Banting's Bend," and about this time we came out of the rain and there opened before my eyes a most unforgettable prospect. Mile upon mile the Kurdish mountains stretched, in soft distant colours, with curtains of cloud around and above them; in some places sharp and well-defined, in others misty and so obscure that whether they were cloud or not I was left in doubt. And to the north-east I saw the snowy top of Pire Makrun rising pyramidal and kingly. And though I thought he would be lovely, when I saw him, in fact, he was five times more lovely, and as I gazed, he became all misty. There is something about a great mountain in the distance that is almost overpowering. So aloof and majestic in the atmospheric vesture, washed pure by the rain.

For a space we followed the Shatt el Adhaim, and then flying along the line of a disused railway, or rather to the left of it, we came to and crossed the Jebel Hamrin. It is a low serrated range of hills running north-west and south-east, orange in its main hue, but on closer inspection revealing all the ochres down to deep Indian red. And it is like a great slab, extending beyond eye-reach and tilted up, its north-eastern edge the highest, all cut up with wadis into an infinite variety of patterns. And to look at it makes one imagine the falling of the waters of a thousand years.

Then we flew on again into a plain, cut by the numerous tributaries of the Shatt el Adhaim, running from the great watershed of the Kurdish foothills. The flat plain terminated abruptly in a wall of hills, again like slabs steeply tilted up in strata, warm ochre and orange in colour; and behind the wall the hills fell away only to rise in serried ranks, layer upon layer, bluff upon bluff, as far as the eye could see, right up to the rugged ranges of mountains under the grey ceiling of cloud. These hills looked like a great army suddenly arrested on the march, and flanked by the plain. And the plain was by no means bare. For it held the imprints of a hundred civilizations; old towers stood on mounds, the mounds of the crumbled edifices of the past. Built and built again on their own ruins by successive communities, they had witnessed life's little round, grim and quiet, until it was finished, and restarted, and finished again. And there were dim markings on the face of the plain that were a mystery known only to the ancient hills that looked down upon them through the changing seasons; that saw the plain baked and parched in the scorching summer, and give forth its young herbs in the springtime, until purple and green glowed round the beds of the chais,[2] running past the old dreamy towns. And where the chais, in their broad beds now but winding streaks of silver, and yet anon to come rushing down in spate carrying even bridges before them, came to the wall of hills, they had forged wide gateways, having eroded the rock century by century; and the hills looked as if they stood apart to let the water through. And at such entrances were Tuz and Tauk and Kirkuk.

We flew over Kirkuk and I saw the aerodrome. The main part of the town is on a mound on the south-east side of the chai; another and a lesser part is on the north-west side, with the aerodrome by its olive orchard. Then we turned eastward into the warm ochre-coloured hills, keeping a little south of the chai until they seemed to calm down into a plateau, although this was broken and rugged. I saw the little town of Chemchemal, and before us rose ever nearer the mighty Pire Makrun. Not alone was he, set as he was among his peers. To the north and to the south were snow-topped mountains like a thousand spires, but he rose above them all. And below him I saw the famous Bazyan Pass like a dark V in the mountains.

We flew on, and by and by we were flying through the Pass. I looked down and saw the winding Kirkuk-Sulaimaniya road through it. To the left the rugged knife-edged hill rose nearly to our level (5,000 feet); to the right the mountain was a little lower, stretching away a mass of dark snow-dappled rock to the Kara Dagh. The Turks controlled all this country by a wall which they built across the Pass, and at which they took toll of all who passed through. And there were round heaps of boulders on the sides of the Pass with zigzag pathways to them, where brigands might shoot down on to the road far below.

Then we passed into the kingdom of mountains. All around they rose, staring at us like colossal giants, detached, aloof, inscrutable. South we flew, until we came to the Tasludja Pass, a haunt also of brigands, scene of desperate "hold ups" in, the lonely solitudes of the gaunt mountains. We turned to the left through this Pass, and then I saw the thin ribbon of road stretching straight across the Sul Valley to the opposite wall of mountains, at whose feet nestled Sul itself. And the road crossed a chai with a little stone bridge; and in the bed of the chai were osiers, I think, making a soft misty look, and Maitland told me that many Armenians were there massacred. The valley, whose bottom was about 3,000 feet high, was undulating, and offered little prospect of good landing ground. Then we arrived over Sul landing ground and I saw two D.H.9as thereon. It is very small and slopes down away from the town across one diagonal The road runs by one edge, and there is a white "V" marked, across which the road runs. You can touch the far side of the road and run across it, so long as you are within the arms of the "V." There is another similar "V," on the side away from the town. Into this, after having thrown out a smoke candle, we landed. As we glided down, I saw Maitland turn red and bite his lips, remembering, as doubtless he did, the many crashes here. For you could not afford to make a mistake.

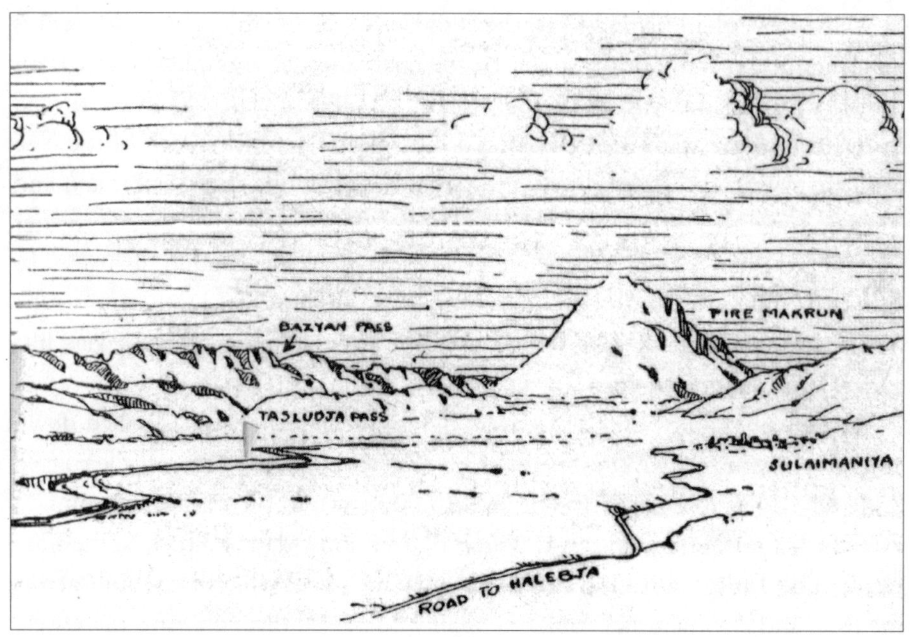

VIEW UP THE SULAIMANIYA VALLEY

We lunched with MacGregor, and sat out on his delightful verandah looking out on the beautiful mountains. And the birds were singing with their hearts full of springtime oxen were ploughing in the fields, and cocks were crowing and the air was full of country sounds, very pleasant to the ear. MacGregor told us that Sheikh Mahmoud was behind the next range of mountains, only about 20 miles away The Boundary Commission was due to turn up the next day, and the whole town had turned out to see us. Doubtless, by my brass hat, they took me for a Turkish expert on the Commission. I paid a visit to Chapman, and I found him sitting in his office in what was once Sheikh Mahmoud's throne house. And I saw the bomb holes, but recently filled in; a grim record.

Sulaimaniya to Kirkuk. After lunch we flew back. Pire Makrun's summit was now capped in cloud. It is funny taking off the ground with a wall of rock a few miles away. You feel you are never going to get out. We rose up, flew back through the two passes; and at the bottom of the Bazyan Pass I saw the ruins of what I took to be an old town, not far from the road. As we approached Kirkuk, I saw black lowering clouds ahead, and sullen spots of rain, began to fall. We landed just before the storm came up. Vincent was waiting on the aerodrome. Robb was at Hinaidi, so I slept in his room at No. 30 Squadron.

When we came into the Mess they gave us an excellent tea with two eggs. Good eggs are not to be had south of the Jebel Hamrin.

Kirkuk to Kingerban. Next morning a flight of 30 Squadron was to make a demonstration flight at the back of Sul. The line of D.H.9as. running up on the aerodrome with their softly sobbing engines, and in full war plumage with shining machine-guns, reminded me so much of the old days in France. We took off after they did and flew south past Tauk and Tuz, leaving the mountains gradually behind us. There was a certain amount of high drifting cloud which moderated the sultry warmth of the sun. Tauk looked particularly picturesque, with its springtime greens and purples on the plain at its feet, and its quaint walls, and broken silhouette and flat roofs touched and picked out by the sunlight. It looked so much like those little towns you always see in fairy books; and one can imagine knights riding towards it over the plain, and sentinels standing on the walls. Anon the knights would wind a mighty horn, which would echo against the mound and summon the township to surrender! And spears would glimmer in the loopholes in the parapet; and a hymn of war would sound dimly down the old streets, till, gathering strength, it would swell to a crescendo and make the old buildings ring.

Then we flew in a more south-easterly direction following the road to Kingerban, and the wall of hills as it curved round to the south-east. Then I saw Kifri, again skirted with green, against a doorway in the hills. Flung out as an outpost on the plain was the old town of Kingerban on its mound. The railway ran past it, and strings of laden camels and donkeys were winding across the landing ground to Kifri. When we landed we were met by an armoured car, which took us to the little Mess of the detachment. Straight, it might have been three-quarters of a mile; but a stream intervened and we had to follow a rough road about two miles round, running up and down over hillocks and stream beds, splashing now through a stream, tilting now at one angle and now at another. Sitting on the back of an armoured car was no easy matter. And I looked back and saw the plain, faintly tinged with green, and far hills toward Kifri, and Table Mountain, and Kingerban on its mound; and "Argo," our aeroplane, standing by herself on the plain, would appear and disappear as the car rushed up and down over the undulating ground. They told us they had heard on the wireless that the R.A.F. had beaten the Navy at Rugger by 3-0 at Twickenham the day before.

Kingerban to Hinaidi. And so home! We flew south-west, over winding rivers, till we crossed the Jebel Hamrin lower down. It got quite warm and bumpy and there was considerable glare. Then the Diyala appeared with its dark

A CITY OF MESOPOTAMIA

cultivation; and we came to the neck at Baquba, and so between the two rivers, over Khan Beni Said, until Hinaidi came in sight. The thing that impressed me most about the trip was the astounding change between the plains of Baghdad and the mountains; and only between two to three hours apart by air!

TRIP TO EGYPT TO FETCH BACK SECRETARIES OF STATE TO IRAQ (MARCH, 1925)

Hinaidi to Ramadi. Trip to Heliopolis to fetch back the Secretaries of State. We started off in beautiful weather; and it was a nice sunny morning as we taxied out to the bund. Embry, on J 7143, the Ambulance,[3] Summers and Maitland came with me. I arranged to stick with Embry, as he had no wireless. As we left Baghdad behind us I noticed for the first time, I think, the sun shining on the golden cupolas and minarets of the mosque at Kadimain up the Tigris.

Ramadi to L.G. D. We had a tremendously long and exhausting trip. It was fairly fine when we started; blue sky and high cloud, with variegated formations of cirrus. Beyond *L.G.* V alto-clouds began to appear. Here Summers and Maitland drew ahead, and left Embry and me. As we were passing *L.G.* VI I saw rather a wonderful sight in the way of clouds. There was to the north an enormous lenticular patch of very high white alto-cumulus, which threw a dark-blue shadow on the desert, an exact image of itself. As we passed out from the "Kingdom of What Wasn't" on to the "Upland of the Winds" the weather turned stiflingly hot, and a sort of dusty haze developed with bad glare. All to the southward you could see long trails of dust blowing up, and in places dust devils reared themselves upwards like grey-white wraiths. There was one particularly bad kind of dust squall that we struck, and it was very bumpy. Finally we came out of the "Land of Conjecture" over the plain towards *L.G.* D and saw Summers and Maitland there. They lit a smoke candle and I glided down through the warm thin gusty air and landed. It must have been the Hamsin,[4] for at *L.G.* D it was disgustingly hot, and the hot air blew up from the basalt boulders and seemed to strike you on the face hauling the petrol drums over from the dump, and refuelling, was no joke. We found that there were bullet-holes by the keyhole in the dump. Maitland and Summers went on, as soon as they were finished, and left us.

L.G. D *to Ziza.* When we had refuelled we made our way across the "Plain of Sorrows," past Kasr Kharana to Ziza. It was still hot and very bumpy, and I had to climb again to o'ertop the Jebel Mugher. But as we approached Ziza the sun was sinking and the air was settling down.

At Ziza. Maitland and Summers got away quite early, but I had to wait for Embry, as he had some trouble with a leaky float. When we did get away, we climbed up a bit, and were just preparing to push off to Ramleh, when we had a message from Amman telling us not to go because of the weather. It certainly looked very misty over the hills.

Ziza to Dead Sea and return. We waited till we had permission from Amman to proceed. By this time we had given up the prospect of going via Ramleh, where I had wished to take Embry. So we set off towards the Dead Sea. We crossed the dreadful gorge of Seil el Mojeb, climbing painfully and steadily. The weather looked thicker and thicker; and by the time we reached the confines of the Dead Sea there seemed to be a solid wall of grey lowering fog on the further shore. As I could not see the opposite cliffs at all, I judged that it would be unwise to proceed. We had also had a message to say that Maitland and Summers were down at Rafa owing to fog. So with some difficulty I managed to get in front of Embry and fire a red light; whereat we both turned back and flew to Ziza in rather a depressed state of mind. We then turned in at the little station in the upper room and went to sleep.

Ziza to Kulundia. During the afternoon the cloud and fog seemed to have lifted a little over the hills, especially on the northern route; so we decided to have a go for Ramleh before dark. We got an affirmative weather report from them in the air. We flew towards the head of the Dead Sea, up over the Hills of Moab, and as we came to the escarpment which falls down in great terraced crags to the Jordan Valley, we struck a colossal headwind, and hardly seemed to make any progress at all. The scene was most impressive. It was late afternoon and the light seemed to be failing unusually early. The Jerusalem Hills stood up silhouetted against the sky, all their forms merged together and simplified into one great shadowy wall ending in a rugged sky line. Far below the Jordan Valley lay deeply veiled in shadow; and I could dimly see Jericho at the foot of the shadowy wall. Over the Dead Sea itself was shadow and gloom; but to the west, over the Judæan Hills, was a line of brightness, made by the westering sun shining through the clouds. In the Jordan Valley, over the other side of the river, a trail of blue smoke was blowing southwards; yet the wind where we were flying, perhaps 5,000 feet above the tortuous river bed, had a strong southerly drift.

I saw the circle on the Jericho landing ground as we passed over, and every now and then I turned round to watch Embry following me. At one moment he would be above me; two minutes later below, cast up and down in the buffeting gusts which were whirling upwards out of the shadowy world below. I did up my safety-belt and told Barrett to do his up also. At last, after a seemingly endless passage, we passed over the opposite wall of hills. I saw the Jericho-Jerusalem road winding up its ravine; but owing to the southerly drift we came out somewhat north of Jerusalem itself. I did not realize this at first and was looking round for some time trying to spot the two towers of the Holy City, until I saw them on my left. Then I looked out towards the sea where I thought Ramleh should be, and behold a great mass of drifting cumulus was rolling up against the westward slope of the Judæan Hills; of the plain, I could see nothing.

What was I to do? Dare I push on, with the southerly wind drifting me northwards and risk coming down through the clouds where I thought Ramleh ought to be? Admittedly I had had a weather report saying that over Ramleh the clouds were 3,000 feet; but … supposing I miscalculated and came down over some outlying spur of the rugged hills? And again; supposing I came out over the sea, with darkness falling? Should I—the thought crossed my mind—fly back to Jericho and land there for the night? I felt that another half hour over those hills would turn my hair grey! Then I remembered that Paget had told me of a landing ground north of Jerusalem by the road. So I flew to Jerusalem, Embry faithfully following, and turned back north up the road along the hill tops. Soon I saw two circles, one on either side of the road,

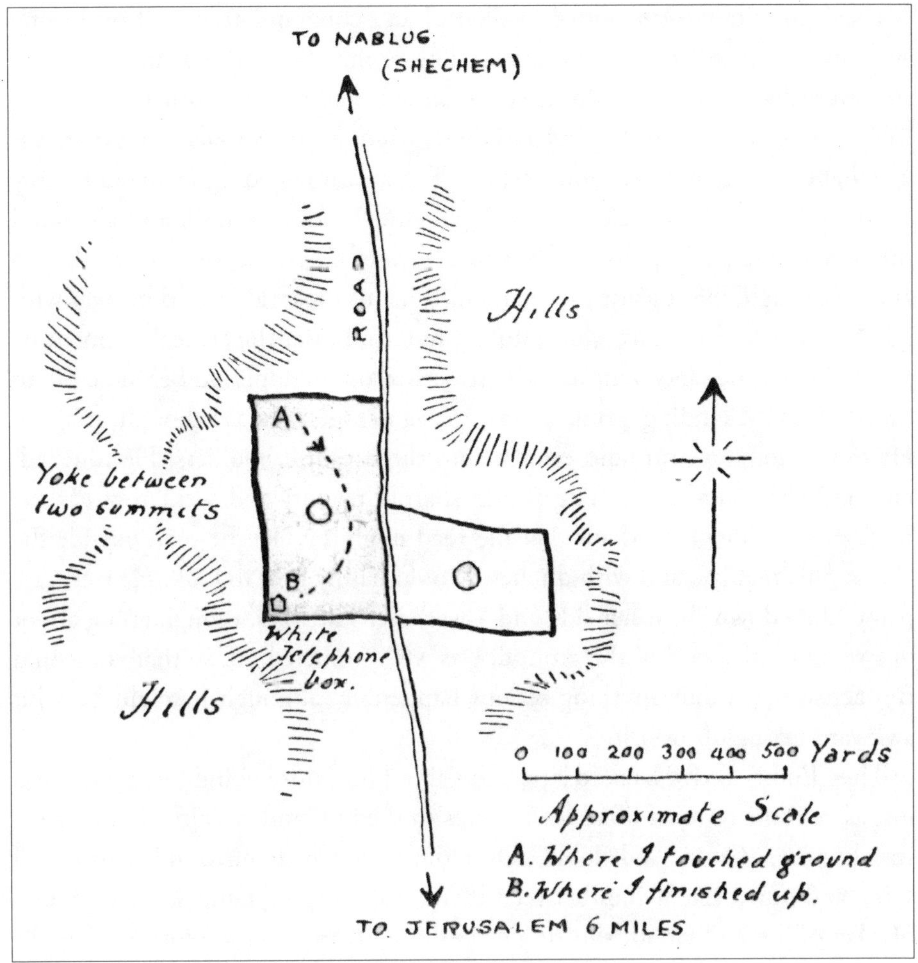

KULANDIA LANDING GROUND

and two green patches, which looked very small but good. I circled round, losing height, and dropped a smoke candle. I then glided down, and realized how small the ground was. I pulled off a slow landing, which was made more difficult by having to approach from the north, half round and half down the side of the hills which sloped right to the very edge of the landing ground, itself 2,600 feet high. I felt that "Valkyrie" was going to drop right out of my hands, but she behaved nobly and we touched near the edge of the landing ground, swung towards the road, and sharply up to the right, ending up near the little white telephone-box at the far side. The ground sloped generally down to my left, so that I first ran a bit downhill and then up again.

I had just time to get out of "Valkyrie" and congratulate myself on having got down safely when I saw Embry circling round above. I lit a smoke candle, and immediately regretted doing so, because I ought, I felt, to have put out a "T", to make Embry land uphill and down wind, for the surface wind then was very light. However, it was too late, and Embry came gliding in the same way as I had done, but too fast and too high. And I looked round, and all round the edge of the landing ground was one mass of boulders, some as much as 3 and 4 feet high, like a giant rock garden. If he hit those, all would be over with the Ambulance. My heart went into my mouth, but at the critical moment he put on his engines and went round. He dashed on, disappeared behind a hill to the south of the landing ground, came in again, even then as I thought too fast. He must surely overrun and crunch into the dreadful boulders. He touched, ran, and then suddenly swung round sharply to port and went towards the road. Now I thought perhaps that the road might be like the road outside the "V" at Sulaimaniya, and with ditches. I could hardly bear to look. He went up, pause, then down the other side and—was safe. The road, though rising a foot or two above the level of the ground, was well cambered off, so that you could run across it without anything serious happening, although it might be a bit awkward taking off over it.

Then Embry taxied back to a position about 50 yards behind "Valkyrie," and just as he came to rest I lifted up my eyes to the hills and exclaimed in an awe-struck voice, "Good God, look!" Over the hills, which surrounded us on all sides, and down the ravines between them, was creeping remorselessly a white blanket of fog and cloud, shutting everything off from view, blotting the hills out as though they were not. And almost before I had finished my exclamation and recovered from my surprise, you could hardly see one aeroplane from the other; and Embry's Vernon had faded to a grey blue. One heard men's voices talking in the mist like disembodied spirits. Anyway we were down and safe.

When Embry and I got together and were exchanging congratulations on our safe arrival, crowds of Jews came up, and in a way I was surprised to see them. After all it was Jerusalem, but still I was somehow surprised. There is a little village of Kulundia, which was then hidden in the fog. Just then a Ford car dashed up with four men with rifles in smart dark green uniforms: the Palestine gendarmerie who happened to be out on patrol. Winston Churchill made them out of the R.I.C. (Black and Tans) in about 1922 apparently.

They were most hospitable. I took Padre Still, and left Embry and Barrett and the crews in the fog. The Ford took us to Mount Scopus, a spur of the

Mount of Olives, about a mile outside Jerusalem, where the headquarters of this company of gendarmerie was. It was Sir Henry Tudor's old headquarters. I believe that it was on Mount Scopus that the Emperor Titus pitched his camp when he besieged Jerusalem.

It got dark, and what with the fog and cloud I could hardly see anything. Then I phoned up Flying Officer Andrews, in charge of the Armoured Car Section at Jerusalem, and he said he would send out a Rolls. The officers of the company of gendarmerie consisted of a Major whom I did not see, Captain Burke, and two Lieutenants. I had a spot of tea and a whisky. They had quite a nice little Mess of wooden huts, some of them lined outside with petrol tins filled with earth.

Jerusalem is all on hills, and the ground sloped away from Mount Scopus and up again to Jerusalem. I heard the grunting of the Rolls outside on the gravel, and on going outside I saw the misty glare of its head lights. I left the Padre and we purred away. An armoured car is the most desperate thing to sit on. You are squashed into a sort of biscuit box in the back and are in imminent danger of falling off at the corners. The fog was awful and we had to go dead slow for fear of getting off the road. In one part they were making it up, and had left three motor rollers at intervals along the roadside without any lights. There was one place where the road turned sharply round at the bottom of a steep hill and over a little bridge crossing a wadi. A filthy place in a fog. I could not help wondering what would happen if we shot off the road, which we apparently nearly did more than once; only pulling up with much grinding of brakes. We eventually got on to the landing ground and wandered about guided by voices in the obscurity, trying to find the aeroplanes. In the end we all packed off, with the crews as well, and the Palestine gendarmerie left a guard. I went to bed on a camp bed in Burke's sitting-room and slept like a child. I thought of Swinburne's lines:

> "That no life lives for ever,
>   That dead men rise up never,
> That even the weariest river
>   Winds somewhere safe to sea."

So much had happened that day…

I woke up in the morning to the sweet lilt of the birds, and saw the sun dimly shining outside the window. I looked out and there was a verandah, and beyond, a garden with rich red earth like that of Devonshire, and lots of flowers, geraniums and wallflowers, and fir trees and bushes; then a valley, and up on the other side the Holy City: a priceless view. And to sit up in bed in the morning and see it all in a flash! At first Jerusalem looked like an English town; it might almost have been in the Stroud Valley, terraced up on its hills, and the long white road leading up to it. But if you looked closer you saw that it was Eastern. It gave me a strange, exalted feeling, and a feeling of awe. The Bible suddenly came home to me in a flash. I thought of Christ on a hill looking at Jerusalem, and being tempted. All the beautiful language and imagery of the New Testament, and the Sermon on the Mount (of Olives, wasn't it?) perhaps quite near where I lay, seemed to fit in magically with the scene in front of me.

The hills, with their boulders and vivid green grass and myriads of rock plants, like a vast rock garden, and thousands of different-coloured wee flowers, were full of the mighty story of the past, two thousand years ago. Perhaps some of the very same boulders, and the ancestors of the same flowers, had lain there or had blossomed just the same. Then all of a sudden the clouds rolled up and blotted it out in two minutes; and what I had seen might well have been a dream. It is extraordinary the way the clouds come up in those hills.

I had an excellent breakfast. Then I went outside, and the weather had cleared again. Looking to the right of the Mount of Olives one sees the two towers that I had already noticed from the air. They are both German and relatively modern. One is a convent, I believe, and the other the Residency. Embry and I climbed up the hill at the back of the Mess, over sort of rough boulder-strewn mounds, rich with grass and flowers; and everywhere were old bits of ruins, some half sunk in the ground; remnants of arches, and things that looked like cellars, and odd pieces of chiselled stone. This stone is too soft to use on the roads, and they say that stone has to be carted from Syria.

There was one thing that was secretly worrying me to death. We had got into Kulundia. How the devil were we ever to get out? It was 2,600 feet up and surrounded on all sides by hills coming almost to its very edge. There was indeed one outlet, along the road to Jerusalem, that had looked possible. But would the wind be favourable? After thinking things over I came to the conclusion that in order to get off we should have to jettison pretty nearly everything. I had got in touch with Gallehawk at Ramleh, and he had sent a lorry, grinding up the 27 miles to Jerusalem, with empty tins and two 50-gallon Bowser petrol tanks.

The lorry arrived at about ten o'clock. We went up a Rolls armoured car to Kulundia, and there things were even worse than I thought. I looked round

BOULDERS ON THE EDGE OF KULUNDIA LANDING GROUND

THE AMBULANCE VERNON AT KULUNDIA

blankly at the heights and shivered. They looked so menacing and seemed to grin at me. We spent most of the morning emptying out petrol, which is a long and tedious business. Meanwhile the Padre was taking panoramic views of Jerusalem from the Mount of Olives with a special camera. I began to feel absolutely sick with worry about the business of getting off. Embry and I paced the landing ground and then looked at the hills, and back at the landing ground, and our eyes met; we each knew what the other feared. Then I decided we must lighten still further. I told Andrews of the armoured cars that our second pilots, passengers and kits must go by road to Ramleh, and that we would make the attempt just with our crews.

The wind was blowing strong from the west, at right angles to the way I wanted to take off. I looked to the west and there was a sort of yoke between the hills, that in the face of a strong wind one might climb over. But it was hideously doubtful. And yet … if one attempted the crosswind take off down the road, one might be swept into the hillside. I had almost decided to have a stab at the take off over the yoke, when over the hills came the clouds and rain, and I saw that we must shut up for the day.

Sir Henry Tudor had made Kulundia landing ground sometime, I believe, in 1923. It was full of boulders, and it cost about £6,000 to clear it.

We put all the covers on our Vernons, and decided to start at the crack of dawn on Saturday, firstly because there would probably be no wind, leaving us free to take off in the direction we wished, and secondly because it would be cool and those terrible down currents that you get in the hills would not have formed. So we drove back to Mount Scopus and had lunch.

Embry and I and three men were the only people now left. In the afternoon Burke took Embry and me into Jerusalem. We saw a lot of American tourists in horn-rimmed spectacles. Jerusalem is a weird mixture. A good deal cleaner than Baghdad, and in many ways than Cairo; and mostly grey stone, which, if it were not for the Eastern architecture, would give it a curiously Western smack. Some of the shops were extraordinarily well appointed. A good Kodak shop, and some quite decent drapers, with good-looking silk stockings in the windows. There are some very impressive buildings, massive and old. The tomb of David is a colossal mass, rising up high like a great fort. There were many signs of previous Turkish occupation and stars and crescents.

We wandered about in the narrow streets, up and down hills, which reminded me of Clovelly in a funny way; and what struck me most was that every other shop was a carpenter's shop, with an open front and the resinous smell of cut wood which is so dear to my nostrils, and the sharp stimulating sounds of planing and sawing. We then found various boys chasing us, wanting to show us things; and finally one of them collared us and took us to the Church of the Holy Sepulchre, which is about six churches in one with six sects: Russian, Greek, Coptic, Roman Catholic, and I do not know what. Sometimes a scrap starts and they belabour one another with sticks in the church. There is a kind of central round nave, rather like that of the Temple Church in London, only bigger, under a dim lofty dome; but it is filled with shrines and chapels—filled stiff. We were each given a candle, Embry and I, which we carried to light our way in dark places. We first saw the stone where they were supposed to have laid Christ when they took Him down from the Cross. Then we went into a little chapel about 8 feet long by 3 feet wide with a big fat priest in it. There was a woman praying, so we had to wait till she had finished before we could get in. Our guide apparently wanted us to push in quite regardless! Here was a slab of marble with a great crack out of which they told us the priest annually struck holy fire. Then we roamed about in dark passages which led off the main building, and saw the tomb of Joseph of Arimathea; and one was in constant danger of falling down dark holes or hitting one's head.

After that we went upstairs into a chapel, amazing in its dark brilliance, and saw an image of the Virgin Mary in a glass case covered with a profusion of jewels, ranging from whacking diamonds to cheap trinkets and wrist-watches. These were the gifts of pregnant mothers who were desirous of an easy time in their dark hour. We descended again, and almost suffocated by the pungent fumes of incense, we heard slow and melodious Latin chanting, rising and falling, and echoing in the grey building. This was emitted by a great procession of Roman Catholics. They said they were going to close the church for half an hour while this lasted, so, seeing we should be caught, we made a somewhat hurried exit, not however without vociferations from our guide who wanted money for (1) candles, (2) priest, (3) church, (4) … (5) … (6) … which I cannot recall. I gave him ten piastres, about two shillings, and told him to retire. We walked away, followed by the lad, who had now trebled his volubility, and was inventing more things that we appeared to be under an obligation for. After we were nearly forced to become rude in order to shake him off, we strolled through more alleys, coming on some picturesque corners, under archways, and seeing most wonderful bearded gentlemen with pale ascetic faces, large spreading hats and white raiment.

We were a bit lost when we fell on a native policeman who had the face of a child and soft cow-like eyes. We entered into conversation with him. I asked him if he had aught to do in this city; and he laughed loud and long and thought it a great joke. I asked if the inhabitants were peaceful, and his truncheon, did he often have to use it? He said, "No, they are very peaceful." He then asked if we were Americans. I replied, "No, English." "But," he said, "you are brothers, you and the Americans?" "There are many who call us so," I answered. Having directed us on our way be took his leave, moving away like a cow, softly smiling to himself.

After a space we boarded a gharri, and told the insignificant driver to drive his poor starved makeshifts of horses to Mount Scopus He tried to gallop the tired brutes up a steep hill, whereat I rated him soundly and told him to walk them. He said, "I Jew, Sabbath start at sunset. Must be back in stable by then." What a weird idea, maltreating your horses to keep the Sabbath!

When we got back to the Mess we had tea and sat I listening to the rain pattering down, and wondering how the Vernons were getting on up at Kulundia. We went to bed early, for we wanted to get up at 4.00 a.m. I had arranged with Andrews for a car to call for us at 4.30 a.m.

Kulundia to Ramleh. Next morning we got up in the dark, feeling rather cold and sticky. Outside, the moon and stars were still shining faintly, and I heard 4.0 o'clock strike on a deep bell somewhere in Jerusalem; the sound came ghostlike and muffled across the valley to us. It was not long before the Crossley tender glided up, its headlights making strange shadows. As we drove along the road to Kulundia in the half-light we passed a camel and its driver plodding along silently up the hill. I was so sleepy that I fell to dreaming. I thought somehow I was in Williams' old bus driving back to Hartland in Devonshire. I was roused by the first miraculous light of dawn breaking over the hills. By and by the light strengthened, and the lamps of the tender burnt feeble and dim on the white road. At last we were climbing up the hill which rises to Kulundia. The sky was full of faint clouds which veiled the dying stars; and the hills showed up more plainly, wet with the night's rain. The air smelt balmy and soft; and it was still, ever so still.

Now we saw the two Vernons with the wrapped up figures of the native police by them, silver grey in the dawn. The warm madder earth of Kulundia, the colour of Worcestershire earth, was all sticky; and I looked at "Valkyrie" and the Ambulance and then at the paltry length of run and then at the hills, and my heart quavered. However, the aircraft were dead light; so a stout heart was the only remedy! The air was cool, and the light of the coming sunrise was glowing behind the grey stone hills with little buildings perched airily at their summits. Andrews tried to telephone to Ramleh from the little white telephone box to ask for a weather report, in case it was misty on the plain below; but he was unable to get through. So we did not wait. We ran up our engines, and I taxied up the northern end of Kulundia, slightly uphill, right into a little patch of some sort of vegetables, to get every yard of run I could, and turned "Valkyrie" round to face the hazard. My heart was beating hard and fast and I felt a hot feeling in my chest. Then I steadied myself and opened the throttle. Slowly we gathered speed—already the morning airs were beginning to waft across the landing ground, and I was none too soon—and I did not come unstuck until about two-thirds way across diagonally At last I came off and hopped over a wall, saw the boulders whizzing underneath, then over a projecting spur and along the Jerusalem road. By this time the roaring engines had got into their stride and lifted the great silver aeroplane clear of the hills which sank beneath me, their menace gone, their power destroyed! And I drew a great deep breath of satisfaction as I circled round and the golden sun peeped up over the rugged sky line

I had a glimpse of the hills terraced down to the plain below, running out in ravines and spurs, elbows and ridges, of the soft green plain all bestrewn with blue morning shadows, stretching away, far away to the sea. And to the eastward was the dim Jordan Valley, mysteriously lit by the sunrise. I circled round and Embry made no move. What could have happened to him? I had no time to waste as I had only just enough petrol for Ramleh, so I flew west and saw the hills subside, and the winding Jerusalem-Ramleh road in its cut through the hillsides, and the headlands projecting out into the flat green of the plain. The road then struck out straight and I saw Ludd, the railway junction, but could not at first pick up Ramleh. At last I saw the three red hangars, and glided down into a pleasant land of green fields and trees.

I shall always remember the scene as I glided down over the railway to approach Ramleh. The clear morning air was like a crystal; sky blue as blue at the zenith, coming down to pale gold over the blue, now faint, line of the Judæan Hills to the eastward. At their feet, between them and the great plain, was a garment of pale silver mist, so that they stood up out of it into the morning air. And the scene was a wonderful symphony of blue, green and gold, enough to gladden the saddest heart. Near-by was the old town of Ramleh, famed of Crusaders, with Italian work predominating over that of

Palestine, and a campanile lifting up its straight finger to the sky. To the west was the infinite blue of the Mediterranean Sea. This was a delectable spot, like a fair garden.

Ramleh was reputed to be a difficult aerodrome as it all slopes up to the north-west, where there is a sort of convex rise. The rise is really the head of a spur on which the hangars are built. All along the bottom is the railway, and running more or less east and west, and cutting across the aerodrome, is a little wadi. As Gallehawk had promised, a "T" was out and a smoke candle alight. Whereat I landed, quite well. At the aerodrome he was waiting for me. He took me in, gave me a good bath and breakfast in the nice clean, airy Mess. The Mess buildings are somewhat like those of Aboukir.

Meanwhile Embry had arrived. He had been delayed in leaving Kulundia by one engine, and, when he had taken off the ground, this engine started vibrating very badly! Terrible position. He staggered up to 6,000 feet above the hills, and, as the engine still continued to go, he made for Ramleh. We examined the engine as well as we could externally, and poked bits of wire down the plug holes to feel the pistons, and could not find the trouble. Nevertheless the vibration was bad when the engine was run up. Gallehawk wired to Heliopolis for a new engine; and, as Embry was in such good hands, I decided to push on and leave him. I took on his passenger, Padre Still, as well as mine. The difficulty was to get off Ramleh. I was loaded to about 12,500 pounds and the morning would be warmish. Young Bonham Carter, who was now at 14 Squadron, took me over the aerodrome in his little car, and I decided that it was preferable to get off down hill and down wind, rather than up hill and up wind, as the country to the south-west was flat plain.

Ramleh to Heliopolis. I taxied over the brow to the north end of the aerodrome, where the ground fell rather sharply for a short distance to a valley which lay between the aerodrome and the town of Ramleh. I thought I could get moving up this little bit of hill, breast the top and take the run down having gained a bit of a start. I did this, and duly went rushing down the hill. The take off was none too easy or pleasant. I flew on low over the plain, passing over the green fields and ragged trees, turned back and flew round over the aerodrome, and then away southwards over against the sea. It was a fine sunny morning with a following wind. We flew down the inland side of the railway to Rafa, passing Gaza on the way. Rafa we passed in an hour. Here I expected to see Maitland on the landing ground where he had been changing an engine. But the landing ground, as I passed over, was quite deserted.

Then I had the most amazing wireless message from my Squadron at Baghdad. "Please say when all machines will be serviceable; shall we send Stand By to Ziza." I was never in a stranger position. Up in the air myself, with half the squadron scattered over 800 miles of desert and mountain and plain, with not the least knowledge of where they were or what condition they were in. Maitland I had no knowledge of. It turned out afterwards that he had got ready and left only half an hour before I came. I heard this on the wireless when I was passing El Arish. Summers was presumably in Heliopolis. Lees and Banting were somewhere coming along on the Mail, perhaps on the southern route between Ziza and Beersheba. As a matter of fact they were ahead of me. And Embry at Ramleh awaiting a new engine. I had to sort out my thoughts as we flew along and try and concoct some kind of message in reply.

Then we had early lunch on board. I happened to see banana peel being thrown out of the window. I sent a stern message back to the passengers from the Captain saying that such practices were strictly forbidden. As we passed Moseifig I noted that the sea had encroached so much that it was practically under water. We made a good trip the rest of the way and arrived in at 3.00 p.m.

Heliopolis to Abu Suweir. I had rather a sticky time getting ready. I had arrived on the Saturday afternoon with my crew fairly tired out; "Valkyrie" had to stand out in the open while at Heliopolis because of all my Vernons there; Monday it blew a sand storm, and it was well-nigh impossible to work on the engines. It was one long rush. A perfect nightmare. Embry only turned up on the Monday, after having had to forced-land because of the driving sand. We had originally been booked to pick up the Secretaries of State at Ismailia; at the last moment it was changed to No.4 F.T.S. Abu Suweir. On Tuesday afternoon we had to leave. When I ran up I found both throttle barrels seized with the sand. That meant off with the radiators, as being the quickest way of dismantling the carburettors. Banting decided to do the trip instead of Maitland, who had engine trouble. So the four of us were: Summers, Banting, Embry and myself. Summers and Embry pushed on to Abu Suweir. Banting returned to change the new propellers he had fitted on for his old ones, and decided to wait for me. Barrett and I had a cup of tea in the little N.A.A.F.I. canteen up by South Camp. Banting and I finally started rather late and wirelessed to Abu Suweir for flares. As we flew up the eastern edge of the cultivation, we crept further and further into the blue evening. The dusk fell suddenly, and lights twinkled in the strip of cultivation along the railway and the fresh-water canal. At last we saw the dull orange glimmer of the flares at Abu Suweir. It was not quite dark when we landed.

Abu Suweir to Rafa. We waited all the morning for the Secretaries of State to arrive. I did not intend to start after 2.00 p.m., as it would not allow a reasonable time to get to Ziza before dusk. They arrived very late. We insisted on weighing all their luggage before they emplaned. Embry took the Secretaries of State and their party as there were comfortable seats in the Ambulance. I took Group Captain Burnett and Captain Wallace, a private secretary. We all taxied out, one after another, myself last, down the "straight." We flew over El Rimel, where there was a landing ground and practice camp, with all the Middle East Aircraft concentrated there. It was a warm sunny afternoon and the desert had a whiteish glare over it.

My port oil pressure had been gradually falling, and was now hovering around 40 pounds. As we approached Rafa it fell to 38 pounds and I decided I must land. What a pity to lose all the height I had so painfully acquired! I wirelessed to the other three to carry on and then glided down over Rafa. I flew round over the green country by the railway junction with the big sheds, threw out a smoke candle on the landing ground, and landed. Rafa has a ridge running from north to south the whole length of it, not steep; in fact, the ground just slopes down from the centre to east and west. I bounced a bit, as I did not allow for the ridge sufficiently. Some donkeys were of course occupying the best part of the landing ground by the circle. When I landed we set to work to try and get the oil pressure right. Summers shortly after came back and landed, not having received my wireless message telling him to push on. He only stayed a few minutes and then left again. We ran the engine up and the oil pressure was no better. So then we exchanged port and starboard oil gauges, and found that it was the port oil gauge that was dud.

By this time it was too late to go on, so we camped down for the night. Group Captain Burnett and Captain Wallace walked over to Rafa station, about one and a half miles away, and bought some eggs from the station-master. It was a lovely evening, and the soft twilight enwrapped the warm green fields in a slumbrous garment. We had a most pleasant supper by the camp fire, and I think G. C. Burnett and Captain Wallace thoroughly enjoyed themselves. I had my camp bed and put it up by the fuselage. During the night I was wakened up by two large white pariah dogs snuffing round; when I sat up they glided away under the plane like pale ghosts.

Rafa to Ziza. We left Rafa as the golden sun came up over the eastern horizon. I took off along the ridge. Some Bedou got in the way, and I had to pass quite close to them. I rose up into the keen cool morning air and saw that around was an extensive layer of strato-cumulus covering a large part of the country. The way to Beersheba looked moderately clear and I steered east as I climbed into the eye of the sun. I sent off a message asking for a weather report from Ziza, for the clouds seemed right up against the Judæan Hills, whose high blue-coloured line in places showed above them. I thought, indeed I feared, that the country over the other side might be covered entirely and that I should not be able to find Ziza, and be flying about over hill country whose height I did not know. However, I failed to get the weather report, so there was nothing to do but to press on.

I gradually rose to 7,000 feet as I was light and the air was cool. I looked back, and through the kingdom of broken cloud I could see the blue mist of the Mediterranean Sea, curving away obliquely. Beersheba itself was concealed under the cloud layer, but I picked up a railway triangle and identified it as just north of the town on a good map of Palestine that I had got in Egypt. Thereafter I flew over clouds till I came to the high hills. Then, of a sudden, the Dead Sea came into view like a polished mirror, and became rapidly larger as the hills moved back beneath me. As I passed over it I consumed biscuits. I was hungry. I had only had a breakfast of tea and bread and jam at Rafa. I passed back a note to the Group Captain with the following quotation from a hymn in it:

> Could we but climb where Moses stood,
> And view the landscape o'er,
> Not Jordan's stream nor death's cold flood
> Should fright us from the shore.

I think that he was quite cheered up with this. Then I passed over the El Lisan peninsula, over "Jehovah's Rest" and the high plateau, and over the great gorge of Seil el Mojeb, where it divides for the second time. This great cut looked rather wonderful in the early sunlight, full of big shadows and rays of sunlight filtering down to the curving wadi in its deep bottom. I throttled down and eased off the engines, picked up Ziza and saw four Vernons there. Horrex had flown over as a Stand By. Then I landed and proceeded to fill up with petrol.

Ziza to Ramadi. The Secretaries of State had gone up to Amman for the night, and after a while the sky was loud with the rumble of the D.H.9as which were bringing them back. Summers, Banting and Embry did not wait for me to finish filling up and pushed on in front. Horrex remained to go with me. I made the best trip to Ramadi I have ever done, with a good following wind.

This is the only time I had got through from Ziza without stopping to fill up. All five of us got through without a hitch.

"Valkyrie" was very slow, and as we crossed the "Upland of the Winds" Horrex pulled ahead. At about *L.G.* N he was a small speck, and as we approached *L.G.* R he was out of sight, but I could hear his wireless, as also that of the other Vernons. He asked if he was to turn and wait for me, or push on. I replied, "Push on." Later on he asked if he might go right through non-stop to Hinaidi, if he had enough petrol. I said he was to do this.

As I approached *L.G.* V I had grave doubts as to whether I should go through, as my petrol consumption appeared to be very high. However, I decided to risk it, and actually did it easily. After *L.G.* V it got hot, and I was so sleepy I could hardly keep my eyes open; for what with my trip over to Egypt and the rush of getting ready to come back in two days, I was feeling rather done. Between *L.G.* V and *L.G.* IV we got one huge bump which banked us over about 30 degrees, and it was quite a business getting back on to an even keel again. I wondered vaguely what sort of a landing I should make at Ramadi, and I was just in that state that I wondered how much control over my senses I really had. However, I made quite a respectable landing. All the others had passed through, but I found Laing there, who was standing by. After filling up and getting a drink we pushed on again in half an hour or so.

Ramadi to Hinaidi. On again, with Laing beside me, over the wide sun-bathed plain with hard horizon, cut across by the winding Euphrates. The blue of Lake Habbaniyah and the river, the white of the hills and distant mounds, the colours of the cultivation have bitten deep into my memory. Once again Baghdad on its river came into view, and I saw my passengers looking out viewing it for the first time. Then round to the east of the aerodrome we flew, glided down and made a good landing near the circle. My face was red and blistered and unshaven, and I was weary, but contented.

1. Marshes.

2. Brooks or rivers.

3. Vernon specially fitted up as an ambulance aeroplane.

4. Well-known hot wind.

CHAPTER IX

TWO MAIL TRIPS IN 1925

MY THIRD MAIL TRIP (APRIL, 1925)

Hinaidi to Ramadi. I flew to Heliopolis with three Vimys flown by Smylie, Glover and Russell. They were taking the Mail. I took my second fitter Sturman. Goldsmith stayed behind for the Inter-Services boxing, in which incidentally he got knocked out. I wanted a rest before the hot weather set in and I was glad to have a short spell in the cooler air of Egypt. I had a good trip over to Ramadi. We took off in a westerly direction, i.e. towards the Tigris.

Ramadi to L.G. D. The Vimys took off before I did. It was scarcely light when we left. The sun only began really to come up when we were passing over the Jebels between *L.G.* II and *L.G.* III. There was a certain amount of alto-cumulus and cirrus, and I looked up and saw the moon fading from lemon to silver and then to white behind the thin moving veil of cloud. The Vimys were drawing further and further ahead, as I could hear on my wireless. About *L.G.* N I saw two specks in the distance coming over the "Upland of the Winds" towards us. These turned out to be the two standby Vernons of No. 70 Squadron, which had gone over with our Secretary of State's party to Ziza, and which were now returning. It seemed strange meeting them above that lonely plain. The two far specks getting larger and larger, the excitement and speculation as to what they could be, the feeling of human touch as they sailed past, and then silence and void as they sped away on their long journey. It was fine weather and we passed over the "Land of Conjecture" quite comfortably. The last part of the trip was pretty bumpy, but nothing out of the way. As we approached *L.G.* D I saw a Vimy on the ground; this turned out to be Smylie. I sailed round and tried to drop a smoke candle, which turned out to be a dud. At last Smylie fired a Very light which gave just enough smoke to give me the direction of the wind. I made quite a good landing. I took in 60 gallons of petrol.

L.G. D *to Ziza.* Smylie and I went on together. "Valkyrie" was very slow, whether due to my old Aboukir propellers, which I had had on since I took her over, or to the fact that she had done nearly 300 hours; and Smylie drew ahead. I more or less cut across from Azrak to Kasr Kharana and did not follow the track closely. I lost some height as I drew towards the fort, and had to open up again to climb over the Jebel Mugher. I had the Vimy in sight until we were approaching Ziza. Although it was quite early in the day Smylie and I decided we would not push on to Heliopolis, but stay and look over our engines. I spent the afternoon re-rigging one of the rudder controls with Corporal Searle, as I found it was crossed between the two pulleys underneath the seat.

In the evening we took a tender and paid a visit to the ruin of Meshetta, miles from Ziza, where the plough track starts off to the Jebel Mugher. I got some interesting photos of the fine deeply incised carving. I also brought a carved fragment back in the tender and left it at Ziza, whence it was ultimately flown over to Baghdad by Lees. It was rather a wonderful view driving back in the tender across the rolling plain of Moab to Ziza. The sun was sinking behind the blue hills of Judæa in a flaming glory, and all the plain became dark and full of mystery. Robert Hanmer was sitting beside me in the front of the tender, and as the almost level rays of the sun struck his face and lit it, I was reminded of driving back from some show on Salisbury Plain.

Ziza to Heliopolis. I made a very good trip down into Egypt, and the engines ran excellently as far as Tel el Kebir, when I felt something happen to the starboard engine and a certain amount of not very severe vibration developed. When I arrived the rotor of one magneto was found to have disappeared. It had evidently forced its way out through the distributor cover, in which it had ripped a hole. The gear in the magneto was also smashed up. I again started from Ziza just behind the Vimys and owing to my lower performance they pulled away from me. They had both the climb and speed of me. I saw them disappearing over the Dead Sea at about 5,500 in a small bunch well north of the El Lisan peninsula. I forged painfully towards the hills, and as I was crossing the chasm of Seil el Mojeb, I took two photographs. I then passed quite low over the plateau by "Jehovah's Rest" and on over the peninsula, on which I was able just to make out a tiny circle. This circle, considering the height it had to be viewed from, was far too small. My engines were full out, and yet my ceiling was only 4,600 feet. This was not encouraging.

As I passed over the hills on the western shores of the Dead Sea I compared the lie of them carefully with my large-scale map (¼ inch to 1 mile) and was able to follow their convolutions fairly well. I picked up the wadi at Tel el Millar, but was unable to see any landing ground[1] marked. This, however, may have been ploughed up. I followed the wadi down to Beersheba and passed south of the town, and away on to the beautiful blue curve of the Mediterranean Sea. I passed over the landing ground at Rafa, which aroused memories of my last trip. Moseifig, as before, was nearly totally covered by the encroaching sea, and the dark circle just showed up in the water.

I arrived at Heliopolis at 10.15 a.m. and Harry Turner was at No. 216 Squadron sick quarters, and sent up for me and took me off with him to No.1 Rue Kafr el Dawar! That afternoon I went with the Turners to No.216 Squadron sports and "Mary" Coningham stunted a Siskin and Noakes did crazy flying on an Avro. He took off Coningham's flying in the most absurd way. It seemed a shock being thrust into civilization right out of the Blue; and to hear the murmur of feminine conversation and to see all the ladies' smart frocks and animated smiles.

Heliopolis to Ziza. We were delayed starting off by the late arrival of the Mail. I came back with Barkley. I brought Phillips back, whom I had taken over on leave for England in February. I flew over Heliopolis and saw little white specks waving good-bye on the balcony of No. 1 Rue Kafr el Dawar. There was a certain amount of cloud. By Bilbeis we seemed to drift into a following wind, but at Tel el Kebir it turned against us again. The weather was simply wonderful, the best I have ever experienced on this trip, and the air was nearly calm. As we flew along, the shores of the Mediterranean the sky was a soft faint blue with a translucent opal mist round the horizon. The sun rays made over the sandy desert with its myriad wind-driven sand dunes a bright white veil. The sea was a deep blue embracing green and violet, and it merged into a blue mist, horizonless. The mist horizon was high up, and out of it one or two wee clouds poked up as out of the sea itself.

We passed Rafa in just over three and a quarter hours and climbed up, up over the Judæan Hills more and more into the sweet sunlight. The familiar picture passed again; the rugged hills split by a thousand wadis; the silver inland sea, dropped down like a pool of molten metal into a cleft in the rocks; the curving El Lisan peninsula; the great gorge of Seil el Mojeb, with its deep clear-cut shadows hiding its abyss, and the brilliant green scrub and bushes in miniature along its curving bottoms; and then the plain of Ziza. As I glided down I tried each magneto, and found one magneto on the port engine had cut out.

Ziza to Kasr Kharana. After landing and filling up I ran up the engines and found that there was some real trouble with the port engine. It was missing and not holding its revs. Finally, we wirelessed to Amman to fly down two new magnetos. All the afternoon and evening we worked away at the engine, and on into the darkness, going down to the little station at Ziza to snatch an odd meal. We finished, tired out, at about 10.30 p.m. Sturman started again at dawn; I got up a little later, as, knowing I should have a pretty strenuous time flying, I tried to get as much rest as I could. A D.H.9a had arrived from Amman with the new magneto, and by about 9.00 a.m. we ran up, and the engine, though a little rough, seemed reasonable enough to go on with.

I took off and saw Barkley was stuck on the aerodrome, presumably with tyre trouble. I waited and flew round for some time, and then pushed on, as I had the Mail. It was already quite warm and I had to go full out to get over the Jebel Mugher. I soon picked up the track. At this point I always expect to take longer to reach the thin white thread drawn across the undulating hills than I actually do. One seems to find it almost underneath one, unexpectedly. I followed the white thread, like a piece of silk, drawn across the long slope down to Kasr Kharana, passed the old Roman fort, little thinking how familiar I should become with it. I passed on and the Pools of Azrak and the "Plain of Sorrows" came in sight.

There were tremendous up and down dunts, and I was ballooning up and down as much as 500 to 1,000 feet at a time, in the hot disturbed air. The engines had been full out, with the heavy load, and I was just beginning to think of easing them down, with the grey "Land of Conjecture" tilted up on the eastern horizon, when a terrible vibration shook "Valkyrie" from stem to stern. It took me some moments to appreciate what had happened, and I heard vaguely and confusedly a series of whirrings and harsh bangings. Then I shook myself up and the realization came to me that my port engine was a hopeless wreck! It was on the far side from where I was sitting, so I could not see it without considerably stretching up. Whether I divined it or actually saw it, I knew that there were great holes in the crank-case and pieces of hot metal were flying through and the engine was hurling out its bowels over the waste below. Out of the corner of my eye I could see the header tank hanging stupidly and wobbling with its stays broken.

TRANSFERRING THE MAIL AT KASR KHARANA

I throttled back the port engine and turned back westward for Kasr Kharana, alongside of which Flight Lieutenant Moore of the armoured cars had told me at *L.G.* D you could land quite well. Luckily the starboard engine was my sound engine, and this is the one you can fly on more easily, owing to the Vernon's tendency to turn to starboard. Which way was the wind? Landing across winds of any strength in exposed places might easily spell disaster. I got Barrett to throw out two smoke candles, but, as I was slowly working round to starboard, neither he nor I could see the little thin wisps of blue smoke on their impact with the ground. Their important message was thus wasted on the desert air. Then of the weather report at Ziza I bethought me. N.N.W. the surface wind, it had said. I would chance it at that.

Now I was approaching the Fort from the south-east; and as I glided down the contours of the ground stood up in relief, small details gave the desert reality, and I exerted my judgment to the uttermost. I looked keenly for folds and holes in the ground, in order to try and clear them. I saw I was going to land on a sort of little plateau which was raised somewhat higher than the level of the 10-mile broad valley, bounded on either side by range upon range of hills stretching away beyond knowledge and sight into a soft dim glow. On its southern edge was the Fort; its northern edge sloped away to a more defined wadi, the track spanned it and camel-thorn covered it with a ragged vesture. Now I was gliding on past the Fort, the ground rose up, reared up in front of me; with satisfaction I noticed that I was not drifting; then a violent flatten out and with a bounce I was down. "Valkyrie" ran a little: stopped. Then silence, save for the soft crooning of the desert wind. The struggle for safety was at an end.

When one forced-lands in the Blue, instead of one's troubles being over, they are just begun, and one knows that one has a hard rough time ahead. Usually starting tired, one has to work till one is so weary that weariness can do no more. It is a whole world of weariness and thirst. And through it all the spirit must not flag, but drive on the tired body and mind to action and thought.

I got out and found the engine in a terrible mess, dirty hot oil dripping from the gaping rents in the crank-case, in which there were six holes, two between the three blocks of cylinders, two larger ones on either side, and two more at the bottom angles of the sump. Bits of steel and aluminium and pieces of connecting rod lay on the planes. Within an hour of landing Searle had the ground W/T set up, and we were in touch with Amman sending out our signals of distress. As I ground the handle of the Hand Generator propped up on the seat inside the hull, till the sweat ran off me, I felt a lump in my throat, and felt near breaking down; partly from the reaction after the strain, and partly from the marvel of our little message, being tapped out and travelling hundreds of miles from that lonely spot.

Searle was sitting inside the hull, and as he lifted his dirty, ugly begrimed face moist with drops of sweat, and gazed out of the window at the sunlit distance, a far-away look came into his eyes; and almost as soon as he turned the tuning knob with his right hand, he said, "Amman's got me," then, "Heliopolis acknowledging," a faint thin high note, like a hair; then, "Abu Suweir," as they picked the message up, and then Amman's powerful station relaying the message to Baghdad. In ten minutes every Mail station knew that His Majesty's Mail was down and in urgent need; and there were we, apparently alone, far from civilization, on that plain haunted only by the wonder of the past, with a few electrical instruments.

By this time it was high noon, and the flint-covered sand plain warmed up. Three hundred yards away stood Kasr Kharana burying its secrets. We unbolted the engine ready to take out, and dismantled the header tank, and wirelessed to Amman to fetch the header tank stay to be mended. We also wirelessed to Egypt for a new one as well as an engine. About 3.00 p.m. the air became vibrant with the sound of an engine, and as we looked towards the dim line of the Jebel Mugher, over which we had come, we saw Barkley. We lit a smoke candle and he came down and landed and took over the Mail. In three-quarters of an hour he was gone again eastwards.

While he was down, the sense of loneliness disappeared, and we seemed in touch with humanity once more. When I saw him disappear as a faint blur over the horizon of hills, I felt the savour had gone out of life. We knew by wireless that Amman were sending out cars, and we scanned the extent of the plain against the westering sun for any signs of them. I had an unpleasant feeling of apprehension as we were right in the Wahabi area; they had told me that the Wahabis were expected up the Kharana track next time; and three weeks before there had been a rumour that they were approaching Ziza, unfounded of course. The worst of it was that we had no rifles; and so we were helpless, with a broken engine and no means of escape. And what could four white men avail against the hosts of Ibn Saud?

I strained my eyes towards the south-eastern horizon, where the plain faded away under infinitely receding headlands of Jebels, some shining curiously white, others yellow and grey; and saw the plain as a dim sea with no boundary except the pale sky. What would I see? The distant column of dust, perchance six leagues away, lit to gold by the sun, not moving at first, but taking shape and form; after an hour or so moving, yes, moving … Then the glimmer of banners, and swift horses and camels ghostly in the dust, and the shining of steel; then warriors of blood arrayed in battle white with banners of green, and the distant battle song rising and falling over the plain, rising to a pæan … could that be real? And I turned and looked at the Vernon, and our dusty begrimed workaday mechanics, and tools lying about, just as they might be on the aerodrome at Farnborough, and I felt bewildered by the riddle of life.

And when the sun was low and the day far spent, after many false alarms, we did make out something in the distance where the darkening plain met the now dimming blue of the Jebel Mugher. The plain looked real, the hills unreal beyond, like a blue cloud. And against the blue rose a golden cloud, a column of dust, which never seemed to grow larger, nor yet smaller. After a quarter of an hour or so it detached itself into three columns which we saw at last were drawing nearer and nearer, speeding fast, though slow at the great distance, across the plain towards us. And I have a memory of the faces of the watchers turned towards the golden sun lit up with an unnatural brightness. At last a little dot appeared at the head of each trail of golden dust; first a sleek Rolls armoured car, with its wicked-looking Vickers gun peeping out of its turret, then two desert tenders. And we ran out on to the track to meet them, joyfully.

Barkley had taken over Phillips at Ziza, as his passenger had got out there, but he had left Phillips again, at his own request, to help me, when he took on the Mail. Barkley got, I think, to *L.G.* P that night.

I remember the scene at dusk. The Roman Fort four-square and ghostly in the background, "Valkyrie's" faint yet massive silhouette and the dark mass of the cars parked together. Before turning in, I looked at the turret of the armoured Rolls with the faint illumination inside made by little lights, and heard the click of the bolt of the gun, as it was put in and the gun trained ready, pointing out south-eastwards into the darkness. A Lewis gun was also made ready and laid in the back of the car. That night I turned in on my little camp bed by the hull and lay and watched the stars in the deep blue velvet night. A faint cool wind blew across the desert at intervals and fanned my hair. It became quite, cold. Maitland told me afterwards that a pilot who had had a forced landing here told him that in the night he heard strange noises, and was certain that he

KASR KHARANA AND THE AIR MAIL TRACK

CHANGING THE ENGINE AT KASR KHARANA

heard the tramp, tramp of the Roman legions going past; and so the old spirit of 2,000 years ago must till be lurking there, of the fierce Roman legionaries, of the terrible discipline of the Eagle. Out at Kasr Kharana and its sister forts Kasr Amra and Kasr Azrak they were probably colonials, used to some extent to the awful privations and hardships and the grim struggle for existence; perhaps Scythians. But I heard not a sound. That night the legions passed in silence. I did not even hear the rattle of the shield of the Roman sentry on the roof of the Fort, as he stood peering perchance into the darkness.

I woke up with the false dawn, that vision of amber over the eastern hills. As the upper sky brightened to lightest violet, the amber faded; and the sun rose in glory and lit "Valkyrie" to silver. Searle came and brought me my cup of coffee as I lay in bed. About 10 a.m. the two Vimys came and Squadron D'Albiac in a D.H.9a from Amman. We had watched the Vimys' progress on the wireless. Squadron Leader Willock and Sergeant Bennet, who brought the engine, came in the Vimys.

Of that day, the grime, the sweat, the afternoon heat and the thirst, I cannot record the details. It is a confused memory, with a few details standing out clearly. Willock standing up in his Vimy consuming a large bottle of beer, the silver undersurface of the planes reflecting white light all over him; the struggles with the sheerlegs; the beam that bent in a sickly manner as we tried to lift the engine off the Vimy; how we nearly dropped the engine as we were getting it off and on to the petrol drums in the back of the armoured car; the finding of the cracked induction pipe to the Duplex carburettor; meals taken sitting on valises and trunks; working on into the darkness with the light from a wandering lead and the armoured car's head-lamp shining on the engine and the faintly lit figures of the tired workers, tools being lost and found, strolling around talking over many things with Willock; the D.H.9as return with the repaired stay; all these were but incidents in the long toil, to get the new in. What made it much more troublesome was having to change the propellers over in the metal bosses, and put the carburettors on. It was extraordinarily lucky that someone found the cracked induction pipe, for otherwise we might have got it on and the radiator fixed up, and then found that the engine would not run. Up at dawn the next morning, a snatch of breakfast, and by 10 a.m. we were ready to run up. Bennet had left in his Vimy fairly early to reach Ziza and get filled up.

On the afternoon we arrived I found an insect running about among the stones, about one and a half inches long, called a Praying Mantis. It had a head like an ape, and it sits up and prays. It, used apparently to be regarded as a sacred insect. Twice I went with Phillips into the ancient Fort. I felt I could not face it by myself. Ruined in a way, yet parts of it were in remarkably good preservation. The roof, quite flat, was on one side whole. The building is square, of three stories, each of less depth than the one below, with a courtyard in the centre which you approach through a barrel-vaulted archway. At the level, of the first floor there were signs of a gallery, and all the chambers gave on to the courtyard. There were real marble steps of slight slope running up, and below burying themselves in the thick layer of rubble. Who knows but that there is not a wonderful tiled floor beneath? Three or four of the vaulted chambers were in a good state, and had fine dog-tooth mouldings round the arched windows and recesses. The outer walls were of immense thickness and slotted diagonally with loopholes. There were some fine medallions on some of the walls, of two sorts: one sort with a bold chrysanthemum design, the other with more delicate flower tracery. All were relatively deeply incised. The place was terribly haunted and you could have cut the atmosphere with a knife. We found several nearly whole skeletons in the rooms with rags covering them, which looked like Arab clothing, and many more isolated bones. One robe, bleached white, and by itself, looked as if its owner had been decapitated. The part round the neck was all brown from what looked like blood-stains. There was a dry eerie acrid smell about the place, which made me shiver in spite of the fact that it was hot. What strange dramas has that place, lonely sentinel of the desert, been witness of? What human agonies unrecorded in the dark annals of history?

In the morning after breakfast I wandered down the wadi with its green vegetation, and I found Painted Lady butterflies and a species of Small Blue, which I do not think was quite the same as our English Small Blue.

Kasr Kharana to L.G. V. I ran up both engines, and the port one (new one) seemed harsh, but I decided to push on with it. Then we found the header tank itself was leaking where the stay had broken. Off it had to come, and Tuck soldered it up. I was very worried, as I thought it would never hold up. However, it did. Then I took off, leaving the covered-in pit which we had dug to empty out the old oil from the engine. If anyone had fallen into that ghastly black mess our troubles would have been complete! I had to take off westwards; and I ran a long way before rising; slowly "Valkyrie" lifted but hardly climbed. At last I was able to turn, and I saw the Vimy, with the little grout standing round her, get smaller and smaller as I gradually lost sight of her and Kasr Kharana in the far distance.

The new engine ran all right, although it is always worrying dashing straight off into the Blue with an untested engine. In one and three-quarter hours we were passing *L.G.* H with a wind behind and going strong; in one and a half hours more we had crossed the "Up land of the Winds" and were making across the "Kingdom of What Wasn't" to *L.G.* 8. We had passed by "Grummet's Grange" and "Wu's Wallop." There were two camps of about 200 tents each on the Wadi Hauran. The food that the Turners had given me had been very welcome on this trip: two chickens, cooked potatoes, bread and a jam roll. The jam roll we now ate. At last the mud flat at *L.G.* V showed up very faint and dim just below and parallel with the horizon, and I landed for petrol. There was a hot wind blowing here, and I was feeling tired and worn-out. We had trouble with the tank. We only got 20 gallons out and then the pump jammed, and I cut the palm of my hand messing about with it. This was unfortunate, because D.H.9as were coming on the next day from Amman and would want petrol. Sergeant Major Copper went out the next day in a D.H.9a, met them and made a temporary repair.

L.G. V *to Ramadi.* On again, bound for home. Now it began to be very hot, and one felt the approach of Iraq and its sun-scorched plains. The sun was getting lower and all the plain took on a sienna tinge. The port oil pressure was getting a little low, and I suspected the gauge again. As we approached Ramadi I tried the switches and found the starboard engine dud on one magneto. As we landed the light was just failing, and I hardly saw the ground, which had turned from sienna to grey, as it rushed up. I touched outside the edge of Ramadi at the south-west corner. The landing was not too bad.

Ramadi to Hinaidi. When I landed at Ramadi I asked Sturman if he would rather work on the engines, and look them over, and fly back that night, or give up work and wait till the morning. He was looking absolutely washed out and dead-beat, and he had been feeling sick and had eaten nothing since leaving Kasr Kharana. He said he would like to work. So we changed the oil gauges, and found that my suspicion that it was the port oil gauge and not the port oil pressure that was dud was correct. He also worked on the magneto of the starboard engine. Pitt laid out the flares, which had to be across the landing ground and gave me a very short run before the trenches on the opposite side. I found it hard to see the flares when taxying out, owing to the dust. I plunged off into the blackness and just pulled "Valkyrie" off before the trench. I made away over the river, so as to get over the desert and away from the cultivation, and soon the moon rose and reflected its in molten gold in the Euphrates.

DOORWAY ON SOUTH SIDE OF KASR KHARANA

These moonlight nights in Iraq are wonderful for flying, after the heat of the day. I watch the moon reflection in streaks of gold against the jet-black desert on the distant reaches of the river, and the glow and searing flame of my exhausts, and the little sparking at the plug terminals.

As we passed Fellujah we saw the first rocket rise and hang in the sky, and I switched my dashboard light on for Barrett to write a W/T message. I let Barrett fly most of the way. Then came the twinkling lights of Baghdad, shining doubly in the Tigris, and the stronger glow of Hinaidi beyond. I glided down and flew low past the flares, fired a green light, was answered, and then circled in over the red lighted wireless masts, for the wind was N.E. here. I flew "Valkyrie" in, as I was too tired to do anything else. I watched the great black shadow of my wheels getting closer and more defined after I put on my Holt flare; and met the upward rushing, orange-lit ground, all speckled with faint shadows, with a sharp pull back on the control wheel. But not enough! Then a bounce, a burst of engine, and "Valkyrie" sank to rest. I taxied in, rather vaguely at first, not being sure of my direction; then I picked up our sheds and as I approached them I saw figures waiting and Uncle Lees signalling me in with outstretched arms. "Valkyrie" had done over 300 hours, and this was her last flight with these wings. Now she goes in for complete overhaul. I had had a long day. Worked on the engine from dawn at Kasr Kharana, and had then flown 500 miles, the last 75 at night. I arrived home at 9.30 hours, had a warm bath, and supper, and sat up till 1 a.m. reading my letters which I found waiting for me at Hinaidi.

MY FOURTH MAIL TRIP (JULY, 1925)

Hinaidi to Ramadi. The weather was intensely hot, and at the height of the burning Iraq summer, pitiless and scalding. That day it blew dust at lunch-time and I wondered if we should be able to start. I got one and a half hour's sleep in the afternoon before starting. Maitland and Horrex started with me. About 4.45 p.m. I ran up. Each engine ran up beautifully and the revolution indicator needles stood steady as rocks at 1,800. The dust had died down on the surface, but hung as a heavy haze in the sky, while the sun burned through the yellow grey pall as through ground glass, and the wind was as a hot hand pressing on the temples.

Away we went into the thin tortured air, climbing slowly and rolling about. At 1,000 feet it was like a hot furnace and it felt stifling in the cockpit, as hot wafts of air found their way in and out. We crossed the Tigris and you could hardly see 2 miles in places. Every now and then the dust haze thickened up, and then cleared somewhat. About 20 miles from Baghdad we saw the lorry with planes lashed on going out to a Vernon which had been crashed at Fellujah on the Monday before, landing at night. This was to be rebuilt. At Fellujah we had to veer a bit to the north, as the dust was very thick, and looked menacing. But towards Ramadi I began to see the Euphrates more clearly, and at last the weather cleared and the visibility improved. I watched the red-hot sun sinking over the desert as I crossed the river. The other two had landed when I got there. I made a perfect landing down the hill, if a trifle fast.

Ramadi to L.G. V. We slept the night in the open at Ramadi, having the beds put outside the serai at the foot of the Wireless Mast. There was a warm breeze, which, however, kept things tolerably cool. Horrex complained of pains and chilliness, and I had to signal for Laing to come on. It turned out that Horrex was starting a dose of Sandfly,[2] and Embry came and fetched him back in the Ambulance Vernon the next day. Maitland and I set off together. At 1,000 feet the layer of atmosphere was very hot. The sun was just about to rise as we started. There was a severe head wind, and we had to land at *L.G.* V for petrol, as we took over two hours to reach it.

L.G. V *to L.G.* D. After spending an hour and forty-five minutes at *L.G.* V we pushed on. Maitland filled up before us and was also having a bit of trouble with one carburettor, which we waited for him to attend to. Freddie Stent and I sat down in the shade and ate hard-boiled egg and biscuits and drank cold lemonade out of my Thermos. I have no very clear memory of that trip to *L.G.* D. Stent did quite a lot of the flying, between the times when he was taking notes of R.P.M.[3] etc. I was flying in my shirt and I wound my handkerchief round my neck to protect it from the sun. I had had a larger peak made to my flying topee by the tailor, but, though I had fixed it with a paper fastener, it was too flabby and blew up. What I do remember is the pitiless sun burning, burning down with an intolerable stare. And my shoulder, which was not covered by my spine pad, felt all stiff and bruised where the rays of the sun had fallen on it. I felt pretty worn out and tired, but still plugged on. Maitland drew ahead somewhere on the "Upland of the Winds" and I saw him no more. "Wu's Wallop" I did not see, but "Grummet's Grange" between O and P looked like a gaunt white skeleton. The glare was pretty bad, and one certainly did feel the effect of the roaring engines, the stunning effect of the sun rays and the bleached desert.

I made quite a good landing at *L.G.* D, on the all-weather landing ground, across the short way of that part which is clear of camel-thorn and which is roughly elliptical shaped. However I nearly ran into the camel-thorn at the other side and just managed to swing in time. We took in gallons from the newly installed tank, which is like that at *L.G.* V. The pump was horribly stiff, and Stent and I each took one end of the handle. It had a way of catching you in the small of the back when you pumped. And it was pretty hot at D, although not so hot as the eastern side of the desert.

L.G. D *to Ziza*. This trip was a tremendously bumpy one. It was high noon. We struggled away from *L.G.* D. Maitland had gone straight through and we heard he had landed at Ziza. Across the "Plain of Sorrows" we flew, over Kasr Kharana, which I saw they had marked with a circle and called *L.G.* B, since my forced landing there. I had to climb a little to o'ertop the Jebel Mugher. Then the usual scanning of the vast Plain of Moab to spot Ziza, which I usually pick up by the Persian ruin[4] which looks like a dark spot on the plain. I made a nice approach up the hill, and a perfect landing.

Ziza to Heliopolis. When we reached Ziza we filled up on the landing ground, and we found, on getting out of "Valkyrie," that the air was fresh and cool; cool as cold water on a hot day. I nearly skipped about for joy and took great draughts of refreshing air into my lungs. One felt it was a joy to be alive. The act of living and breathing was an ecstasy. I felt as if I had been living in an oven for an interminable time, farther back than I could remember, and now I was released! And my body felt lighter, and my limbs exhilarated. I had a bath by the wall behind the station in the pleasant sunlight. This consisted in standing by a zinc basin and letting the cool wind play on my wet skinny limbs! How excellent it was! Simple joys are always the most perfect. That night I slept out in my camp bed by "Valkyrie," and woke up in the night with cold feet. Laing had turned up just before dusk.

The next morning was quite windless. Our Vernons were down by the station. As I taxied up to the landing ground the wind blew the dust, such little wind as there was, all over the road up to the landing ground and over the landing ground itself. I had to peer out into the fog of dust—and in this Stent helped me—to stop myself taxying into holes. And the dust kept coming forwards over the Vernon and on ahead. At the top of the slope I throttled down as much as I could to stop whisking up the dust and waited till it should subside. Then I thought I had better take off up the hill, so started taxying down. Then I changed my mind and took off into the dust cloud with some misgiving; for I thought that I might have to fly round and round in it if my climb was very bad, and not be able to climb out of it. However, by the time I had turned back to the aerodrome, I had climbed out of it and saw it lying like a local fog. The other Vernons, to their hatred and disgust, were prevented from getting off for about a quarter of an hour.

It was quite cool and I was flying in my blue Burberry. We climbed up over the Wadi Seil el Mojeb, and I tried to get two more photographs of it. They never seem to come out well, though. Then, up over the plateau, which I carefully examined for promising landing grounds. I asked Stent to sketch in the plateau on the Jerusalem map. We had climbed to quite a good height, and I spotted the circle on El Lisan as we passed over. Then over the opposite hills, and towards Beersheba. It was perfect weather, with a gentle blue sky; and as I looked back the Dead Sea appeared like a molten mirror with the shadowy hills standing up in a golden sun haze behind it.

I was keen to find Tel-a-Rad, the new landing ground that had been marked out between Beersheba and the Dead Sea. I think the village of Tel.-a-Rad is on a little hill, closed in by the jut of hills standing out from the western wall of the Dead Sea. There is a sort of plain, which forms the end of one or two wadis running in the Beersheba direction. I had to circle round quite a lot before I suddenly spotted the circle. This I found when I had located one or two aeroplane tracks on the ground. Then we went south of Beersheba, past Rafa.

We had quite a pleasant breakfast off l egg and biscuits and tea, as we approached El Arish. We sailed down the shores of the Mediterranean and the rest of the trip was uneventful. About Kantara the starboard engine began to run a little roughly. This turned out to be one magneto cut right out with a broken rocker arm. We cut across the desert south of Tel el Kebir, making a straight run across the arc of the Nile cultivation. From a long way off one can see the patch of white hills north of Heliopolis. All the way it was pleasant and cool. As I passed back the final message "Approaching Heliopolis, winding in," I saw Searle read it and wind his arm round to the rest of the crew, who suddenly cheered up and ground their arms round too! I approached down the aerodrome past South Camp sheds, and ran a tong way down the hill. It is extraordinary how, in approaching this way, one has a tendency to come in high. At any rate, our overhauled engines had carried us to Egypt, and had run passing well.

Test at Heliopolis. On the Tuesday after we arrived it was discovered that our port engine had developed an internal water leak, so it had to be changed.

However, as E.R.D.[5] were in the process of moving from Abassia to Aboukir, and a new engine was not immediately forthcoming, my stay was prolonged to a fortnight, which gave me a very pleasant rest in the land of the Pharaohs. I finally got it installed ten days later. I did a test in the afternoon and walked to the aerodrome from the Turners'. The walk up to South Camp is hot anyway, and by the time I got there I was in a simply shocking state, and absolutely running with sweat. But above 3,000 feet it was delightfully cool, and very pleasant. I took *Lord Tony's Wife* by Baroness Orczy, up with me, and read it while Stent flew. I also showed him how to turn against the starboard engine.

There was a shiminery whitish glare over the desert, so characteristic of Egypt. The Nile cultivation and Cairo were spread out like a vast picture, the Nile disappearing southwards into the distance between the Moqattam Hills on one side and the Libyan Desert on the other. I could see little Ma'adi nestling in its green, and to the north the cultivation looked like a huge floor of brown and green parquetry, with the Nile winding through it. There was a mist horizon with small cumulus clouds straying unevenly about its edge.

Stent brought "Valkyrie" down in a fierce spiral. I asked him to desist, in deference to the crew, especially those towards the back of the hull. After we had landed we had a very pleasant bathe in No. 216 Squadron baths. Russell came up to South Camp to fetch us in his car, which was very nice of him.

While we were flying over to Egypt, on that very hot run from *L.G.* V to *L.G.* D, my left wrist got terribly burnt where the sun fell on it. My hand was mostly shaded by the lip of the fairing; but where my wrist was exposed, up to my sleeve, with a neat image of my wrist-watch left out, the skin was dull crimson, as if it had been seared. The great thing is to protect yourself against the power of the sun, when it is as strong as that. Shorts and stockings are very unwise. It is best to fly in a tunic if one can stand it.

Heliopolis to Ziza. The return journey. As I had stayed a week extra waiting for the engine, Maitland and Laing had gone off the previous Thursday. This time Flight Lieutenant Geoffrey Hornblower Cock, of No. 8 Squadron, had to accompany me with D.H.9a J 7017, as he had no wireless. He was one of the party who had brought Air Vice-Marshal Ellington on leave from India. Cock's tank had split, so the others had gone back without him.

When we started there was a layer of low cloud, about 500 feet up, as there frequently is in Egypt in the early mornings. However, we started off. I seemed rather heavy. I got off on the South Aerodrome, parallel to the sheds towards

El Maza, the place where that splendid officer General Groves was killed. I swung to the right a bit and noticed how difficult it was to stop a right-hand swing at full load; and how with absolutely full left rudder, the Vernon took a long time to get in hand. I soon found it difficult to see the D.H.9a as it kept getting lost in the swaths of the floating grey canopy of cumulus. I also found it difficult to make a good course when flying so low, as, if you cannot see much of the cultivation at once, the irregularity of its contours tends to confuse you. About opposite Bilbeis, I saw the sun trying to break through the clouds, and orange shafts of light shone wanly on to the undulating sand hills to the east. Then the clouds gradually lifted and broke, and crossing the desert between Tel el Kebir and Kantara I climbed up to 2,000 feet and saw the great white cloud sheet from above. There were gaps in places, but not very large ones. The weather report said it was clear over Palestine, and I wondered when the clouds would end and if it was safe to try and steer above them. I hardly saw the Canal: just one glimpse of its parallel sides through a gap in the clouds. But at Romani the cloud sheet dwindled and passed behind us. From there onwards it was perfect weather. The glare of the eastern sun was rather intense.

We passed along the coast, with the myriad sand dunes on our right, like a pattern of infinite complexity dotted all over with little bits of scrub and odd palms. Away to the south were the grey lines of rugged hills, lying like dark fish in a whitish golden haze. But their outlines were clear cut though faint. In three hours we reached Rafa, and were climbing well. Up, up we toiled towards the broken hills, with the mountain of salt on our right that, by legend, is Lot's wife. Then the Dead Sea sprang out of its deep gorge, reflecting the morning sunlight, and I saw the highest point on the hills beyond over which we must pass. It always seems to take a long, long time to get over the rugged parts; they look so fierce and inhospitable. Then over the Wadi Seil el Mojeb once more, on to the rolling plain, the engines eased now with the lightened load, sliding gradually downhill. Once or twice I looked round and could not see Cock for some time, until I had turned and viewed all the sky. Then would I see the D.H.9a in some quite unexpected place. We circled round Ziza while Searle got off the message announcing our arrival and wound in. Then we glided down, landing up towards the smoke candle. We found one of the Amman Bristols there.

Attempt to get off Ziza. What a great deal is summed up in those five words; what excitement, what fear, what concentration of effort, what ultimate relief!

When we had both filled up, I decided to push on, along the track. I thought we should have a good deal of difficulty getting off, but did not bargain for what actually fell out. I also wanted to show Stent what it was like getting off a high aerodrome with a heavy load in high summer. It was, for Ziza, hot; about 90 degrees.

I taxied circumspectly right down to the bottom of the hill, past Cock, who only went a little way. He then got off, leaving a trail of silver dust. I turned "Valkyrie" round, tested the controls, looked at Stent, who nodded, and then I said "Right!" and opened the throttles. Up the hill we ran, slowly, slowly gathering speed. Just about opposite the ancient Nissen hut we came off, and for a moment seemed to climb well, to about 70 feet. But short-lived was to be our triumph. The ground fell away, and we fell with it, sucked down. Soon I must turn, or strike rising ground; moreover, I must get round inside the little foothills to the right. As I turned, so I sank, in fact and in heart. The dipped right wing sang over the ground, 50 feet, 20 feet, 10 feet below. I was rushing down wind now, at perhaps 95 m.p.h. ground speed. I must raise my right wing, or it would hit. Then "Valkyrie" drifted, turning flat. Great God! Must I hit? I prepared to make contact, for all appeared up. My one main idea was to get that drift off, so that if strike we must it should be without that sickening sideway. With all my might I heaved on the rudder to neutralize the skid. "Valkyrie" shuddered and straightened; but the crisis was past. The down current had done its worst.

We shot up again and flew on. My heart beat once again. Then for twelve agonizing minutes I battled and fought, fought for "Valkyrie" and for safety. Always seeking, seeking for the up currents, watching the trembling needle of the statoscope. So we circled round the airlocked basin, ducking up and down on invisible waves, helpless in the grip of the forces of nature. I looked at Stent once or twice; and he seemed grey and grown old. The leap and collapse of the air currents was a perpetual miracle; and o'ertop them as we would, we were caught by the inexorable vortex. Once we rose to 200 feet, but at the end of a quarter of an hour we had barely 50 feet. The engines had had enough. We were beaten. The umpire held up his hand. But it is no easy matter to effect a landing from that height, as when you cut the engines off near your "ceiling," as one is in conditions like this, the Vernon falls like a stone. I stuffed the nose down to 80 m.p.h. and cautiously eased back the engines, ultimately landing with about one-third engine. "Valkyrie" bounced sulkily and came to rest. The struggle was over.

I had never had an experience like that in all my nine and a half years' flying. And in that quarter of an hour I learnt more about flying than in many moons. I taxied down to the station, Cock having also landed, and went to sleep for the afternoon. And I could not help thinking what might have happened if we had struck the grey mud plain with its little odd desert lilies, at that speed, making drift, and down wind. "Valkyrie" would have shivered and fallen in a crumpled heap, amid the grinning dust genii of the desert.

Ziza to L.G. E. The next morning we pushed on. I love the white sunrise lighting the hills at Ziza, cool and pure. And we got off in the eye of that sunrise. The air was still warm above the ground, and I had to circle for some time before I could rise over the Jebel Mugher. Then across to the thin white track, with the D.H.9a at my heels. Over Kasr Kharana I looked for my tracks of two months before and saw them. South of Azrak, across the "Plain of Sorrows," littered with its million memories, over *L.G.* D, with the twin mud flats, the hills to the south set in gaunt array like a blackened ice-field.

As we passed the outpost wall of the "Land of Conjecture," Goldsmith sent me a note to say we had an oil leak in the port engine, and would I land? I turned to port towards *L.G.* E, with its wavy parallel lines of scrub, fired a green light, dropped a smoke candle in the middle of the mud flat, and landed hard by the lazy trail of hanging smoke. One has to be very careful landing on these mud flats in summer, as they are light-coloured and smooth as an eggshell, and one is apt to misjudge one's height badly, in the same way as over glassy water in a seaplane. The trail of smoke often gives a good indication of the ground level. Down we glided and touched on the perfect surface. Cock followed. We found that a sleeve on one of the camshaft drives of the port engine had screwed back and was letting out the oil. Goldsmith screwed it up. I was interested to see *L.G.* E from the ground. All round the edge one could see the gentle rise of the boulder-strewn margin of the basin, and to the south were flat-topped basalt hills like grim sentinels, all gnarled and scarred from exposure to the centuries of time.

L.G. E *to L.G.* F. After a delay of an hour and a quarter I got off again. I flew low over the flat-topped black basalt crags, and saw plainly the ancient traces of fortification and all the remains of the little boulder walls in variegated patterns. I came on the track winding through this quiet grey land sooner than I expected, and had just started along it, when I looked round—and no D.H. 9a. After a little I turned back and saw it on the mud flat in a different position. Before I had got away Cock had to change a tyre, and my fitter had put his spare wheel back on its mounting under the exhaust pipe, the wrong way round. When Cock took off the hot exhaust pipe burnt through the tyre and made a frightful stink; so he had to land and change it round. As I arrived back at E he moved off and followed me. I then cut back towards the shark-toothed hills and soon saw the hill at F and the kidney-shaped mud flat.

As I passed along it Goldsmith sent me another note saying that the oil leak had started again and asked me to land. I groaned in the spirit and threw out a smoke candle. The surface wind was very light and variable. The smoke now meandered up and then in a north-westerly direction. I decided to land on the mud flat and came in to the left of the hill. I was a bit high, and owing to the weakness of the wind I found myself overrunning. I swung to the left and ran round the boulder-strewn edge of the flat, until I was nearly pointing in the direction from which I had come. Then a jut of boulder-strewn ground projected into the flat, so I switched off and just stopped in time, a few yards short of the boulders. This time Goldsmith screwed up the sleeve which had come adrift again, and wedged it with a Melville clip. I was beginning to be fed up and the sun was rapidly strengthening. It was now 9 a.m. I thought our troubles had really started, and if we were going to do 400 miles hopping from landing ground to landing ground, we should never get there. After forty minutes' delay, I taxied very carefully out through the odd boulders, Stent and I having shifted a few big ones, and took off along the length of the mud flat.

L.G. F *to L.G.* V. This proved the end of our troubles. We made quite fair headway now. I told Cock he could push on ahead when we came to the Nairn track. He had to S-turn[6] a good deal to keep with me, which must have been very boring, but I did not want him to leave me till we came to the Nairn track, as otherwise I should have been debarred from taking my short cuts along the armoured-car track, in case he were down anywhere.

I was slogging along over the "Upland of the Winds," with "Jacob's Pillow" standing up out of the Blue well away on my starboard, when between K and L I saw a black speck in the far distance. Nearer and nearer it came, and I knew it was the outgoing Mail. Banting and Embry. As the Vernon passed, someone, I believe Banting, waved his long farewell. He was leaving the Squadron and going home. This farewell salute in the vast spaces of the desert touched me deeply. It seemed impressive, the two Vernons meeting in the Blue, and the lone human touch in an infinity of waste. Just the salute, and the aeroplane was gone on its far journey.

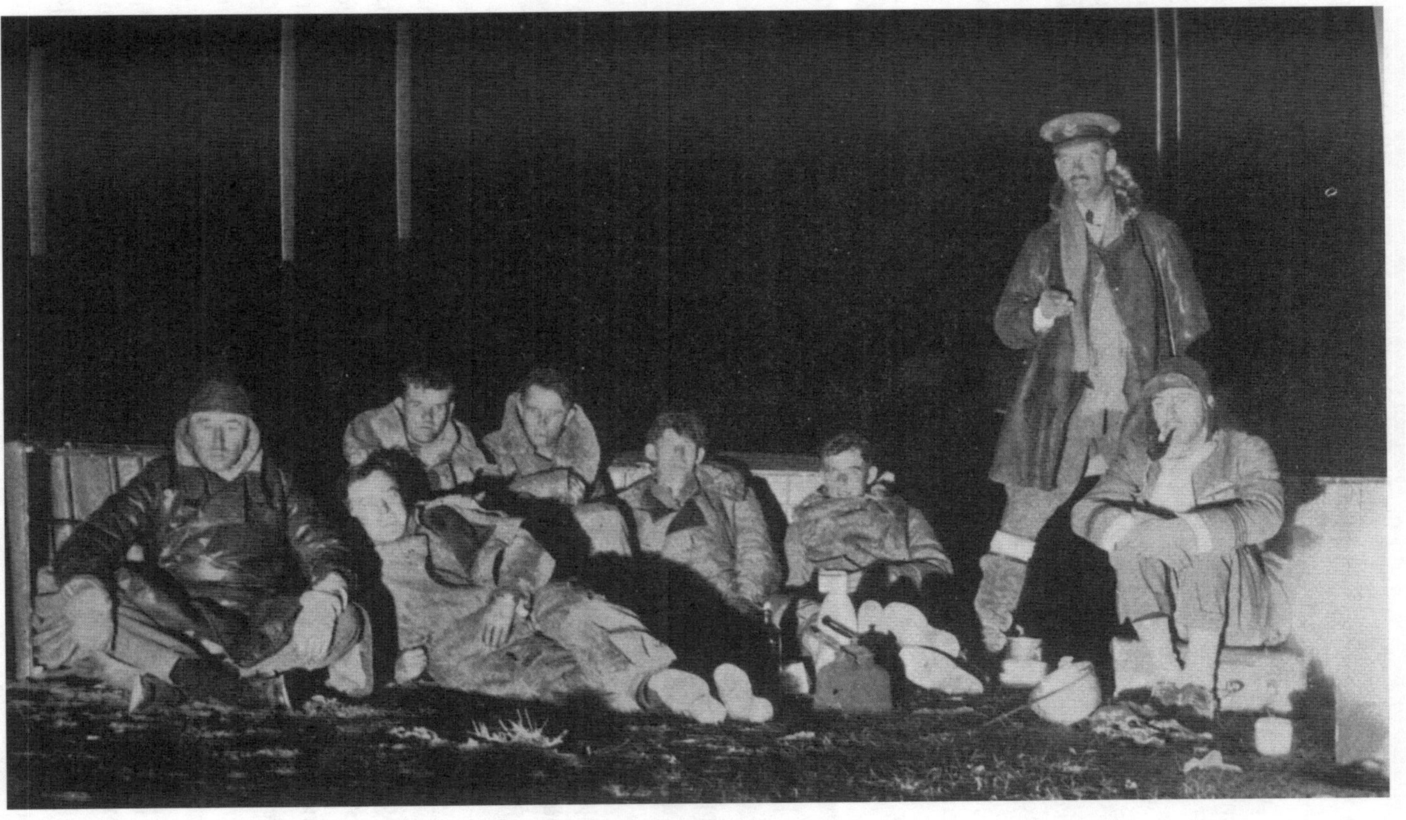

AFTER SUPPER NEAR LANDING GROUND IV

And so onwards, until at *L.G.* H I passed Kelly, following the first Vernon. In just over two hours we were cutting up the Wadi Hauran south of the turn of the track through the "Kingdom of What Wasn't." I remember noticing the myriad camel-tracks up the wadi, and the little black goat-hide tents of the usual camp by Rutbah Wells. Here Cock left me and disappeared in the atmosphere. We slowly pushed on past the hills and across the wadi at *L.G.* VII until, in the far distance, we saw the thin yellow line of the mud flat of *L.G.* V perched high up on the horizon. When I arrived there I saw Cock landing; and taking the wind from his dust I landed also. He did not fill up, but took off some cowling which was blowing loose. He said he would arrange a late lunch for us at Ramadi. I took in 80 gallons, taking it in turns with Stent to pump. We arranged "Valkyrie's" nose so that one could get in the shade, as one pumped.

L.G. V *to Ramadi.* And now, as it always does, the heat began to grip us. Between *L.G.* V and *L.G.* IV we got one enormous bump—I have had the same sort of one before just about here—and Stent was flying. It swung us through about 45 degrees to starboard and the nose went down and we actually started a spiral! When we got through the little jebels, the "Hills of Lost Thoughts," we began to strike dust. There were dust devils and sheets of dust blowing along up to 1,500 feet. This, together with the heat, was very unpleasant. I began to run with sweat, and my chest was a running river. I kept putting my hand inside my shirt, pulling it out all wet, and holding it up outside the cockpit to get it cool by evaporation.

As we approached Ramadi I saw dust devils blowing across the aerodrome, and I flew round and tried to land during an interval when all was clear. I just got down before one whirled across the landing ground right at us. I made a perfect approach, though through under-estimating the wind I thought I should not get over the trenches; and a simply priceless landing. I hardly ran more than a few yards. We filled up with 40 gallons of mixture and 20 gallons of oil. Stent and I lunched off the remainder of a chicken that the Turners had given me, and a tin of fruit.

Ramadi to Hinaidi. And now for the last stage of our journey. The dust had cleared off, but it was very hot. All the country seemed warm and ruddy under the golden light. The heat lifted up the horizon and the cultivation seemed tilted up at odd angles. As we approached Fellujah we had a good look round for the Vernon which we supposed was being rebuilt. No sign of it. It had been flown back nearly a week before, having been rebuilt in heat and almost incessant dust in eight working days. With a good following wind, it seemed but a step to Hinaidi. Once more the sight of the ancient city, the familiar cantonment, the sheds, the bund. I flew up the back of the line of sheds as usual, turned in from the Diyala and made a nice landing.

1. A landing ground in use for a short time.
2. Sandfly fever.
3. R.P.M. means engine revolutions per minute.
4. Meshetta.
5. Engine Repair Depot.
6. A D.H.9a flew faster than a Vernon.

CHAPTER X

A MAIL TRIP AND A RESCUE JOB—1925

MY FIFTH MAIL TRIP (SEPT 1925)

Hinaidi to Ramadi. It was very hot, though bright and clear, and not hazy and dusty as on my previous trip. I flew along with Embry and Paget behind; and when I had crossed over the junction of the streams beyond Fellujah, Paget came up and flew in very close formation behind my port wing tip. The glare was pretty bad, especially towards the end of the trip, when the sun curving round low over Lake Habbaniyah took one full in the eyes. I had to land in over the graveyard for the first time; and I landed just parallel with the track across the landing ground, as this would allow one to overrun between two lines of trenches. We found Maitland there with the Overland cars. He was leaving the Squadron, and I bade him a long farewell. We had our beds put out that night in the usual way, and it was not too hot. Someone began talking in the night about Bedou prowling around the serai, but I think he was dreaming it.

I got up in the dark after Tahah, the boy, had brought me a cup of strong tea in bed. When I get up very early in the morning, my eyes are so sleepy that all the electric lights appear to have coloured rings round them. This has been worse in the summer, so I suppose it is a certain amount of eye fatigue, due to glare.

Ramadi to Ziza. We started away in the grey dawn. A faint light was brightening in the east, and touching a few clouds in the eastern zenith. Embry taxied out first, and the light was so dim that I could hardly see him when I got into position. I took off, and my exhaust flames glowed red to the heavy boom of my exhaust, which always sounds a bit irregular at first until the engines settle down to their appointed work. I worked round to the left over the edge of the lake, showing with a luminous faded blue in the early dawn. I found it, as I always do, a little difficult to orient myself, and to pick up the serai in the soft greyness that enveloped the little town by the river. Every moment the dawn was coming nearer, and the grey to eastward turned to grey violet haze, which, when I had climbed a little, I saw had a soft horizon.

I set out along the track, flying low with a good deal of southerly drift, so that my nose was pointing more or less across it. Embry followed on my right. Then the brightness seemed to intensify in one place, as if hidden fires were reflected dimly in the sky above. Anon the flames seemed to burn brighter, and the patch brightened yet more, pale rose and amber. And through the purple mist, as I looked back between my wing struts, I could see the dull red crescent of the half-obscured sun in his arising. Then for a space he was hidden, only to burst again over the haze horizon in a flood of roseate glory, spreading a warm light over the misty desert and reddening the struts and silver planes, lit up incarnadine, where the light caught them. Little did I think that the same sun would rise up, during the long hours of that day, peep up over my top planes, hang hours overhead, and sinking, I should see it set in orange smouldering flames, in the bosom of the Nile. Yes, rise over the Euphrates and set behind the Pyramids. There seems something wonderful about that, something which it is not easy to grip. To be sitting in the cockpit, between the roaring engines, with the needles of the instruments photographed again and again on the mind, the landscape passing, ever passing below, the sun striking his course overhead, till nearly one twenty-fourth of the circumference of the world we live on has slipped by. And yet it happened quite naturally.

I shall always remember the flights up the long, imperceptible slope to *L.G.* V. Although you cannot see any vestige of hill, and the whole desert looks like a flat table as far as the eye can see, one does very much get the sense of climbing uphill. Then the thin faint line of the great mud flat appears on the horizon, and you are there. Although at *L.G.* III we had been making 88 m.p.h. ground speed, at *L.G.* V we had fallen to 74 m.p.h. The ground speed is found by taking the times between landing grounds and referring to a convenient table in the Red Mail Book, from which you read the ground speed straight off. We passed the hills of Cain and Abel, going strong, rounded the bend, and flew through the "Kingdom of What Wasn't." As we were approaching *L.G.* XI I decided that we would have a second breakfast of biscuits, hard boiled eggs, tea out of my Thermos flasks and bread and jam sandwiches. I wrote out a menu with the Squadron crest on top, with a note at the bottom saying that "Messrs. Napier's orchestra will oblige."

I saw both "Wu's Wallop" and "Grummet's Grange" as we passed them, and soon in the far distance across the "Upland of the Winds" over which we were passing I caught sight of three little sword-points of white flame in the desert. Gradually we overtook them, and found it was the Overland Mail with Maitland aboard. We passed them by the mud flats at *L.G.* M. One car was stopped temporarily, but the others must have been doing 65 m.p.h. easily, as we only passed them very slowly, with their long curling trails of sunlit dust. I glided down fairly close to one of them—Embry was now flying ahead—but I could not see if Maitland was aboard. Then, just as slowly we left them behind until they looked like the little sword-points of flame which we first descried. By the time we reached the "Land of Conjecture," "Vaivode"[1] had climbed to 5,000 feet, and I looked up and down its eastern barrier with my field-glasses which I had brought with me. No trace did I ever see of "Esmeralda," the dream village. We cut more or less straight across to *L.G.* E, rather behind *L.G.* F, with its line of shark hills to the south of it.

We had had a pretty strong head wind most of the way, and I began seriously to wonder if I had enough petrol to carry me through to Ziza. Just as I was making rapid mental calculations and consulting Sergeant Ballantyne as to the amount of petrol left in my top tanks, for they were not yet calibrated, I received a wireless message from Embry, who was now about 2 miles ahead, asking me if I was going to land for petrol at *L.G.* D. I wirelessed back to say I would let him know in a few minutes. A little later I signalled to say I would carry through. When we had passed over the twin mud flats at *L.G.* D and were breaking through on to the "Plain of Sorrows," Embry was drawing farther and farther ahead, and was becoming a faint speck in the sky, so that I had great difficulty in seeing him at all. As I had the Mail, I did not want him to leave me, so I signalled to him to turn round and wait. He replied that as he had only just enough petrol to get through to Ziza, might he push on? I replied "Yes." So for the moment he pushed on and was lost to my view. The next thing that happened was I saw a low purple mist haze on the western horizon, out of which little white tops of clouds appeared as white horses suddenly break out on a restless sea. By and by white detached cumulus came drifting towards me, below and just above me—was flying at about 4,000 feet—and the air became terribly disturbed and bumpy. Ballantyne was unfortunately sick over the side.

We passed south of Azrak well on our course, but I could not for the life of me pick up Kasr Kharana, which has a knack of ensconcing itself in the shifting shadows of the desert and hiding itself in a cloak of invisibility that is quite uncanny. As a matter of fact I did not see it until I was nearly on top of it. Then, as I looked up the long thread of track which led up to the sky line of the Jebel Mugher, I saw Embry again, flying quite low and working away to the south of the track. I followed him and saw him going in very low over the hills rather to the southward; then again he disappeared.

I came rather south of the wadi through the great irregular crescent-shaped zone of the Jebel Mugher, and looked blankly round for Ziza. There is no reference point by which to orient oneself in this tract of country as in many other parts of the desert; and one is apt to get quite a wrong sense of direction. One imagines a certain place will be in a certain direction, and one finds it is almost at right angles. Every little black spot on the plain seemed to me in turn to be Meshetta. Then I suddenly saw a little dart of fire in an unexpected direction: the sunlit dust of Embry landing at Ziza. I followed it and landed, and taxied up to the men waiting by the little dumps of petrol drums. D.H.9as and Bristols were there from Amman and Ramleh, and Flying Officer Andrews, who looked after Embry and me at Jerusalem. It was warmer than usual at Ziza.

Ziza to Heliopolis. We stayed two hours for lunch, although as we were following the sun this only counted as one. Mackenzie, Butler and I had our lunch out of my desert box under the port wing tip, which was only interrupted once by a D.H.9a taxying round and trying to cover our lunch with dust. There were tall dust devils hurrying across Ziza. Ziza is a great place for these genii; and one seldom goes there and does not see these wandering spirits rearing their slender wraithlike bodies out of the dusty plain. Embry was very anxious to push on, so on we went. I taxied right down to the far corner up to where the ground becomes rough, and took a long run uphill. I came off at the top and climbed better than I thought I would; but "Vaivode" has, of course, a better performance than old "Valkyrie." Still, I had to keep my engines practically at full throttle till I was over "Jehovah's Rest." The port engine I had,—English airscrews—was doing nearly 2,200 r.p.m., which I did not like.

I climbed away over the rising hills, keeping to the right of the confused crests which surround the wadi that runs away south-west from Ziza, gaining height pitifully slowly. I left Embry rather a long way behind: he told me afterwards that he had no difficulty in gaining height, as, seeing a kite soaring, he followed it into the ascending column of air, and gained 1,500 feet in an astoundingly short space of time. It was very bumpy as I approached the Wadi

Seil el Mojeb, and I actually lost height. I crossed the great wadi where it forks for the second time. I saw the road descending the opposite side from the south, in sharp zigzags, until it emerged on to a great outstanding spur, like the lap of a seated giant. Having made its way over this, it disappeared into a tumbled mass of crag and spur. Over I went, the hills heaving themselves up under me, on to the plateau of the Circassians, with its rectangular cultivated fields perched on that rocky eminence; and soon the Dead Sea burst into view to the left of the ragged whale-back peak of "Jehovah's Rest."

Flying over the hills here is like flying over the edge of the world into nothingness, into a blue void possessed by emptiness; flying out over the grey lips of the wall of Moab into sheer space. Then far below is spread out a dim picture, looking unreal, of the El Lisan peninsula fitted like a cameo into the hushed and patterned cerulean of the sea, with its thousand ruffled wavelets like handfuls of scattered tinsel on the palest blue tapestry. And beyond, tier upon tier rise the Judæan Hills, sometimes sombre grey, sometimes lit by the sun into their rich galaxy of colours—reds, ochres, purples, slate blues; and away to the south the jagged salt mountain, its skirts covered with salty rocks like cream-curds. The tiers of rock on this wall look like the rising seats of a spectral amphitheatre, unsubstantial and floating like a dream between the soft sky and the sea of forgetfulness. Perchance a white-barred vulture wheels in the sunlight, passing below one's wings in his dizzy flight. This was rather a wonderful afternoon. I do not think I have ever flown this way except in the morning time with its somewhat more garish light. Now the countryside was imperceptibly softened and warmed by the friendly sympathetic light. It somehow made me think of the lights and shadows of my dear English countryside. Out to the undiscovered ends of heaven, light drifts of cumulus laughed gently at perhaps 7,000 feet above the sea. The touch of the air was full of the distant sea, of the spices of the mountains: it was like the touch of a friendly hand, and it seemed full of music.

I had left Embry some long way behind, and kept looking and sometimes turning round to see if I could see him. At last I did, rather south of the peninsula, a faint speck in the sky. I saw the little hill on which Tel-a-Rad is perched, looking like a broken molehill in the kind of basin between the broken mass of hills to the south, and the long spur that juts out like a protecting arm from the hills rising higher to the north. After looking round for a bit I saw the tailskid marks of Bristols which accentuate the landing ground, and then, dimly, the circle, almost obliterated. Over the end of the jut of hill I flew, and over Beersheba facing the long line of the blue Mediterranean, receding away in its infinite perspective. A steady wind was humming against me, and it took two hours and five minutes to reach Rafa, an exceptional time. As I was approaching Rafa I saw Embry closing up, and flying higher than I was; after that he closed up altogether and flew on my right rear nearly all the way to Heliopolis. We flew on together into the afternoon, and I could see that the sun was getting perceptibly lower. The landing ground at El Arish was covered with tailskid marks. Two Vimys had forced-landed there recently, and it looked as if they had been holding a sort of gymkhana there, so faithfully does the salty sand reproduce and hold the trace of what has happened.

I watched and watched the little white breakers on the Mediterranean shore, which runs mostly in a gentle curve, but with every few miles a miniature promontory of sand. I scanned them with my field-glasses and I would see the little waves draw in, turn over and gently subside in milky foam, ripple forward again, pushing the line of disappearing foam ahead till it dribbled away on the beach and followed the recession of the waves, sucked back under their followers. And toy palm trees stood up out of the sand. I was beginning to feel the strain of the long day's flying. Ballantyne, I could see, was tired also, and when he was not flying, would keep nodding off to sleep, and wake up with a start when I asked him to write a message. I kept looking at the thousand variegated shapes of the sand dunes, little cliffs casting queerly patterned shadows, holding palm groves in their shelter, the rest of the land bare. I believe in places these cliffs are quite sheer and perhaps 100 feet high. So descriptions of them and their shadows tell me, I had asked Mackenzie to supply us with tea "on the bridge" about 4.30 p.m. Just after 4 p.m. as we were approaching Kantara we had it. There seemed quite a number of trains; I passed one going west and one east. Perhaps they go on Fridays, and I usually pass this way on a Saturday morning. The meal freshened me up a bit. All to the south-west a haze had now thickened, and being shone into by the sun, became an opaque vesture. I set a compass course from Kantara for Tel el Kebir, but did not allow for southerly drift, and found myself quite close to No. F.T.S., where the industrious Officer of the Watch lit a smoke candle, thinking we should land. The smoke blew out grey and ragged.

The day was now far spent and the light failing. A chill crept into the air, as the sun sank into the mist, its dimming golden glory shrinking behind the veil over the river cultivation. Every moment it got darker, and we passed along the cultivation from Abu Suweir and then swung away to the left over the desert clothed in twilight mystery. Opposite Bilbeis I changed my tinted for my plain goggles, which I got out of my haversack from under my seat, as I knew we should have to land in the dusk. I was now getting cold and my teeth were chattering. Ballantyne could hardly keep awake. As the blurred outline of Heliopolis came into sight the last rays of the sunken sun were being doused by the fingers of night. Embry came up and tried to fly in formation just before we got there, but had the last of the sun in his eyes and had to give it up.

I circled round and prepared to land from the far end of the south aerodrome. I glided down; and as so often happens when one is at the end of a long flight and one's senses are numbed, the ground seemed to hurl itself up towards me. I seemed to be falling down on to it instead of gliding. I flattened out somehow and made a passable landing, and taxied round the serai and between the barriers. I was very tired. I seemed always to have been flying, ever since before I could remember. I had been in the air that day just a quarter of an hour under the twelve hours. Embry landed about three minutes after me. Some ladies who had been playing tennis at the Heliopolis Club had come up to meet the Mail. They looked so fresh and dainty all in white, and they somehow reminded me of a country house party. And there was I, tired, sun-scorched, dirty and unshaven, chilled and from a strange land that I had only dim memories of: as if I had come from another world. I handed over the mail-bags to Sutton in the Heliopolis Details Guard Room.

Heliopolis to Ziza. The return Mail trip. The three of us climbed more or less together along the side of the delta. It was a beautiful morning with a fresh glow of light. I made some notes in the air on the look of things as we swung up towards the sea. There was a purple mist horizon with a little false veil of transparent indian red-grey across it and slightly above it. To the south was a warm white mist horizon, brighter actually at the horizon, but with soft blue showing through it. The upper sky was flecked with razor backed cirrus; some with feathers longitudinally, others diagonally or transversely. The Mediterranean was as calm as a mill-pond. The desert of sand was all drifted and blown. The prevailing aspect of the land was as if covered with speckled scrub, like dry coffee spilt at random on a tablecloth. Then there were the little dunes, bare, smooth, queer-shaped like droll question marks with occasionally a date-palm grove settled where it could find shelter and showing black against the sand.

After Kantara we were all three flying in the loose, open formation, of a triangle. The Mediterranean fades into its purple mist with the little tufts of lemon-white lining showing. Between Moseifig and El Arish a bright luminous cloud floated gaily and unconsciously past us at 3,800 feet. Then more detached little bits of cumulus with the sun shining through and into them floated under us. The sea had the most diminutive wavelets. To the south, the layer of diaphanous mist was surmounted with the faintest figurings of the contours of the pale purple grey northern Sinai Hills, looking like an effect on a Japanese fan. Here the sand is much more thickly peppered with scrub. There are two patterns on the face of the land, one more dominant than and, as it were, superimposed upon the other. The dominant pattern is the wavy one of the dunes, the under pattern consists of man-made little rectangular plots, where in the spring he may cultivate. Seen from the ground I fancy the relation of the two patterns would be reversed.

As we passed Beersheba I turned to see if Embry and Summers were there. Embry was flying along a good way to the south, a course which he maintained till nearly over the wall of hills which flank the Dead Sea. Summers was first below me on my left, then afterwards on my right. "Vaivode" had such a good performance that she climbed high easily, and Embry was weighted down with his load, although his was a Mark III[2] Vernon, Maitland's old aeroplane. When flying high above the Dead Sea I did a complete turn to see where the other two were. Then Summers got slightly in front of me. And I glided down a bit more or less to his level, towards the gnarled ridges of the "Vision of Israel," and we flew together fairly low above the mountain tops. As he was crossing the Wadi Seil el Mojeb I took a photo of him. And I looked down into the close-walled bottom of the gorge to see if I could see the oleander trees that Powell had told me of when I met him at Ma'adi. He said he had been across there by land just after Allenby's push, and that there were trout in the ancient river and oleander bushes growing beside. When I looked down from the air, I did not think I could see any water, and the wadi appeared to be dry. Perhaps in the springtime there may be some.

We flew across the shelving plain to Ziza and found three D.H.9as just landing. Summers and I followed them and both rather overshot. Summer came after me and I turned round and watched him trying to work off his height by side-slipping. He finally made a very nice landing. It was warmer at Ziza than I have yet known it. We waited till next morning to push on, and taxied our aeroplanes down to the station. We had eleven passengers between three Vernons, two of whom were acting as second pilots. This, I thought, was pretty good. But the crowd at Ziza was some thing terrific. Andrews, from

Amman, was there and he made quite a jolly time, and rigged up an extension to our supper table by getting the top of another table and propping one end on our table and the other end on the window-sill. I slept outside in a little bed placed against the building used as a W/T hut.

Ziza to L.G. V. We all started off together, but I was able to climb much better than the other two. I circled round for a bit to and fro over Meshetta, and then made away up the wadi in the Jebel Mugher. I took rather longer to reach the track than I expected, and was beginning to wonder where it had got to, although I felt sure I could see the reservoir and ruined white castle where the track goes over the hills. I then looked round for the other two and for a bit could see no sign over Ziza across the line of the hills. The air was quite empty. I circled low over the track, which pointed away into the rising sun, and after a bit I saw first Summers and then Embry as little black midges, following after. Poor Embry crawled over the hills at an altitude of 100 feet, and I circled till both caught up. As we passed Kasr Kharana and on to the oasis of Azrak Summers climbed and eventually got to my own height or slightly above, but Embry kept quite low and I often had to turn and look down, as one does to find something one has dropped on the floor. We were making pretty bad headway, as the wind was against us. I passed a little south of *L.G.* D from which I could just see the shark-toothed hills south of *L.G.* F. I circled and waited again for the other two, coming into the outer wall of hills of the "Land of Conjecture." Embry was still flying so low I found it hard to pick him up. No one seemed to want to land, so on we went. I never saw Embry again. The sun was rising up in the heavens, bright and flaring, a flashing disc. Over *L.G.* H I was again ahead, now at about 5,000 feet, and I turned and flew back towards the advancing speck of Summers' Vernon. Then we stuck more closely together.

About *L.G.* K I saw four cars parked together, facing Ziza, with people standing about and various articles spread out behind the cars. I looked at them with my field-glasses and circled over them, but could not quite make out whether they were effecting repairs or picnicking. I made a note of what the great "Upland of the Winds" looked like between *L.G.* M and *L.G.* O. Its colour was almost that of a slate with a dull polish, with great tiger skins flung across it. There was a bad head wind and it took us just two hours to cross the "Upland" into the "Kingdom of What Wasn't." Summers cut off rather more of the corner than I did, and got ahead of me. I was anxious to see *L.G.* IX which I had never yet seen, and was this time rewarded by finding it in the angle made by the convergence of the track round the end of the spur of hills and the track that cuts across them.

When we started off from Heliopolis, Corporal Searle had been suffering from a boil on his ear, and the doctor had come to the aerodrome just before we set off and told me that he ought not to work wireless. However, about half-way across the "Uplands of the Winds" Searle could not resist it any longer and sent me a message asking if he could carry on. I replied, "Yes, if you feel well enough." During the next few minutes I got a perfect flood of messages, intercepted and otherwise. That Sueida, the city of the Druse, was still burning, and that Air Vice-Marshal Brancker was coming along with two D.H.9as. We kept hearing their messages all the way along, and I tried to calculate when we should meet. I was well on the left of the track at about 7,000 feet approaching *L.G.* R when I caught sight of them flying fairly low down on the other side of the track. As we passed the Air Vice-Marshal I fired a white light, but whether he saw it or not I cannot tell. Anyhow he made no reply.

Summers and I both flew round *L.G.* V preparatory to landing, and both threw out smoke candles. We had to land across the track from the north in a south easterly direction. I stupidly ran through a large patch of camel-thorn, the result of which was that after I had filled up one of my starboard tyres was flat. I replaced it with my own spare wheel. Then, on taxying away, I ran the inner wheel very carelessly over the lid of the tank, and burst that tyre too. I had to stop my engines and borrow Summers' spare wheel. All this took time, and we were two and a quarter hours at *L.G.* V. I taxied up beside Summers before we got off, then he taxied out into a clear avenue, took off, and I followed him.

L.G. V *to Ramadi.* Summers and I made the journey on to Ramadi without incident. When I was at *L.G.* IX I heard on the wireless that Embry was down somewhere near M with oil trouble, that he could repair the defect, but was not proceeding till later in the day owing to the strong head wind. It turned out that he had the old oil-gauge trouble. I should think the fact that the oil-gauge is mounted on the front inner engine bay strut shakes it up. Anyway, the trouble is one of a particularly offensive sort, as you very often dare not risk pushing on in case your oil pressure is down, or else you stop and adjust your relief valve when it is unnecessary.

I had jokingly warned Summers of the bump between *L.G.* V and *L.G.* IV, but on this trip I myself did not experience it. It was tremendously bumpy from *L.G.* V to Ramadi, and it was so hazy that there was no horizon, and flying was not at all pleasant. Previous to *L.G.* V I had for practically the first time, owing to the better performance of "Vaivode," been able to fly high above the bumps and heated belt of air. This made an enormous difference to the comfort of the journey. On nearly every other occasion I have had to grind along in the bumps, and in addition, in summer, the heat. I landed after Summers at Ramadi, and had to come in from the direction of the Bitumen Pools. I used engine to help me over the last trenches, but otherwise made a gentle pleasant landing.

Ramadi to Hinaidi. I decided to finish up at night. Summers could not come on with me, as he had no night-flying gear on his Vernon. It was just getting dusk when I started off. I was in my shirt-sleeves and pretty dirty at the end of a long day's flying. I took off, as I landed, in an easterly direction, without flares. I made across over the river in the blue-grey falling twilight and watched the sky fade from blue to grey, and grey to an indefinite dimness, an indistinguishable haze of obscurity. The visibility, apart from this, was actually very low. It was dark enough for the lights of Fellujah to shine out as we passed it, and then I set off by compass. It was by now quite dark and the stars had come out, but Orion's belt, that I used to fly by last year, did not appear to be there. I set a compass course for Hinaidi. On, on I went in the darkness, which hooded me with a blindness that was, in a way, menacing. The horizon was not clear, and it was a bit of a strain flying. Occasionally I looked round at my second pilot's form dimly silhouetted beside me, with the tiniest reflection of light on his face from the instrument lights. I tried to pierce the obscurity to see whether I was over cultivation or desert. I wished I had asked them to fire up rockets at Hinaidi, as I did not realize that the visibility was going to be so bad. I thought at times I could faintly see the Baghdad-Fellujah road, though it may well have been a trick of my imagination.

I was beginning to get seriously worried that the lights of Baghdad did not appear, and to think of edging a bit north, so that in any case I should strike the Tigris. The time of waiting when one's nerves are tense always seems far longer than it is, and by and by a faint twin glow suffused the dark gloom. Was it? For a little time I wondered if my imagination was playing tricks again. Yes, it must be. And the faint glow on the left was Baghdad, and the wider spread one was Hinaidi, 7 miles beyond. Then, from about 5 miles off, Baghdad came out of the haze. And soon the black floor was studded with twinkling gems, and we passed over the river and saw the yellow flares on the aerodrome like cressets of coal. I fired a green light as I came over and saw my call sign and "O.K." winked out by the Despatch Officer at the flares. I flew in over the road to Lancashire Bridge,[3] glided down, saw the orange-lit ground rise up, flattened out, thought I was too high, and to my surprise subsided gently and made a nearly perfect landing, which was not bad at the end of just over nine hours' flying.

After I had checked the Mail in the Orderly Room it was found that a small letter that I had been given at Ziza was nowhere to be found. I had to go back and search the aeroplane, and eventually found it in one of the racks above the windows between two enamel plates.

TRIP TO *L.G.* X AND BACK (NOVEMBER 1925)

Hinaidi to Ramadi. This was a rescue job to take radiators and water out to Alger who had forced-landed at *L.G.* X on "Vagabond" J 7135 on the return Mail. He had had an appalling time; first forced-landing on the plateau of the Circassians just east of the Dead Sea, then at *L.G.* F with a broken engine, and finally at *L.G.* X. I got up in the dark and started off before the dawn. I failed to get oil pressure running up, because the oil was not properly warm, and this delayed me a quarter of an hour. I met Sergeant Page in the dark between our two hangars going towards the Vernon. The first hint of breaking light trembled in the east, and the bund lay like a faint shadow at the far end of the aerodrome. The lights burned wanly in the extremity of the dawn. The presage of the day was everywhere perceptible to the senses, but day was not come. I noticed some thin nebulous clouds apparently rolling up from the west, and I wondered what sort of a day it would be. When my engines were running up satisfactorily I moved away from the ghostly sheds. I had two radiators and 30 gallons of water in drums, besides a case of beer for Ramadi. As I taxied out and got away from the lights I could just see the dim grey surface of the aerodrome, and I seemed steering out into an unknown sea. When I turned round at the far end of the aerodrome, I could see the hangar lights in the blue greyness which was every moment becoming less sombre and more luminous.

I took off and saw Hinaidi and Baghdad before dawn, a sight which I had never beheld before. It had a peculiar atmosphere, as every time of the day, and the dawn and the dusk, I think more particularly, has its own atmosphere. The lights burnt yellow in a plain of pewt and the scene looked full of romance. So I sped away on the wings of the "false dawn." I had a bit of difficulty climbing, and I circled round over the rifle ranges before flying away over the river. As I passed over the loop of the Tigris the sunrise started. When I looked back from Aqqar Kuf the Pusht-i-Kuh made a defined and rugged skyline, violet against the pink flush that held the eastern horizon. And whence the sun was about to come was a bright flame like a scimitar of fire. The desert was not dry and wore a more subdued mien than in the glare of summer. The soft greens of the cultivation, still somewhat indistinct in the dawn, might have been taken for English heath-land.

As we approached Fellujah the low hills or cliffs beyond shone orange red in the eye of the rising sun; and behind them, looking as if it were balanced on a low tableland, lay Lake Habbaniyah, pale green: above grey mauve stratus, then a faded bronze sky with a wonderful Turneresque gradation to dim violet, in which hung high a paling and three-quarter moon. As the sun rose, the whole desert reddened, even the greens were gilded by the warm glow—and the threads of the rivers and their tributaries, meandering amongst confused mounds which cast a pattern-work of weblike and vague shadows, or through cultivation of faded greens, the little fields seeming like leaves branching from a curving stem, made strange contrast with the long straight remains of ancient canals on the face of the desert. The sun rose yet further—I looked back on its bright radiance, casting arrows of fire into my eyes—and the purple grey of the eastern horizon was streaked with horizontal layers of mist like silken strands. I curved round the lake to Ramadi, and when Sergeant Maclaren had wound the aerial in, I landed down the hill towards the serai. Here we had some breakfast.

Ramadi to L.G. X. I took 30 gallons of petrol with me in drums, having got rid of the case of beer. It had turned into a lovely day, and I had a wind following on my starboard quarter which made things all the more pleasant. The track was not really very easy to see at the start—in fact, I am never quite sure of myself until I reach the Bitumen Pools—and the rain had darkened it, and made it less prominent. It is also much widened out after it leaves Ramadi, because the cars have not been particular to keep to the same track. I passed over the "Hills of Lost Thoughts" and found I was getting more familiar with the track in its convolutions through these little hills: how it runs parallel to a wadi for some distance and then goes round a flat valley in the shape of a "V" with its apex to the northwards. Just before I got to *L.G.* III I saw a Vernon returning from taking the engine out to Alger. He was flying high and on the other side of the track. Then I bore out on to the great flat "Plain of Unfulfilled Desire," where the track straightens and runs for miles with hardly a bend, up a vast ascending plane ending only at the unbroken horizon.

At *L.G.* III I took my hands off the wheel to write a message and found that the Vernon was quite stable and doing an undamped stable oscillation between 60 and 62 m.p.h. with a period of 10 seconds, which I timed. I was so interested that I let it carry on, and actually flew all the way from *L.G.* III to *L.G.* V without ever touching the wheel with my hands. Page, my second pilot, was astounded and could not make out what was the matter. The Vernon was even competing with small bumps, which threw it back to 55 m.p.h. and down to 67 m.p.h. The oscillation always reasserted itself after the disturbance had passed. I was able to steer with the rudder as long as I did it very, very gently; for a turn would immediately drop the nose slightly; and if I had turned too sharply I do not think the nose would have risen again.

At *L.G.* V there were some armoured cars probably taking in petrol. I circled twice round them and tried to drop a message, which I found afterwards, when I had landed at *L.G.* X, had caught on one of the wires of my tail plane. They fired a white Very light. Then we continued onward in the blue and golden light of the morning.

The visibility was simply astounding, and one could see the outposts of the hill country to the south of *L.G.* VII jutting northwards in myriads of flat-topped spurs, and to the right, unreal and detached in the luminous distance, the hills of "Cain" and "Abel." Soon after I could see the faint blue outline of the "Kingdom of What Wasn't," just beyond the confines of which lay Alger. At Rutbah there was a small camp and I saw the rectangular outlines of the foundations of a building which they appear to be putting up by the wells. I went very low over the hills at *L.G.* IX, just to the left of where the track curves round them, but I passed over *L.G.* IX itself without seeing it, perhaps because I was so low. It felt curious passing just over the flat tops of the black hills, which looked rather like the crassiers in the French mining district of Artois, They glided past underneath like a grim picture. Then I followed the track down the wadi where it crossed over from one side to the other, and told Page to keep a look-out for Alger.

I saw him first, far away on the great plateau, just a wee black speck. I wondered why it should look black and not silver. However, I did not risk a mistake and still kept to the track, which swung out to the right. Soon I saw a dull silver scintillation on the black speck, and gradually it took the form and features of a Vernon, just like a dull grey beetle. I flew along over it—it was not far from the "X" just on the right of the track—and saw they had a "T" out, and there were little black expectant figures. Then they fired a Very light and I curved round and glided down. I made rather a heavy landing, though not too bad. The ground seemed to rush up, or rather the Vernon seemed to fall instead of glide; and whenever I get this feeling I find it hard to land. I do not know what quite to attribute it to, but it often comes when I am tired. This time I had quite a bad headache which came on after I left Ramadi.

Alger looked quite cheery, but a bit thin and worn. He had been out for thirteen days in the Blue, and I saw that nameless look in his eyes which so often one sees in the eyes of men who have been exposed for some time in the desert, and which I can only describe as "fey." I immediately got Page and Maclaren to make up some tongue and sardine sandwiches, which I fancy the beleaguered crew appreciated, having been on bully and biscuit for three or four days. Alger said they had had a terrible thunderstorm at *L.G.* F, and in a few minutes there were 4 inches of water on the mud flat, and he was wading about over his ankles. And they were frightened to get inside their Vernon because of the lightning. I can just imagine the "Land of Conjecture" in its blackest mood, lit white with the colossal lightning flashes and showing the lava hills crouching like black demons.

We changed Alger's two radiators. He had repaired his own most ingeniously: red lead, fabric, chewing gum and what not. This had enabled him to stagger on from *L.G.* R, where he had landed the day before, and made my problem of getting to him and back on my petrol far easier. I found that one of my starboard engine water pipes had chafed through and my fitter had to have the radiator off and cut it and work a rubber joint on. I walked round and inspected a dead camel, of which there were two in the neighbourhood, and took photographs of a cairn and some circles of stones. I looked at the track running straight over the mighty plateau till it rose over the shoulder of a distant hill and was lost to sight. We did not see a living soul there.

L.G. X *to L.G.* V. I let Page sit in the first pilot's seat. Alger took off first and we taxied slightly in behind him, as there was a little rise in the ground in front of us. I rather lost my bearings at first, for we were flying straight into the hills of the "Kingdom of What Wasn't" very low. In a moment I saw far away the little shapes of "Cain" and "Abel," which gave us our exact direction. We cut up the Wadi Hauran and passed some armoured cars going westwards. Alger flew away on our port beam and higher. And so we continued until the mud flat at *L.G.* V came in sight. It hardly showed up from the rest of the plain. The camel-thorn preceding it was really a better landmark. Alger landed first without a smoke candle. We dropped one and Page made a good landing into a stiff east wind. Alger filled up at the tank, but we managed on the 30 gallons in our Vernon. I saw now that we could not get further than *L.G.* III in the light and suggested we should camp there for the night, but both Page and Alger wanted to go on.

L.G. V *to Ramadi.* We duly set off. The sun seemed unreasonably high, seeing how soon it was due to set, and I thought perhaps we should have a bit longer daylight than we actually did. Before starting, Sergeant Maclaren tested my flares, and I wirelessed for flares and obstruction lights at Ramadi, and rockets to be fired every ten minutes after 17.30 hours. Just after we had passed *L.G.* III the last light faded and we dropped into a half-light that seemed to continue for a long time. I gradually switched on my lights, but strained to keep my eyes on the track. The stars came out, one by one, in the blue velvet sky, rich and luminous. All through the "Hills of Lost Thoughts" I somehow followed the track, half, I am sure, by instinct. It would lose itself in confused shadows and crossings of wadis, and somehow I would find it again. Alger's lights followed on my starboard quarter like twin stars. Away in the west was the last dim afterglow. Then more and more I lost the track and less and less I found it again, until I relied on the faintly lit compass bowl.

I was a bit worried because I did not see the first rocket till six o'clock. I passed over the Bitumen Pools, which showed me my course was right, and then I saw a light that I thought might be Ramadi, but it was north of my course, so I paid no attention to it. It is fatal to follow these will-o'-the-wisps of the desert. It may have been some lonely hut on the Euphrates. Then the rockets shot up and hung in the sky, motionless stars, and by and by I saw the flares. Then I began to experience a shrinking, for I liked not the thought of landing at Ramadi in the dark. However, I had to pull myself together. My approach—I flew in—was a bit undecided and wobbly—maybe because I was not very well and had been suffering from a headache all day. I glided down, caught the ridge short of the flares, and bounced a bit. And then I had landed and taxied down the flare path very thankfully. I found Eldred there, who was on the way to refuel *L.G.* V. Alger made a really beautiful approach and landing, on which I congratulated him heartily. I had my supper alone in the little room where I had had breakfast that morning.

Ramadi to Hinaidi. Between the Bitumen Pools and Ramadi I had been flying at 1,000 feet by my aneroid[4], but I could see practically nothing of the ground, just a dim veil of dark grey, sombre and impenetrable. I had a ghastly feeling that my aneroid might be wrong and I might hit the ground at any moment.

RESTING UNDER THE PLANES IN THE HEAT OF THE DAY

THE OFFICERS' MESS

And I strained to catch sight of any feature in the ground to see how fast it was moving under my plane. I thought I could make a little out, and what I saw moved slowly. And yet I could not shake myself free of the feeling.

I told Alger that when we left Ramadi he must keep close to me and follow my tail light. I bore away over the river in the starlight, and I was soon destined to behold one of the most wonderful sights I have ever seen. The visibility had improved wonderfully since after sun down, and everything was sharp and clear, though unreal in the garment of night. It was a picture in black and grey and blue and silver, still as death and shrouded in the wizardry of the East. Suddenly and breathlessly there was a flash of golden light in the east—I can describe it as nothing other than a flash—and a moon, red as blood, shot up over the horizon with incredible speed. You could see it lifting itself up and flooding the night with an eerie radiance. All at once you realized there was a horizon, and winding rivers; and the moon was reflected many times in the winding rivers, so that it looked as if molten metal were running in pools and rivulets over the deep blue plain, for as we moved along, so the reflection moved and the light filled the winding mazy patterns of water and created this ethereal illusion. It was marvellous, and made me hold my breath.

Before we got to Fellujah, where we sent a W/T message, I could see the lights of Baghdad, and to the right of them, those of Hinaidi, so I let Page fly and just point towards them. I rested my head on the side of the cockpit arid dozed a bit, for I was very tired. Alger's lights were close behind, faithfully following us through the night. As we approached Baghdad and the river with all its thousand soft lights, I could see the dim form of Alger's Vernon close behind on our port side, and he was flying in beautiful formation, and thus did we come over Hinaidi. Page fired a green light and we glided down, and I made an excellent landing though short of the flares. Half the Squadron was turned out to welcome Alger home.

1. My new Vernon, which replaced "Valkyrie."

2. Later type.

3. A bridge over the Diyala just where it flows into the Tigris.

4. Instrument which records height.

CHAPTER XI

THE NIGHT MAIL AND A FLOOD

MY SIXTH MAIL TRIP (NOVEMBER, 1925)

Hinaidi to Ramadi. We started off on the Mail trip in wonderful weather. Burnett came with me on "Ancaeus." I ran up my engines and owing to the direction of the wind it was not necessary to taxi out to the bund. My crew signalled "O.K.," and I taxied out towards the circle and took off parallel to No. 8 Squadron. Burnett came on some way behind me and a good deal lower down. He apparently could not get enough height to cross the Tigris safely, so he flew up north of Baghdad and came back again. It was a beautiful evening with sweet mellow light, and the air was calm and steady. After Fellujah I did not go north of the river as usual, but crossed it and flew along by the edge of Lake Habbaniyah over the Fellujah Ramadi road. I looked down at its windings through the low foothills, which encircled little sloping flats, and I wondered if one could land on them.

At Ramadi I had to land in over the graveyard, and there was quite a gathering of natives strolling about outside Ramadi like an English village on a Sunday afternoon. Of course one native was walking along the track right in the middle of the landing ground, just in the place where I wanted to land. I half flew in and made quite a decent landing. Just as I was landing I saw Embry take off. He had been out filling *L.G.* V. Burnett landed a minute or two after. That evening we went into Ramadi village—this was the first time I had been in there—and it looked rather impressive in the grey blue moonlight, with its quiet streets and unexpected archways. I thought it consisted only of mud huts and was greatly surprised to find what looked like mediæval buildings. Little groups of natives, half seen, and donkeys, lurked in the shadows by the walls. We went to Jimmy James's house and sat and talked round an oil stove in an upper room.

At Ramadi. It looked a fine morning, but there were plenty of alto-clouds in the twilight of the early dawn. The stars were fading as we ran up our engines. We had considerable difficulty in getting up the oil pressures. When I had taxied out and Burnett and I were in position, I found a tyre had gone which I had to get out and put right. Then I took off, and almost immediately the starboard oil pressure fell away, so there was nothing to do but to land again. We took out the filter and ran up without it, and then put it back again and the pressure came up correctly.

Ramadi to Point between L.G. IV *and L.G.* V. Again Burnett and I started off. This time my oil pressures kept up. I soon found that there was a strong southerly drift. I never feel sure of that track till I reach the Bitumen Pools; it ought to be clear enough, but it always confuses me. As we approached the Bitumen Pools I tried signalling to Burnett by means of an Aldis lamp operated by Maclaren out of the window, but it was not very successful. As I passed through the hills between *L.G.* II and *L.G.* III I saw the faintest blue-grey line on the western horizon. Could it be ominous weather? We flew on, and gradually it was borne in upon me that there were clouds ahead. The sky above and around looked serene and joyous. Imperceptibly the blue-grey line approached and formed itself into a bank of cloud, or rather a stratified layer with its top at about 2,500 feet. I well knew the ground was rising all the time on the long upward slope to *L.G.* V. The cloud layer seemed to extend to about 20 miles north and south of the track, beyond which it seemed to be clear. But obedience to the track forbade me to go above the cloud layer, or circumvent it in this region devoid of landmarks.

At about *L.G.* IV I plunged just beneath the roof of the cloud, Burnett following. Light grey cloud wisps drifted past and below, and I kept as high as I could consistently with keeping sight of the motor road below. But the ground rose steadily and the ceiling of cloud remained at a constant height, and so I was driven nearer and nearer the ground. A slight rain sprayed the wind-screen. Flying began to get extremely uncomfortable. I kept peering ahead to see if I could see any light which would indicate a lift in the cloud. Two or three times I thought I could see light ahead, but I was disappointed every time. Then it began to be practically motoring and I judged I had had enough, as it is dangerous flying a heavily loaded Vernon so low down. Once or twice I had caught sight of Burnett coming on behind, and I was almost frightened to turn lest I should collide with him. I did turn, however, and got Maclaren to wind in the aerial, and then I threw out a smoke candle and landed in a southerly direction, touching just south of the track. I then taxied back to the track.

The sky was grey with low cloud, a strong wind was swishing through the desert scrub and a light rain was falling fitfully. It looked most drear and lonesome; and I had that queer detached feeling one gets on landing in the desert in bad weather. The chilly wind blowing, the gloomy sky, the lack of warm and comforting shelter, the remoteness from the abode of man, all confirm and strengthen the impression of forlornness and loneliness. I waited a bit and Burnett did not land, so I concluded he must have forced his way on further. Then I decided we would push on as soon as the weather showed the slightest sign of improvement.

Point between L.G. IV *and L.G.* V *to L.G.* D. After a wait of thirty-five minutes the weather looked a trifle better, so I pushed on again. My hopes were justified. The clouds lifted and broke a little as I flew westwards along the track, and by the time I reached *L.G.* V I was about 500 feet above the ground. There I saw Burnett on the ground. I was in two minds about landing for petrol, as I had been nearly two hours altogether getting there. However, I decided to risk it. Burnett had two crosses[1] out. As I flew over him I signalled onwards with my hand to signal him on. There were some Bedou and camels round *L.G.* V. As I flew on towards *L.G.* VII the clouds lifted and broke more and more and let the sun come streaming through; and I saw the clean-washed blue sky once again. I climbed, and as I looked back I saw the clouds roll away behind, melting and dissolving like half-forgotten tears, till at last they sank to a silver bar on the far horizon. Now it was warm and jolly.

As I passed Rutbah I heard Burnett on the wireless coming along behind. They were getting on with the foundations of the square building by the wells at Rutbah. There was quite a lot of water in the Wadi Hauran, which clearly reflected the soft blue of the sky. There was also the usual Arab camp at Rutbah, with considerable numbers of flocks. We had breakfast as usual while passing through the "Kingdom of What Wasn't." After that it began to get a bit bumpy. The visibility was perfectly marvellous, and all across the "Upland of the Winds" one felt one could see for 100 miles all round. When I was at *L.G.* M I thought I could see the faint blue grey hills of the "Land of Conjecture" peer up over the horizon, and "Jacob's Pillow" to the south. And before I got to *L.G.* K I could see the shark-toothed hills by *L.G.* F, and so I steered more or less straight across to *L.G.* H, and fell in with the track again as it passed across the orange sand belt. *L.G.* H was largely flooded, and I saw the Nairn stopped before the mud flat facing west. I judged that they would have to make a circuitous and very difficult journey round it.

After that I hardly followed the track at all. I passed over *L.G.* F and again looked with wonder at all the queer patterns of fortifications made by the "old men," as the Arabs say. I passed between *L.G.* E and the hills where the track goes through. They flank the plain at the end of which the twin mud flats of *L.G.* D lie, and I was very seriously worrying about my petrol supply. In fact, I had been doing so for some time, as I thought that if the wind turned badly against me I might have to land at F and wait for Burnett to land at D and bring me back some petrol. It might be inadvisable to land at E if the mud flat was wet, whereas at F you can land along side the mud flat with reasonable safety. However, I managed to reach *L.G.* D all right. I saw an armoured car there. This turned out to be with a convoy which had just left on its eastward journey. I had missed it because I had not been sticking very closely to the track.

I filled up, and just as I was getting ready to push off, we heard a faint hum and a little speck appeared in the sky. It was Burnett, and a cheerful sight it was to see him. I put out a smoke candle for him. He did some rather violent S-turns before; landing, and it looked as if he dropped "Ancaeus" into a large patch of camel-thorn. He was some way away, and I could not be certain. I taxied clear of the tank to let Burnett fill up.

At L.G. D. I taxied out along the landing ground towards the letter D and took off just past Burnett's Vernon. As soon as I turned over the mud flat I noticed that the petrol float valve was not lifting. I thought that it was probably stuck, but as it might be the pumps I decided to land again. I turned round and made the most perfect landing; one of those when you cannot feel the precise moment of touching the ground. While Goldsmith was operating on the petrol valve, I went across to Burnett's Vernon and had a ham sandwich or two.

L.G. D *to Ziza.* There was now only just time to reach Ziza comfortably before nightfall. I did not want to approach Ziza in the dark, for I knew by experience it was very difficult to pick up. As I followed down the wadi which curves round from *L.G.* D I kept looking behind to see if Burnett had taken off, but when I last saw him he was still on the ground beside the tank. I was even more anxious that he should not be caught in the dark than for myself. At the same time I knew he would land at our old friend Kasr Kharana if darkness came down upon him.

After this I suffered from a piece of over-confidence. The sky was covered with a sheet of various forms of alto-cloud, which brought the twilight on earlier. The sun sank in bronze and red through the grey and purple clouds. A solemn hush crept over the sombre landscape, which I felt even through the insistent boom-boom of the two Lion engines. I was accustomed to get my direction from *L.G.* D by pointing at the southern end of the pools at Azrak, which brought me out at Kasr Kharana. I did this, not realizing that the autumn rains had swollen and extended the pools far south of their normal orbit. I had a feeling that I was going too much south-west, and my compass also showed this, but, like a fool, I did not trust it. As the desert was rapidly getting dimmer in the failing light, I should have been wise to stick faithfully to the track, even with the difficulty of following it up to the landing ground at Azrak and out of the loop again towards Kasr Kharana. Anyway, I left Azrak behind and made towards the darkening ridge of the Jebel Mugher.

Now the curious thing about this tract of country is that its conformation is spiral, like a maze, and there is no line by which one can orient oneself. One looks and makes sure from the line and flow of the hills that Ziza must lie there; and one looks again, and it might be in a dozen directions, and when one finally does light upon it, it is usually as much as 30 degrees off the bearing one has made certain it lies on. On this occasion I kept looking for Kasr Kharana, thinking that some last ray of light would bring it out of its hiding-place. But I did not come to it, and after a bit I knew from the time it must be behind me somewhere. And then I thought I caught a glimpse of the white cliffs to the south of it away behind me on the right. I turned therefore slightly north and pushed on over the brow of the hills into the darkening plain beyond, where the lights of lonely Bedouin camp fires were beginning to twinkle. I tried to search the contour of the distant hills by the Dead Sea to give me a sense of direction, but I could not make out much. I realized that night was coming on so quickly that if I did not pick up Ziza in about five minutes I should have to make the best of it and land somewhere out on the plain for the night, before it got completely dark. Being sure Ziza was to the north, I flew up northwards and was much relieved to pick up the little Nissen hut on the edge of the landing ground.

When I landed there was no sign of Burnett over the dim line of hills. I began to get very worried about him. They had had a message from him saying he was passing Kasr Kharana. I got the officer from Amman to light a petrol beacon, and for about an hour I walked up and down in the gathering shadows wondering what had happened to Burnett. At last we got a message from Burnett to say he had forced-landed O.K. about 10 miles west of Kasr Kharana and was short of oil. I knew his port engine was throwing out a fearful lot of oil because at *L.G.* D his fitter had transferred some of the oil out of the starboard into the port tank, which was short. Later, apparently both engines suddenly lost revolutions and Burnett simply shut off and landed where he was. He said it was possible to land in quite a number of places on the gentle eastern slopes of the Jebel Mugher, which I was rather pleased to hear, for I had the idea that the nature of the ground was, on the whole, very bad.

Ziza to Dead Sea and Back. When we got up at Ziza that morning it was indeed a gloomy prospect. Low clouds driving along from the south-west, and a hint of coming rain. Again and again I looked out of the little window in the upper room to see if I could distinguish the whale back of "Jehovah's Rest" in the looming greyness over the Judæan Hills. I went up to "Vaivode" and started her up; and just when I was ready to go it came on to rain quite hard, so I had to get out, have the covers put on, and go back to the Station. Well do I know—it is bitten into my mind—the feeling of those days of bad weather at Ziza: the prospect of dim uncertainty over the Dead Sea, the thought of Egypt and civilization beyond compared with the bleak discomfort—almost squalor—of Ziza station. On this occasion we had a second breakfast, and it was not till ten o'clock that I started off, even then in grave doubt as to whether I should get through. I was not certain whether the cloud ceiling was blotting out "Jehovah's Rest" or not. After my previous bad experience in February, 1925, I had decided not to try and push through if "Jehovah's Rest" were covered.

I climbed away towards the Dead Sea, and seemed to plunge towards waves and waves of grey cloud, though it was not below but above me. The cloud kept me so low that I could see plainly all the little wadis and paths and scaly crests of the mussel-topped hill country; and little flat greens and sandy places enclosed like pools in rocks. I got as far as the crossing of the Mojeb, and then I saw it was a hopeless proposition. The clouds were right down, and on my right and left there were fierce rain showers. So reluctantly I turned back, throttled down my engines and set a compass course for Ziza. As the view was so intermittent owing to the clouds, I had some doubts whether I should get back without wandering. However, I spotted Ziza beyond where the hills and wrinkles of wadis smooth themselves out into the wide plain.

Ziza to Rafa. We came back and waited about two hours. Meanwhile Burnett turned up, the oil having been taken out to him in cars from Amman. I was very glad to see him again. It was now getting doubtful whether it would be possible to reach Heliopolis that night, for the day was wearing on. However, it looked a little brighter over the hills, and though I was still extremely worried about the prospects of getting through—the low clouds over the hills, the unknown factors that always tested one's determination—I heard that a Vernon was coming the other way, and I thought if it got through and I did not it would be an eternal shame to me, so that settled it and I decided upon another attempt.

The wind was blowing strongly from the Dead Sea and it seemed an age till I reached the Mojeb. Then I looked ahead and saw that "Jehovah's Rest" was covered, and the clouds rose from it as from a mighty volcano smoking. Now, according to my previous reckoning, I should have turned back, but the thought of that other Vernon spurred me on, and it dawned on me that I should have to fly out to the sea over the wadi, in the same way as I did last February, only not below the level of the hill-tops. This time I knew where I was going, whereas before I thought I had come to the wall of the Dead Sea. So, instead of crossing the wadi, I turned to starboard, and tried to climb a bit, working backwards and forwards across the great bluff that ends in a head which splits the great divide further west. A I reached the triangular head I was perhaps 1,000 feet above it and near the cloud ceiling. To the left, "Jehovah's Rest" with the black cloud seated upon it; to the right, mass upon mass of rising cloud; in front, ten minutes of flying over nothing but crag 3,000 feet below. I screwed myself up to the ordeal. I hardly dared look down. I composed a little limerick.

Slowly the minutes wore away, and the marching panorama opened, unfolded itself, widened and showed the sea. Round the steep cliffs slowly moved the peninsula, and I mentally measured my gliding distance as it came more and more underneath me. I came well out over the rocks where the wadi breaks into the sea through its mile-wide cleft, turned south, hung over the peninsula against the rushing wind, and looked back at the dark menacing hills enwrapped in towering cloud, by which the gap I had penetrated seemed sealed up. Before me were clouds again over the opposing cliffs, but not so dense. I could now throttle down, and steering so as to avoid the denser masses, I floated slowly down towards Beersheba. I circled a bit to make sure of passing over Tel-a-Rad, and had some difficulty in finding it. A half sunlight was now filtering through, with intermittent rain showers. Far away I saw Beersheba, through a pattern of mingled lights and shadows.

After that I passed through quite a sharp rain shower, flying at about 1,500 feet. Then Goldsmith passed me a note saying that the starboard radiator stay rod of the port engine had broken. I asked him if it was advisable to land at once. He replied that it would be advisable as soon as conveniently possible. This had gone because the port engine had started a slight vibration; and if you get vibration, even ever so slight, something is sure to go. The clouds had broken and a warm early afternoon sunlight was caressing the green and brown fields of Palestine. When I arrived at Rafa—I had come out somewhat north of it—there were as usual crowds of donkeys and flocks on the landing ground. As I circled round the shepherds began driving them off. I landed towards the Mediterranean. I always think Rafa rather a friendly place with its quiet green fields. In half an hour Goldsmith had replaced the radiator stay and I took off again. I went slightly outside the markings, as the run is really very short in that direction. You have to go down into a dip, up again on to a rise past the circle, and get off as the ground falls away to the edge of the landing ground. I flew along by the sea's edge, still getting a little vibration, probably from the port engine.

Raja to Abu Suweir. I was making better headway now. I thought if I could reach Abu Suweir by dusk, I might do the rest of the journey by night. It would be dark about five o'clock. There were high alto-clouds all over the sky; and in the west the sky looked like the fretted dome of some vast cathedral, and had, something of its mystery. Red gleams of the falling sun, softened through the grey, seemed as if they might have been stained-glass windows. There was a low haze, as there very often is. As I approached Romani, I looked back and upwards, and saw, with a thrill of pleasure, a full pale glowing moon, showing through the high clouds. Gradually I watched it brighten as the dusk imperceptibly crept over and through the desert.

When I reached the Suez Canal, my radiator thermometer began to fluctuate, and gradually got worse and worse. The oil pressure and temperature remained normal. Soon I could see spray escaping from the header tank vent on the starboard engine in gusts every minute or so. I knew there must be something wrong, and wondered if I could make Abu Suweir before I lost all my water. I cut across south of Kantara, anxiously watching the needle oscillating between 75 degrees and 95 degrees. I gradually turned on my little cockpit lights, as darkness had now definitely overtaken me. It was tempered by the mellow moonlight. The air had the brightness of lilies, and the dimness and mystery of deep woods. And little by little the dimness became afire in a thousand directions, as if illumined by fairy lamps. And I came to Abu Suweir and my engine was still going. I could see the smoke candle burning that they lit for me and asked my second pilot, as he knew the place, and I had only landed there once before, what was the best place to land on. He said, over the sheds, but to be careful of the wire fence. So over the sheds I glided down and made a perfect landing without a flare, by moonlight.

I found that the starboard radiator had developed a bad leak. Williamson, whom I met there, said he would get it repaired for me, which was very decent of him, considering that it was a Saturday night. So, while I had supper and met many people I knew, the radiator was removed, repaired in the shops and replaced. I had taxied "Vaivode" in through the wide swinging gates of the fence, using my Aldis lamp as a spot light.

Abu Suweir to Heliopolis. The last stage of the journey. I was pretty tired, but I had that exalted feeling that one gets after difficulties surmounted and the safe end of a long journey in sight. In this state the river of confidence runs freely. I was tremendously thrilled with the idea of taking the Mail in at night. I taxied out of the gates, and asked for no flares. As I left I heard the strains of dance music in my ears, for they were having a dance close by. I swept off into the grey-blue moon light; and from the moment I rose from the sand, I felt like a disembodied spirit somehow finding itself in an element for which it has long yearned—finding its own. The orange, blue, gold and pink flames of the exhaust, the interminable thunder of the engines, the silent land of the Pharaohs, full of the ghosts of the past, had never filled me with such breathless wonder as it did then. It was an ecstasy indeed.

I flew along by the cultivation, flecked with faint lights, and saw its grey pencilled edge against the desert which shone like tinsel in the full strong moonlight. The clouds had cleared away and had left a turquoise sky. So strong was the moon that the landscape was full of colour, rich though subdued. And a faint haze only served to heighten the beauty of the night-filled desert. I could even see the dark and light patterns on the desert dimly glittering, and felt I could choose a firm piece of ground should it become necessary to forced-land. I felt, too, that I was helping to make Kipling's "Night Mail" come true. I could almost see the circle at Bilbeis, at any rate I had a good idea where it was. And now, my port engine, with which there had been something not quite right ever since Ziza—I am sure the vibration had made both the radiator and radiator stay go—began to misfire, slightly, but very distinctly. Every now and then the throbbing glow from the exhaust would waver and flicker out for perhaps just a fraction of a second. This worried me a good deal, and I kept wondering whether it would last until we reached Heliopolis.

Owing to the haze I did not see the lights of Heliopolis until we were fairly close there. I threaded my way round the jut of cultivation by Abu Zabal and arrived over the town just about on the stroke of midnight. When I got over the aerodrome I saw a great to-do going on—there seemed to be a number of flares, but it was impossible to tell which direction they were supposed to be pointing in. We had had a W/T message to say that we were to look out for working parties on the South aerodrome. It turned out that the wadi above had flooded all over it; and though I did not know this, I was reluctant to land there by night. The flares were on the North aerodrome, and as I flew round I decided, if my port engine failed, to risk it and land on the South aerodrome.

I kept firing green lights for permission to land and was answered by red. At last the green light came, and I saw that the flares were across the narrowest neck from "Vimy Ridge" to the road between the Squadron and South Camp. I flew in very gingerly, and, on the ground, swung to port to the left of No. 6 flare. Altogether the flares were on the most difficult part they could have been, and the cross distance between Nos. 5 and 6 flares was only about 50 yards. I found afterwards that they had had the flares up and down the aerodrome, and had decided, as the wind appeared to shift, to change them at the last moment. I handed the Mail over to Bryant in the little guard room.

THE FLOOD ON THE RETURN TRIP

Heliopolis to Ziza. Three Vickers Vimys went on this Mail. Goodwin, Mealing and Glover. I went as passenger to Mealing. Passing Kantara we had a following wind. The sky was mostly covered with alto-stratus and alto-cumulus cloud. At Romani we were flying at 2,100 feet and started to climb. There appeared to be a stratified layer of cloud about 4,000 feet. At Moseifig we were still at 2,000 feet. It was more hazy there, alto-stratus and cirrus. The sun was watery with a big sun halo. The Mediterranean was a wonderful aquamarine blue with a misty horizon. The cirrus cloud was all streaky, crossed and feathered. When we came towards Palestine the early spring had already painted in its simple quiet colourings, green and purple madder and yellow lake. In the sea were the reflections of the clouds, warm ochre up to a delicate area of violet blue. Between El Arish and Rafa there was a striking harmony or colour chord derived from the blue of the water and the yellow ochre of the sand. The shore itself is cut out in the shape of a question mark. It was perfect quiet calm weather with a pale sky the colour of faded violets and dead rose leaves. Nature seemed absolutely at peace.

Goodwin turned inland at Rafa till he came to the big serrated wadi, and then turned north again as if he were going to Ramleh. This was apparently because he got a W/T message to say that the weather at Ziza was negative. Then, after we had gone a little way, he received another message saying that Ziza was affirmative, so all three of us again turned west and passed about 15 miles north of Beersheba.

We actually passed over the Dead Sea about 6 miles north of El Lisan. As we approached the western shore of the sea, I made a sketch of the Mojeb. There was now a pronounced sun halo, which probably foretold bad weather to come. As we passed over the Dead Sea the Vimys did not make for the plateau of the Circassians, but passed along, or nearly right over the Mojeb. I was struck by how quiet a Vimy is with its two fairly well-silenced Rolls Eagle VIII's, compared with the Vernon, which nearly blows your ears inside out.

Ziza to L.G. D. When we left Ziza there was a layer of very attractive fracto-cumulus clouds, the shadows of which were violet and their tops flecked by the sun. Glover was unable to get off and we flew round for half an hour waiting for him. The lower sky was amber and copper; the ground green, old gold and madder. The whole was a very rich and soft colour harmony. There was a "Cherub" cumulus sky. All the broken cumulus was like leaping cherubim, dynamic, and full of life and intense rhythmic movement. There was also a light pink flush on the far cliffs beyond the Dead Sea; then in front showed the clear-cut, picked-out shadows in two tones, the soft flat lighted planes and the deeper tones without detail and indued with throbbing colour—of range upon range of escarpments coming down from the sea.

As we passed over the mud flat at *L.G.* D the sky was clearing and was a beautiful and very intense Prussian blue. We flew on for some miles over the plain towards *L.G.* E, and then Goodwin turned back and it appeared that Glover had landed on the mud flat. I thought it would probably be too wet to land on, and that we should have landed on the all-weather landing ground; however, we all got down and it was not too bad. Glover had blown out a plug.

L.G. D *to L.G.* V. After staying for twenty minutes on the mud flat we all three pushed on, Glover flying low and behind. The sky brightened and the sun came out at intervals. The heavens were a soft luminous gentle blue with clouds of great diversity: little white castellated ones, mauve and cream nimbus, all sorts of cumulus and stratus and soft lights filtering through high cloud layers as through the mysterious upper galleries of an immense building. At *L.G.* F we struck a very bad head-wind and this held on through the long forenoon. It also began to be pretty bumpy, and as we toiled across the "Upland of the Winds" I felt very sick, as I seem to when flying as a passenger and with consequently nothing to do. I munched biscuits at intervals. By *L.G.* J Goodwin got a good way ahead and Glover was well to the south. We kept fairly close to the track.

By and by we came, after as it seemed an almost interminable age, to the confines of the "Kingdom of What Wasn't." Here there was a blue sky with alto-cumulus. We passed across just south of *L.G.* IX and at *L.G.* 8 we crossed over the Nairn track and kept well away to the north of it—why, I cannot tell. We saw the building at Rutbah, which was very well advanced: four-square walls with a triangular apex pointing eastward, buildings inside the walls, and a gate that one might drive in by. We saw a convoy of eleven cars going east near *L.G.* VII, a building convoy. As we approached *L.G.* V, Mealing was running out of petrol and was getting very worried. He glided down and landed. We all filled up and by then the day was too far spent to reach Ramadi before dusk. I suggested trying to reach *L.G.* III and camping for the night there. I knew the landing grounds were difficult to pick out, especially in a bad light, so I was reluctant to suggest pushing beyond *L.G.* III owing to the deterioration of the surrounding country. There was a restless, late afternoon wind blowing at *L.G.* V, and I thought that *L.G.* IV or *L.G.* III, being a little lower, might be less exposed and quieter.

L.G. V *to Point 1½ miles West of* *L.G.* IV. So we sped away again eastwards down the track, while the sun sank and the light became uncertain. We were all three more or less together and I was peering out to spot the marked landing grounds beside the track. I saw *L.G.* IV all right, and when we had got there, I thought the light had already faded sufficiently to make it unwise to reach *L.G.* III in the face of the stiff head wind. So I pointed downwards to the marked IV. Mealing circled over the track and finally landed on what appeared to be a very good and flat piece of ground about one and a half miles west of *L.G.* IV and on the other (north) side of the track. One by one the other two Vimys landed behind us and taxied up on our left to make a line. The wind was less and sinking with the sun; but still restless, with a hint of coming rain.

I looked uneasily about. There was no shelter of any sort, and the wings of a Vimy do not afford much. A party of us set to work to pull up camel-thorn to make a fire, but we had nothing but screw pickets to get it up with—and it has tough roots, and grew thinly. After a bit we gave that up. I found a little caterpillar on the thorn in front of our Vimy, with a vivid crimson stripe on its back and whitish hairs. Later we settled down, made an excellent petrol and oil fire in a 4-gallon tin and Goodwin cooked an appetizing supper. After which I took two photos by means of Very lights.

I settled down by the starboard wheels in my valise, and Mealing by the port wheels. Dark confused clouds were imperceptibly banking up like dim menacing shapes in the south-east. But for them we cared not, as we were weary. I propped a bomb bay cover behind my head with my suit-case and, as I went to sleep, listened drowsily to the crooning of the desert night wind. And little by little the rain-drops came: first one, then a dozen, then thousands. Through my sleep I heard the rain pattering down like a low accompaniment, and restlessly the soughing of the wind, coming in weird gusts; now rising to a crescendo with heavy rain; now falling away almost to silence while the rain trickled away off the planes in heavier drops. I believe, during the whole night, that the rain only ceased for about quarter of an hour. With the first pale grey light came the indistinct and slow re-dawn of consciousness. It was still raining, raining, raining ceaselessly.

I sat up in my valise and looked around. It took me some time to appreciate what was happening. I saw Mealing's reflection on the ground: no, it must be water. We were flooding. All around was flooding. As I looked out I saw the thorn and grass peeping up in wisps and hummocks through the creeping flood, which seemed to extend for a long, long way. I, luckily, was on a sort of little islet, and I got my riding crop and with the handle poked up a little bund all round me as the water encroached. Mealing woke up and swore. He was lying in a puddle. I covered myself in my valise, and lay down for a bit, hoping, and knowing well the hope was vain, that it would stop raining. Sitting up again, I saw the water all round my bund, and felt it creeping in along by the wheel, where I could not scratch the earth up properly. So up I got and rolled up my valise as best I could in my cramped space, and staggered out into the rain. It was a cheerless prospect indeed. I had my flying knee boots on and was already splashing through an inch or so of water. It was deeper in places. I found my little scarlet caterpillar drowned, floating aimlessly. No one had moved. Some were sitting up, making exclamations half in annoyance, half humorously. At last one or two people simply had to get up and we more or less took stock of the situation.

I knew a mud flat was not far away to the east, about opposite to where the landing ground ought to be; and this would obviously flood with any amount of rain. The ground we had been unfortunate enough to land on was a long strip with slightly higher ground each side of it running north and south, which was all draining on to our strip which may have been 500 yards or so wide. This strip was now under 2 or 3 inches of water in places, and looked like a large lake with the Vimys in the middle reflected in the water. Through the grey drifting rain the western rise looked the only chance of safety.

It became increasingly obvious that if we were to get the Vimys out at all, we must extricate them within the next half-hour or they would sink. The water had softened the surface of the mud, and a layer of slimy ooze was forming, which was every moment deepening; that is, the hard mud, penetrated by the water, was sinking in level. So we splashed about and gathered our traps and tins and put them in the Vimys.

Mealing got started up first, and after some difficulty forced his wheels forward, turned to the right and taxied away through the flood on to the higher ground. Then Goodwin started, and after greater difficulty, men pulling on each wing strut, he taxied forward. He thought the flood was less deep straight ahead, and so taxied till he came to the track. There it got deeper, so he turned to the right, and as he went, he, not daring to taxi slow lest the wheels should sink in, shot through the flood and threw up clouds of spray like a seaplane. Just as he came to the edge, there was a crack, and up he went on his nose. His front skid dug hard in, but saved him; and after a second or two his tail fell back. There he waited with engines running till we splashed through the flood to pull on his wing tips. After a bit we got him on to dry land, and he taxied up by Mealing.

Even the high ground was covered by myriads of rivulets of running water. I remember noticing many of the scarlet-striped caterpillars drowned and dead. The clouds were blowing over from the east, and the rain continued, sometimes coming down heavier, sometimes abating a little, but never stopping. My leather flying coat and the knees of my breeches were soaked, and the water had come through my flying boats and was squelching round my feet.

We then hastened as best we could back to Glover's Vimy, which was in a sorry plight. The flood had deepened, and the ooze thickened, and the Vimy was bogged up to one axle. Glover was standing up in the seat pulling Mail out and getting it put in the back, so as to stop the Vimy tipping up on its nose so easily. One solitary Bedouin had wandered up, with a hammer in his hand, and was sitting quite contentedly on a little island in the flood, with his coarse brown abba pulled right up over his head. We got ropes on to the outer wing struts and worked like madmen. It was now near noon and no one had thought

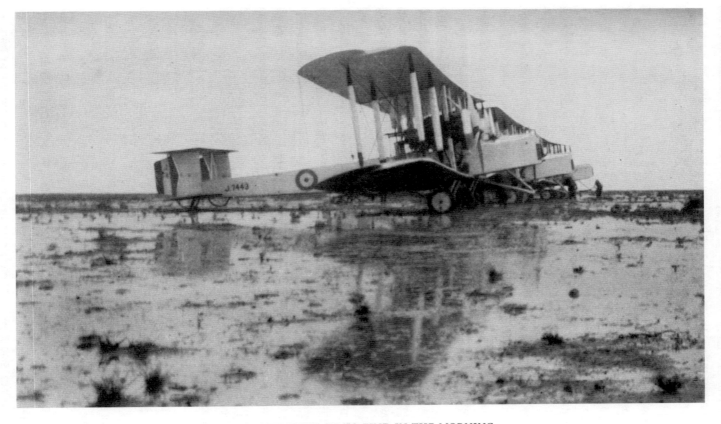

WHAT WE WOKE UP TO FIND IN THE MORNING

of food or drink. We were too wet and tired, and we knew the imperious necessity of extricating the Vimy. Glover ran up his engines separately, and tried to move one pair of wheels forward at a time. Mostly the wheels simply ploughed forward on the hard bottom, which was every moment sinking as it turned into ooze, and pushed the mud forward in a sticky mess, which we kept digging away under the water. At last the Vimy moved bodily forward and we shouted to Glover to keep going and not give the wheels a chance of sinking again in that veritable Slough of Despond. After about an hour he got out on to the left side of the flood, that is, opposite the side on which Mealing's and Goodwin's Vimys were.

How we ever got him out, I cannot imagine. At the time it seemed an absolutely hopeless task. For one thing you could not get any firm ground to pull on, as your feet sank in. Men sank down, fell down in the mud and water, cursed, got up and struggled on. But for pure pluck and determination not to be beaten on the part of the men, and a grim cheerfulness withal, I think we should not have got that Vimy away for a fortnight. Goodwin told Glover to try and take off and fly over to where the other Vimys were. So we splashed through the flood yet once again on to the higher ground and laid out a "T" just by the track, about 600 yards south of the two Vimys. Glover, when he saw from afar off, perhaps half a mile, that we were ready, took off across wind to the north-west, flew round low over us, and nodded as he passed over. He then landed on the "T" and ran straight into a little circular bog about 25 yards in diameter, went up on his nose and stopped dead!

We now betook ourselves to the other two Vimys which were a little lower down the slope and sat under the planes and ate some wet bully and biscuit, our first meal that day. Goodwin was looking wretchedly ill, white, and his teeth were chattering. It is difficult when one is at home to picture how absolutely pitiless the desert looks under circumstances like this, the grey circular horizon roofed far and wide by low cloud, and the rain pouring down without relief. The humans are merely pigmies, unutterably insignificant in a waste of rain-swept dreariness. The rain almost stifles thought and feeling. One hardly knows whether to crouch sodden and shivering beneath the planes and freeze, or to get out and tramp up and down in the rain and get more wet. Goodwin was squatting down under the planes and, as the beads of rain trembled on his eye lashes, he looked out over the plain towards Ramadi 85 miles or so eastwards and said, "It would only need an earthquake to finish this!" And indeed it felt so. Then we went back to Glover's Vimy to see what could be done about it.

Meanwhile the wind was backing round to the north, and blew bitterly cold. The rain had not penetrated much above my knees, which was a mercy: but my leather coat was sodden, and the wind made one's bones rattle like a highwayman hung up on a gibbet. As a matter of fact the thing that absolutely saved us was the fact of having to work so hard during the rain. If the rain went on the next night, I could not bear to think of what we should do. One had the sort of feeling of standing on the edge of a blank void and, being forced to go on. The ground was a running stream and too wet to lie down on. It was too cold to squat beneath the planes with that damp chilly wind. It was hell outside. No, one dare not contemplate the prospect.

Hour after hour we worked at Glover's Vimy. We collected armfuls of stones, dug away the mud from in front of the wheels, and tried to make a causeway, which, of course, became immediately filled in with water. Then Glover would run one engine full out and the Vimy would keep tipping on to its skid, but would nevertheless move forward a foot or so, and force all the stones out. As yet there was no firm ground to stand on, and the ropes were wet and slimy. About four o'clock the rain gradually ceased—then stopped, after twenty hours. And the wind blew cold and strong from the north and started drying the ground. We got our wireless working and Ramadi was under heavy rain. They could hear us talking, but not what we said. We many times repeated the operation on Glover's Vimy, and as dusk was setting in, we got it nearly to the edge of the bog, that is, we had moved it forward about ten yards. Then we taxied the other two Vimys up on to higher ground near Glover's Vimy. The sun had broken through the layer of driving cloud, and oh, what a blessing it was to see that faint gleam, what an absolute benediction! And as the sun set it made a long bright streak against the shoulder of the rising ground. Then night came down and the clouds rolled back to either horizon, leaving the grey blue arch of heaven full of dim stars.

We got a fire going, cooked some supper and stood around it trying to dry ourselves till about 1 a.m. We arranged all our things round it, and stood first back and then front towards it, and I took my flying boots off and changed my socks. It was the night of the R.A.F. ball at Baghdad and all the Vimy pilots had brought over their Mess kit for it. Mealing put on his dancing pumps. The ground was now tolerably dry where we were, and we spread our valises and slept. Mine was about the driest, as I had been on an island in the flood and had rolled it up before the water got to it much.

Next morning dawned clear and fine. During the night high white cloud in small drifts had passed across the moon on a westerly wind, but had faded away.

The wind was now west and following. After about an hour's work, the bog having dried somewhat we got Glover out, but he had used up a lot of petrol running up his engines. Goodwin was in doubt whether one Vimy should not go back to *L.G.* V and fetch more petrol; but the disadvantage was that so much more petrol would be used up in flying the 50 miles there and back. So in the end he decided that we should all push on to *L.G.* I, land there and see how much petrol we had, and then decide what to do: whether to redistribute it, or for one Vimy to go into Ramadi and fetch some out.

Point 1½ miles West of L.G. IV *to Point near L.G.* I. We left the ground last, the other two Vimys flying on ahead. I had some fresh socks and shoes on, as my flying boots were too absolutely sodden to put on again. My leather coat was partly dry, and I was not feeling any the worse for my experience the day before. It was a fresh sunny morning, with a wet, clear-washed blue sky after the intense rain, and a west wind. The desert looked a marvellous sight, one mass of lakes and pools, reflecting the clear blue of the sky, and in the distance lit to gold. The track was in many places one long strip of water, wherever the ground dropped to a lower level. The light was, however, so good that it was very easy to follow. After passing through the jebels between *L.G.* III and *L.G.* II, we saw, far ahead, a Vimy landing, which was Glover, then Goodwin circling over him and landing. We went on and landed there too. It was so soft that we hardly ran any distance at all. We pulled up a little way behind the other two. This was a flat though slightly undulating plain: beautiful landing ground. It was, I think, just west of *L.G.* I. Mealing and Goodwin discovered that with the following wind they had enough petrol to push on to Ramadi, but Glover had not. So Goodwin said he would fetch some back to Glover.

Point near L.G. I *to Ramadi.* This was Mealing's first Mail trip and he did not know Ramadi aerodrome, so I had drawn him a pencil sketch map of it and had asked him to look particularly carefully for the markings, as they might be indistinct after the rain. We left before Goodwin and soon the old familiar landing ground came into sight. This was perhaps the last time I should approach "Ye old windinge Inne" from the Mail Route. When we landed, Dearlove met me and took me to his rather pleasant house in Ramadi, where I had a shave, a wash and tiffin. Meanwhile Goodwin landed and took petrol out to Glover and eventually later brought him back.

We had really had a pretty bad time getting off from near *L.G.* I. The ground was very soft and we had to have men on the wing tips to start us off. We took a tremendous time to get up speed, and every now and then the Vimy curtsied as if she would tip up. It was lucky that there was such a tremendous run. Unfortunately it was slightly uphill; and what I was frightened of was that we might suddenly strike a wetter patch and tip up at speed, which would have meant a baddish crash. When I looked at myself in the glass at Dearlove's house I could hardly recognize my face: indescribably dirty, my hair matted, and covered with black from standing over the fire the night before trying to get dry. Before we left I went to call on Major Wilson and his wife. He said he had realized the plight we were in out at *L.G.* IV and had thought of trying to get out on camels to help us. It was pleasant to feel that friends had been thinking of us out there, sodden and alone.

Ramadi to Hinaidi. We made a very good trip on this last lap, all three flying in good formation. Goodwin led, we came on the left, Glover on the right. There were huge lakes all over the place. The aerodrome was rather wet, but we all landed safely.

1. Meaning "Do not land, but go on."

CHAPTER XII

MISCELLANEOUS FLIGHTS IN 1926

A TRIP TO MOSUL AND BACK (FEBRUARY, 1926)

Hinaidi to Mosul. My first trip up to the famous and much-discussed city. I only heard fairly late the evening before that an Ambulance aeroplane was wanted to fetch a cot case from Mosul. I spent some time getting my maps ready and plotting out the courses and distances between the various landing grounds. I started just before sunrise and bore away to the Tigris above Baghdad. The whole desert was lit with an elusive light. When I had crossed the river, a golden glow appeared in the east and gradually flooded the country.

All the way up to Beled station, after I had picked up the railway, the country was indescribably wet after the rains and was full of lakes and pools. It looked almost hopeless if one had a forced landing. Before starting I had had a report to say that Mosul aerodrome was mostly under water, which was not very encouraging, considering it was my first trip there. I looked round for Beled landing ground, but failed to spot it. I believe it is somewhere near the station, which is 2 or 3 miles from the town up in the shoulder of the river. Then I crossed the river; and perhaps 30 miles away I saw a tongue of flame in the desert, which was the golden-domed mosque of Samarra. The risen sun had now climbed well above the mist layer and filled the sky with a haze of opened-out glory, and the struts and silver planes and metal parts of "Vaivode" were lit up against the cold soft blue of the atmosphere. All the pools and lakes in the dark amber of the desert looked like moving pools of golden light, a pattern of wizard design.

When we passed over the river we came into the land of the dead cities. We followed up the left bank of the Tigris. Before Samarra and just after you have passed the river you see mighty remains in the desert, like a great pentagon. After Samarra there are miles and miles of dead ruined cities, with long colonnades and huge avenues, the vast and pathetic relics of civilizations long gone by. They are planned on a huge scale, but hardly any walls remain. Only the desert holds the imprint, the weird ghost of what once was. There are various cities on the Tigris bank which one passes, nestling on low cliffs on the banks, Tekrit and Baiji.

By and by one sees a faint ridge of hills in front, and the great winding river leads towards them. This is the Jebel Hamrin, which runs diagonally across the line of flight: from south-east to north-west. The river pierces it through the famous Fatha Gorge, where the Turks made their last stand in the War, before being forced to retreat by Allenby on their flank at Aleppo. The position looks almost impregnable and their extensive lines of trenches and works remain probably almost as the last man left them. The Jebel seems gradually to rise and become more massive as it extends north-west. It looks reddish in colour, green slopes leading up to it, and giving way to broken outcrops of rock, in the form of enormous slabs, laid one upon another, the planes of cleavage being at an angle of about degrees to the horizontal. This resulted along the summit in sharp serrated ridges, along one or two of which I saw winding tracks overlooking sharp precipices. The gorge is perhaps half a mile to a mile in width, with some quite good landing ground by the river side. I passed through the gorge and found that the right bank of the river seemed for some way to hug the bottom of the Jebel. The railway, which runs as far as Shergat, passes through the Jebel some miles further west.

I then passed the point of junction of the Lesser Zab, which runs away north-east in the direction of Alton Keupri. On my right front stood two great whalebacked hills, rather like a large edition of the Malverns. I could see the river winding away northwards, far, far across the green undulating plain; for one noticed that everything had become greener without any perceptible change. If anything, the Jebel Hamrin seemed to mark the division between the North and South country. Soon we came to Shergat, and saw trucks and sidings. On the right bank of the river, but a little way removed, were hills; but between them was undulating green plain. Sometimes the river came nearer the hills, sometimes it wandered a bit away. I saw on the right bank the ruins of the ancient city of Assur, perched on the side of a cleft in the cliff-like bank. Later we came to Qaiyara of the oil fields. Here the hills were more rugged and came nearer the river in one place, and I saw the aquamarine blue streams of oil running down from the hills. I looked around for the landing ground, but could not see it. Then, further, came into view the junction of the Greater Zab, and I knew we were approaching our destination.

We did not follow the Tigris closely, but cut rather across where I saw there was a road through the hills. Ahead rose the long line of beautiful snow mountains, across which lies the frontier. They make a wonderful background and seem like a wall hiding lands of remote possibilities; they secrete a spirit of adventure; their loftiness is like a distant bugle call heard high above one in the clouds. Then over and among the green, undulating foothills peeped up the white city of Mosul, about which I had heard so much, had seen so often in my imagination. And now that I set eyes on it at last, I seemed to see it anew in all its exciting beauty in that marvellous setting of free mountains, a city of Fable indeed.

Soon I saw the aerodrome and flew round it carefully to take in its limits and dimensions. There seemed a good deal of water on it. I overshot slightly and landed just beyond the circle, coming from the west. I had to swing a bit at the end to the south in the fresh green grass. I was glad to feel my wheels not sinking, for the soil is such that though it may receive much water, yet it does not become too boggy. And from the aerodrome I could see the towers and minarets of the white city standing somewhat above me and beyond them the mountains. Stevenson was away on a reconnaissance over the hills and far away. I had breakfast in the Mess, a Turkish building with a square colonnaded court with a grass lawn. There was a tame gazelle and a tame jackdaw. The flight had taken 3 hrs. 20 mins. I was quite shivering when I got there, as the early morning had been cold.

Mosul to Hinaidi. After waiting for a bit, the "case" was brought to the aerodrome in a Ford Ambulance. I think the man was supposed to be an enteric case. He was pushed in through the hose of "Vaivode" and made as comfortable as possible in the back stretcher position. I had to be rather careful taking off, owing to the large amount of water on the aerodrome.

I flew back fairly close to the river. I passed through a good deal of drifting cumulus, and flew through one or two clouds. Between times I could see the far-off silhouette of the Fatha Gorge against the dim light of the sky, with the sense of great kingdoms beyond. As I flew just over the gorge I could look at the zigzag road on the beetling western cliffs most precipitous, and the flat places around the river as it flowed through the gorge, on one of which I could perhaps land if need be. I flew on southwards: further to the east of the river the ground is rough, and begins to heap itself up to the wall of the Jebel Hamrin. The weather had cleared, and far away I saw the tongue of fire of the dome of Samarra mosque. Then across the river, by the great pentagon-shaped ancient wall, and towards the railway, passing by the little station of Beled, and then another village with green palms in and around it. Again across the Tigris and the domes and roofs of Baghdad were once more in sight … and old Hinaidi, spread out and grey, with the light reflected off multitudinous mud roofs softened by smoke.

A FLIGHT INTO THE SOUTHERN DESERT (MARCH, 1926)

A message had come in saying that a Vernon was wanted to go out to Shabicha to take rations and water to Sergeant Pilot G—— who had crashed there. This was Thursday evening and he had been there since Monday. I decided to leave at 6 a.m. the next morning. My rigger set to work to replace a broken tailskid and the Vernon had to be filled right up, water, rations, machine gun, ammunition, etc., got ready and parachutes to drop the stuff. My crew were given the opportunity to go to bed and let other men get "Vaivode" ready, but they refused to go till all was in order. John David, my bearer, called me at 4.30 a.m. and I had some breakfast in the Mess at 5.15 a.m. McClaughry had told me that if ever I had to go into the Shamiyah desert he would come with me as second pilot if he could, for that is the region in which his squadron do their desert reconnaissances. If you do not know the country, you practically have to take a guide because there is very little marked on the map. As it turned out McClaughry got leave to come as my second pilot and was on the aerodrome by the hangars at 6 a.m.

The morning looked threatening with lowish grey clouds and a certain amount of nimbus about. However, we started at 6.10 a.m. The first part of the way is almost the same as to Basrah. You go direct over Hillah instead of leaving it 12 to 15 miles on your right. Then, instead of continuing down the Hiliah branch of the Euphrates to Diwaniya, you cut across south-westwards to the Hindiya branch, pass over it, and in the distance, 40 miles or so beyond Hillah, you see standing out in the Blue by itself, walled in and bastioned, the Holy City of Nejef. I believe it was built by Haroun al Rashid of the *Arabian Nights*. It is like Samarra, only rather finer. The city clusters round a central golden mosque, which you can see flashing miles away. There is a wall all round with round towers and a fine entrance gate, which stands upon a sort of cliff, as far as I could see from the air, and from which a long straight covered avenue led to the mosque. Outside the city walls are many little buildings and not a few blue-domed little mosques. Inside also were some more blue-domed mosques which struck a fine colour note with the great central golden dome

THE CRASHED AEROPLANE AT SHABICHA

OUR ARRIVAL AT SHABICHA

and minarets. The city and courtyard of the mosque were black with people because it was Ramadan, or Ramazan (the consonant being something between a "d" and a "z"), the holy month of the Moslems. Many people were coming into the gates along the open desert road.

Then we passed on southwards to a little place called Rahaba, with the accent on the first "a". This place was about 25 miles beyond Nejef. It looks like a fortified Khan, or rest house, with a few buildings round it. It more or less stands on the western edge of the cultivation. After this we were to break out into the infinite desert. A few miles south of Rahaba there is an ancient and mighty road called the Darb Zobaida—"Darb," I am told, is pronounced "Durrub," and mean's "road." It was made in ancient times by Haroun al Rashid, and ran from Nejef, through Hail to Mecca, right across Arabia. You can only see the Darb distinctly in parts. It was a holy road for pilgrims, and must have been an astounding achievement in construction. It looks like a faint band on the desert, running more or less straight like a Roman road. No one knows whether it was metalled or not; but it is about 40 feet wide, and looks as if it had been levelled, and in places there are the remains of low walls. Perhaps people drove in chariots down it. And lest the travellers should perish, in the desert, wells were constructed every 30 or 40 miles, and forts, which were perhaps garrisoned. Most of the forts are ruined. One of the wells, Godsave of the Armoured Cars told me, was 20 feet square and 400 feet deep, cut through solid limestone. The ancients were not frightened of building. But the Darb is very faint at first and I do not think I could ever have picked it up from Rahaba by myself. Even Mac had some difficulty. By and by we found it after we had scouted about a bit.

Now we were coming into finer weather. I had brought a Thermos of tea and some biscuits and some meat sandwiches, which, once we were on the Darb, we proceeded to devour. It is a hundred miles from Hinaidi to Nejef and a hundred miles on to Shabicha. At this place the Darb has two branches, and the wells at Shabicha are on the western branch. On our way we had passed directly over the ruins of Babylon just before reaching Hillah. It looks a wonderful place, and covers quite an extensive site, but there do not seem to be many buildings actually left standing. Headquarters were rather anxious about G—— and B——, his wireless operator, because they had been out for nearly a week and their food and water were known to be running out. Godsave had started out to them with four armoured Fords and had apparently failed to reach them. So it was decided to send the Vernon out to make certain somebody would get to them. The crash was alleged to be 4 miles or so away from the wells at Shabicha.

We flew along following the faint band of the Darb slightly west of south, past various wells and ruined buildings with comic names. "Bir," or "Birkat," means a well, and most of these names start with "Bir." One place is Birkat Margritha. When we were going along the Darb I saw a recent car track and thought, "All is well; Godsave has reached them." At Margritha the car-track branched away to the left, and I thought the Darb did too, because if you think a thing is going to do something, you think you actually see it. I was a bit doubtful, so I asked McClaughry. He had a look and showed me the Darb branching away to the right, so I turned, left the car track and followed it. Now we should soon be coming to the junction where the Darb branches into two. We never saw it. We flew on and on, and Mac said we had better continue on, strike the lower junction and turn back up the west branch. By that time we should be in sight of Waksah, the next wells to the south, where there is a ridge of cliffs. Waksah actually came in sight on the southern horizon, or rather the cliffs did, when Mac suddenly spotted the crash just below us. They were lighting a smoke candle. We had actually come down the west branch without knowing it, and I had never seen the point where the east branch went off. These faint marks in the Blue are very tricky.

I flew down low and dropped two gallon drums of water in parachutes, which opened and landed perfectly, not so far away from the crash. Three Fords were there. Then I dropped fifteen rations in two tins and a bottle of whisky and some cigarettes. These also landed well. One of my engines was running roughly, and I was anxious to land and have the magneto looked at, so I flew around for a little and had a careful look at the ground. Mac suggested one likely-looking green patch about half a mile away from the crash. I had one try at this place and got nearly to the ground (which was 1,000 feet above sea level) and then I found I was overshooting. I put on my engines and went round again. I had another try and landed gently.

We were in a sort of down country of bare limestone covered with yellowy white boulders; long uplands with steepish ends, perhaps like the Yorkshire moors. Some of the hollows had become filled with soil and these were thickly covered with stuff that looked like camel-thorn and was something else. It had prickles but not ones that would burst the tyres. It was almost knee-deep. And there was also grass in which were growing millions and millions of every imaginable wild flower, white marguerites and masses of other kinds. Hundreds of butterflies, Painted Ladies and small yellow ones I did not know fluttered in the sunlight, and larks were filling the blue air with song. The air was so sweet and a fresh breeze was blowing. It was only hot if you got out of the wind. It really was a most delectable spot. The desert in spring in parts is really heavenly; so free and open and untouched. And the Darb ran through the flowers and waving grasses not far away. My heart was filled with the beauty of the scene.

It turned out that Godsave had had an appalling trip. He had picked up one guide in Nejef and another somewhere else, and they took him wrong at Margritha. He thought they were wrong, but they would not admit it, till they had led him 50 miles out of his way. Then they offered to show him a way across to strike the Darb. This proved to be impossible ground, and after one of the front wheels had broken off a Ford, he had to leave it and go all the way back to Margritha with the other three. He actually reached G—— and B—— about an hour before we did. It took me three and a half hours to reach Shabicha, which I reached at 10.40 a.m. On our arrival Godsave cooked us a meal.

Near the crash, on the Darb was a circular ruin which looked like an old bath. It had a ledge all the way round and steps leading down. It was dry inside. Great lizards sun themselves on these relics in the timeless desert, among the flowers and the butterflies, under the cloud-flecked blue sky. One feels as if one were in the presence of some great mystery, and one approached them almost reverently.

Even on the place where we had landed there were hidden boulders in the vegetation which might easily break one's tailskid. Mac and I walked over it carefully and removed a number. We got pricked through our socks. He said it was a marvellous place for scorpions, which love to sit underneath the stones, so we were very careful in picking them up. Godsave was going to take the engine out of the crash in bits and burn the rest. He was then going to make

CIRCULAR RUIN BY THE DARB ZOBAIDA

Nejef and return to pick up the other Ford. McClaughry was going to fly down a new stub axle to Nejef and salve the rest of the gear. We took back the pilot, the instruments, all wireless gear and some bits of the engine.

About 1.45 I started up and taxied very carefully back to the other end of my patch. It was surrounded by rising ground strewn with limestone boulders. Mac and my fitter trotted at either wing tip to warn me of hidden boulders. Mac got fearfully hot! Then one of the Fords met me with all the gear at the end from which I was to take off. I did not wish to taxi with the heavy load. Then we loaded up. I had to be careful, because we were 1,000 feet up and it was warmish, so I should not be able to get off with too heavy a load. We said good-bye to Godsave, and I took off. "Vaivode" climbed manfully. We got one nasty down dunt just after getting off, but I pushed the throttles full open and we breasted it all right. It was very bumpy on the way back, but we had the wind astern and it only took two and three-quarter hours, and we got in at 4.30 p.m.

All the way back along the Darb we were ballooning up and down on, the air currents as much as 500 feet. The waves seemed about 3 miles from crest to crest. I would be at 3,000 feet, and then sink to 2,500 feet one and a half miles further on, and then, without altering the throttles, I would shoot up again to 3,000 feet. Each shoot up was preluded by colossal rolling bumps. When I arrived home I had Mac to tea on our lawn. He said he had enjoyed himself very much. The whole day's flying was six and a quarter hours. I felt devilish tired when I got back. I had been flying late the night before, and had not had a great deal of sleep, because I had had so much to arrange before going. But that night I slept like a log.

FLIGHT FROM HINAIDI TO KIRKUK AND BACK (APRIL, 1926)

It was fairly fine after heavy rain two nights before, but the south wind always makes the weather uncertain. We passed over Khan Beni Said and saw Baquba on our right with the big curve and railway bridge over the Diyala. It is in a great mass of palms. Deltawa is in a similar mass on the left, which forms a sort of dark green island between the two rivers. I saw Summers' landing ground N85 and recognized it by the tailskid marks. We then pushed northwards over the disused railway, pointing off to the north-east across the great space of desert before you come to the Shatt el Adhaim, where it turns sharply northwards at Banting's Bend. There is a loop which sticks right out.

Then we flew right on, keeping the narrow wriggling river just below us on the port side till the Jebel Hamrin came in sight, which looks like nothing so much as breakers out in the offing beyond a calm sea. We passed over the Jebel just to the right of where the Shatt el Adhaim curls through it, curving right back in a great "S" through a shallow but sharply cut gorge. These low hills have rather beautiful colours, and the reds and ochres contrast with the slate greys and pale mauves, while the vegetation looks like green liquid spilt in the undulations of the Jebel. The Jebel runs north-west in a whale-back as far as the eye can see, as if the plain had heaved gently up in the middle and cracked in layers.

Meanwhile on our right the dim mountains had come into view like a troubled dream, mauve-grey like a ghostly silhouette. They always give me an intense emotion, when I see the great rugged line, the ghostly eternal wall, mingling its summits, as it did then, with dappled nimbus cloud. I kept trying to see Pire Makrun, but could never be certain whether in the distance I saw the cream-coloured snows or whether it was but hanging masses of white vapour. Across the plain, as the Jebel calmed down in folds of lessening steepness, I saw Tuz by the door in the hills, with its chai running out on to the plain. Up along the hills lay Tauk standing on a mound by its ancient chai. We were flying at 2,000 feet, and I was trying to test a new kind of statoscope, when suddenly the air was full of Painted Lady butterflies. They came whizzing through my wings until one crashed on my wind-screen. I imagine they must have been carried up there in ascending currents of air. It was an extraordinary sight, and I could not believe that they were real at first.

Two whale-backed hills lay like delicate grey-blue carvings on the north-western horizon. After Tauk I got slightly muddled in my direction and saw two or three openings in the hills where I thought Kirkuk might be. However, I made out what I took to be Taza, and cut northwards across the hills, leaving it on my left; for the hills curve outward towards the west. Then I spotted Kirkuk and made towards the aerodrome. The sun was shining through a light drift of broken cumulus and the air was fairly bumpy. I glided down and found I was about 50 feet above the eastern edge of the aerodrome. I think I could have stopped quite easily before the corn at the other end, but I decided not to risk it, so I put on my engines and went round again, this time dropping in lower.

I made quite a decent landing, but a bit on the fast side, I am afraid.

RETURN JOURNEY

As I should have to land at night, I tested a Holt flare before leaving the ground. Some officers and men were playing cricket on the aerodrome. It was a calm, restful evening, although there was rather a black gloom away to the west over the mountains. I flew fairly low down over the chai where I knew that Eric Pollard was having a bathing party with the armoured cars. Soon I spotted the cars parked on a sand bank, and saw the party splashing about in the shallow glistening water. They looked just like tiny frogs in a pool. I flew on for a bit, climbing a little, and then bore rather to the west, following the rugged line of the hills, which led me down towards Tauk.

The sun was shining in a golden haze over the western plain, covering it with a mild glory in which stood the whale-backed hills by Alton Keupri. I saw more butterflies flying through the blue air. Over the mountains in the east it was black; and above the gloom rose the most glorious white cumulus, with sharply cut shadows in its massive structure, pale mauve. The shape of the cloud was a thing of beauty to behold, like a huge white edifice reared aloft in the sky.

When I passed over Tuz the sun was sinking below the horizon; and when I had left the Jebel Hamrin like a troubled line of shadowy breakers behind me, the red ball of the sun dropped into the blue-grey desert, as into the sea. But the afterglow lasted long after I had flown between the rivers at N85.

It is almost impossible to describe the gradual approach of night when one is flying: the imperceptible brightening of the exhaust flame; the folding up of all the tones of the scene into repose; how nature gathers her blue to cast its ghostly radiance over the desert. Here and there a lonely Bedouin fire winked on the haunted plain. Far away to the south glimmered the lights of Baghdad and the pale violet streak of the flood water of the Tigris and Diyala.

In a few minutes I was putting on my Holt flare and sinking down into the hot, moist air of Hinaidi. It was very much fresher and more pleasant at Kirkuk on the aerodrome. "Vaivode," my aeroplane, is fitted up with all sorts of marvellous night-flying gadgets. There were no flares at Kirkuk, so they shone the headlights of the ambulance along the edge of the aerodrome, to show it to me in case I should want to land again.

At 8.35 p.m. I pushed off into the night and soon left the lights of Kirkuk behind. Away in the west I could see the glare of the mighty desert fires about 20 miles away like luminous horseshoes. I tried to pierce the obscurity to find the edge of the hills, and I think I found Tauk, although I am not sure. I was keeping an eye on the little

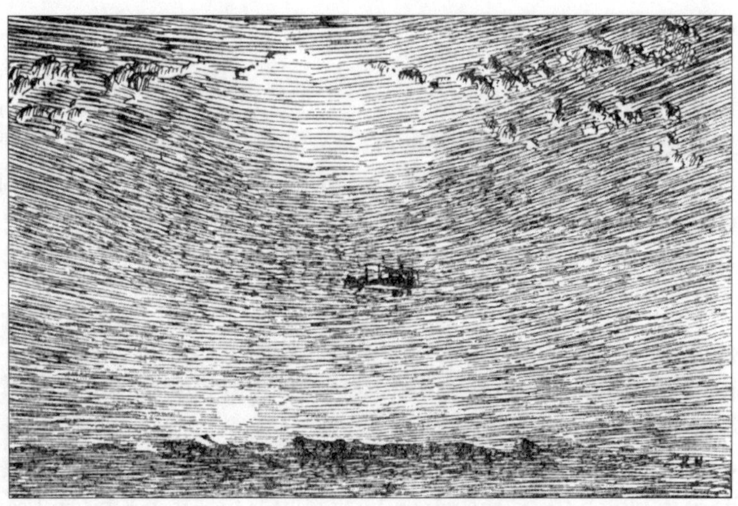

MOON RISING OVER THE PUSHT-I-KUH

illuminated compass bowl, which was to guide me home. Behind me was the Pole star and Cassiopeia, and in front, to the south, was a constellation of whose name I was not sure. I think it must have been Scorpio. Orion was nowhere to be seen. He lives in the east and guides me home on the Mail Route.

I was trying to work out on to the plain; but after a bit wherever I looked down it was always Jebel underneath, rugged inhospitable hills. I had a waking nightmare that my compass might be wrong, and that the hills would rise up all round me like spectres and lock me in. But I stuck on my compass course. I do not know where I crossed the Jebel Hamrin. At one time there was suddenly a smell of burning rubber, and my pelvis nearly fell out. I simply could not land. I would not have dared to, except in extremis, in such rough stuff and at night. However, the smell passed away without anything happening, and eventually I picked up the Shatt el Adhaim near its confluence with the Tigris and knew I was safe. Thirty miles mantle around her and her eyelids gradually sink over her eyes to sleep. As the first star twinkles in the mysterious distance of the zenith, the earth seems to darken and the sky to lighten. Then an orange moon lifted up over the Pusht-i-Kuh, but was almost immediately barred by a low cloud. Soon it came out again to cast its ghostly radiance over the desert. Here and there a lonely Bedouin fire winked on the haunted plain. Far away to the south glimmered the lights of Baghdad and the pale violet streak of the flood water of the Tigris and Diyala.

In a few minutes I was putting on my Holt flare and sinking down into the hot, moist air of Hinaidi. It was very much fresher and more pleasant at Kirkuk.

NIGHT FLIGHT FROM KIRKUK TO HINAIDI (JUNE, 1926)

The night closed down over Kirkuk, a little moon rose, and the six Vernons became grey shadows out on the aerodrome. "Vaivode", my aeroplane, is fitted up with all sorts of marvellous night-flying gadgets. There were no flares at Kirkuk, so they shone the headlights of the ambulance along the edge of the aerodrome, to show it to me in case I should want to land again.

At 8.35 p.m. I pushed off into the night and soon left the lights of Kirkuk behind. Away in the west I could see the glare of the mighty desert fires about 20 miles away like luminous horseshoes. I tried to pierce the obscurity to find the edge of the hills, and I think I found Tauk, although I am not sure. I was keeping an eye on the little illuminated compass bowl, which was to guide me home. Behind me was the Pole star and Cassiopeia, and in front, to the south, was a constellation of whose name I was not sure. I think it must have been Scorpio. Orion was nowhere to be seen. He lives in the east and guides me home on the Mail Route.

I was trying to work out on to the plain; but after a bit wherever I looked down it was always Jebel underneath, rugged inhospitable hills. I had a waking nightmare that my compass might be wrong, and that the hills would rise up all round me like spectres and lock me in. But I stuck on my compass course. I do not know where I crossed the Jebel Hamrin. At one time there was suddenly a smell of burning rubber, and my pelvis nearly fell out. I simply could not land. I would not have dared to, except *in extremis*, in such rough stuff and at night. However, the smell passed away without anything happening, and eventually I picked up the Shatt el Adhaim near its confluence with the Tigris and knew I was safe. Thirty miles away I saw the glow of Baghdad and Hinaidi flaring in the southern sky, and at about 10.30 p.m. I was over Hinaidi, having been on the go for over nineteen hours, which was a good day's work. Afterwards my wireless operator told me that the smell of burning rubber was an accumulator which had gone wrong. Accumulators are not things to be trifled with.

NIGHT FLIGHT FROM *L.G.* V TO HINAIDI (JUNE, 1926)

Bunny and I left Hinaidi at 6 a.m. and arrived at *L.G.* V (180 miles) at 9.5 a.m. As we wanted to leave Hinaidi with full petrol we had to start in the cool of the early morning. We cooked breakfast before the real desert heat set in. Bangers (sausages) and eggs, and afterwards tinned ham and chai (tea), were our fare. Then we prepared to sit it out under the planes till dark. We took with us two big blocks of ice, four dozen lemonades and one dozen beer. We soon saw what was going to be our trouble: locusts. The dirty brutes! For ten hours they gave us no peace. I got my camp bed rigged underneath one plane, but the locusts were so thirsty that if you let them settle on you they bit. I got bitten twice. They were so mad for anything damp that they actually ate half the sack the ice was in. Ooch! there were four or five on my pillow at once. The underneath of the plane, even though in shadow, got so hot that it was uncomfortable to hold your hand against. During the hot hours the wind dropped, and we lay and sweated our hearts out; what little puffs of wind there were, were like a waft from the infernal regions. From about 2 till 3 p.m. the shade temperature must have risen to about 120 degrees, and I wilted a bit, but perked up again afterwards. On another occasion I am always going to have a net. I do not think the locusts would eat it if it were dry.

Strange as it may sound, I simply loved the whole show; loved the heat of the old desert; the silence, the freedom, and the mad spirit of adventure. Of course, I was burnt black, and my eyes always go very blue after I have been out in the desert.

Gradually the evening came, the shadows lengthened and the heat abated somewhat. At 7.30 p.m. we had our second meal: pork pies, tinned fruit, and more chai and lemonade. I must digress for a moment and explain here that Bunny is an Australian, although he loudly asserts he is a South African. Wherever he goes there is an almost incessant brew of tea.

Curiously enough a little grey dove had come in the morning and stayed with us all day hopping about on the planes. It flew away at dusk. A desert lark also came and stayed for a little. They both looked horribly thin and starved. The sun then sank down below the grey green edge of the desert, absolutely whole like a burnished yellow shield, till the last little bit was gone behind the perfectly level horizon; and you could almost feel its absence as if a heater had suddenly been shut off. In the south-east the moon was already up, whole and round, and brightening every moment. A few fleecy clouds looked as if they were pasted on to the sky, rather like the clouds you see painted by old Italian masters. The hush of the dusk enwrapped the desert. The stillness was profound.

We were within a hundred yards of the track. During the day twelve cars had passed along the track, all driven by natives. One of them hailed us to know if we wanted water. The desert felt very different from the last time I was in that neighbourhood, in the terrible flood at *L.G.* IV 27 miles further east.

Soon the desert became a vast grey shadow under the soft opal dome of the sky in which tiny points of fire slowly became visible. As the moon brightened the desert turned to dull silver. We tested our night-flying gear, let off a Holt flare each, and ran up our engines. Bunny took off first, disappeared in a shadow of dust, then rose above it, silhouetted against the moon. I took off rather closely behind him and his slipstream forced my right wing down. I could not tell precisely how far off the ground was, but it was not far; and for a few seconds I was rather worried till I was able to lift the wing up. The air was stiflingly hot as it always is at night; and *L.G.* V is 1,500 feet high. Under these conditions the aeroplane did not climb well at first.

We rendezvoused over the great silver mud flat, on which I had decided to land if it became necessary immediately after taking off. Then I spotted the track where it runs across the flat and found that the light was sufficiently good to follow it. We followed it all the way to Ramadi. Mostly it showed up as a thin black line on the dull pewter of the desert. It was a bit of a strain to follow it, and I lost it once in the "Hills of Lost Thoughts" between *L.G.* III and *L.G.* II, when I dropped a Michelin flare and was slightly dazzled. However, I circled in the usual way and soon found it again.

I was surprised how well the track showed up by moonlight. I had navigation instruments and was prepared to navigate at any point should I lose the track. Flying Officer Gandy was in the hull sitting at the navigation table, and kept a dead reckoning of our progress, informing me every fifteen minutes or so. When we left *L.G.* V I sent a wireless message to Baghdad:—"Vernons … and … left *L.G.* V for Hinaidi O.K. at 20.30 hrs. Can see track. Am following it."

Once again I was speeding through the wizard Eastern night with the full moon and the silver haze and the stretching grey wings lit to pink and gold by the exhaust flames. The heat was colossal and I had mugs of water sent up which my second pilot and I drank. I also dashed some over my face. Just before we reached the Bitumen Pools I saw four cars that had passed us in the evening, dashing along with their headlights streaming across the desert. I glided down quietly behind them and whizzed past. I wonder what they thought of an aeroplane suddenly crashing out of the night on the lonely track. We did not see the flares at Ramadi till we were within 7 miles. I had another Vernon standing by there and flares out in case we should want to land, and I sent it a message telling it to pack up and go home.

Then we flew on across the great rivers till the lights of Hinaidi hove in sight, and I found myself landing down the familiar searchlight beam at 11.30 p.m., just three hours after we had left *L.G.* V. I was feeling rather tired, having done 6 hrs. 5 min. flying and having been attacked by locusts all day. Bunny was absolutely passed out, but blissfully happy. What we had set out to accomplish we had accomplished.

NIGHT FLIGHT BACK FROM *L.G.* 8 (JULY, 1926)

Louis Paget and I set out for Ramadi on Monday morning. When we arrived there we filled up with petrol. We had to work on the aeroplane till 11p.m., so I only got about four hours' sleep at the foot of the wireless mast at Ramadi on Monday night. We had supper that evening with Godsave, who happened to be there with his armoured cars. He had taken a lighthouse over, which was to be installed there. Unfortunately there appeared to be something wrong with its internals; and, as Godsave described it, you had to hold your thumb on it to make it work.

Early next morning "Happy" Horrex flew over with the ice for our trip. He looked like a sort of milk train arriving, with his hull all dripping water. Louis and I had "Vaivode" and "Venus," our two Vernons, run up ready to start. When the ice arrived and was disgorged from Happy's Vernon, we put part of it into petrol tins, which we covered over with sacking, and what we could not manage to cram into the tins we put in a large wooden box.

We made an excellent trip to *L.G.* 8, in three hours and five minutes, and arrived there at 9.5 (local time); no, as a matter of fact, not local time, for Rutbah, which is close by *L.G.* 8, uses Amman time, an hour earlier. It is all rather confusing. If you fly from *L.G.* V where you have Baghdad time, and you have a bit of a following wind, you would reach Rutbah before you started! We found it beautifully cool at Rutbah for the time of year, and a pleasant north breeze was blowing. I should think it was about 90 degrees. Soft white cumulus clouds were passing and casting patterned shadows over the upland.

At Ramadi two D.H.9as had passed overhead. They were taking Sir Percy Lorraine over to Egypt. I believe he was going home to England. We passed over them at *L.G.* V and saw them filling up at the desert tank, and then they passed over us again at *L.G.* 8. After that there were violent conversations on the wireless: for both Amman and Baghdad seemed to have lost track of them. I think they must have landed somewhere away on the route. Anyway I kept being asked where I had last seen them and what they were doing. Eventually we heard that they had landed at Amman at about 4.30 p.m. in the afternoon.

Meanwhile we proceeded to dig two shallow trenches in the ground, wherein we made a fire to heat up water for tea in a kettle. I had taken a clean linen handkerchief to make a bag for the tea. We fried the eggs I had brought, together with the "bangers." Louis and I had each taken a dozen lemonades and we got these on the ice. After we had sent through two or three messages to Baghdad by means of our ground wireless station which we had erected, we started exploring, and B——, who had come with me as navigator, started having dysentery, so he thought. This was not encouraging.

I walked over the landing ground with Louis, up a little hill, to see if we could see Rutbah, which we had seen from the air was not very far away. Then we walked across another shallow valley, up another hill, and there below us lay the Wadi Hauran, and the buildings which had just been constructed to include a police post, wireless station and rest house. The wireless was not yet installed. Beyond the building, stretching vista upon vista, lay the hills of the "Kingdom of What Wasn't," that fascinating country that lies between the "Upland of the Winds" beyond, and the "Plain of Unfulfilled Desire" on which *L.G.* 8 is situated.

On the way to Rutbah we found what we thought must be the remains of an old town, where the traces of walls of buildings could be seen. We eventually reached the police post, and found various natives working on it and a representative of Nairn's, who gave us cups of water. He then ran us out in an ancient Ford, which went along, by the grace of God, to the landing ground which had just been made for Imperial Airways. After showing us round, he drove us back along the track to *L.G.* 8, which was rather a longer way round than the way we had walked. He had some beer with us and shared a tin of blackberries which was our lunch. I had lemonade, as I never touch alcohol till I have finished flying; and I knew I should need every ounce of sense that I possessed for the coming night flight. The Nairn man said that he would run out again that evening in his Ford with some chlorodyne for B——, which was very kind of him.

After that he left us, and I fixed my net over my camp bed by the hull of "Vaivode" and lay torpid. I could not sleep, partly from thinking about the night flight, and partly because the breeze had freshened and flapped everything about. Meanwhile some of our crews took a stroll over to Rutbah. I got up at about 5 p.m. and we did a little pistol and rifle practice on petrol tins. The Nairn man turned up again with the medicine, which B—— took. After that he seemed better.

At about 8.30 p.m., just after it got dark, the westbound Nairn convoy came past—six big cars—and we stopped them on the track by firing up Very lights. A friend of Louis Paget's, the chief doctor of the Anglo-Persian Oil Company, was on it, and John Babington, who was going home on two months' leave, and one or two ladies. We treated them to whiskies and sodas and Kia-ora. I am afraid we looked the most frightful tousled tramps, blatantly unshaven. We were having our supper at the time and our kitchen fire threw a weird, flickering light over the desert. We had a good Machonochie stew with tinned tomatoes and peas thrown in.

From about 10.30 to 11.30 p.m. I lay down again on my bed and fell into a restless doze. I was too excited really to sleep. I began to have misgivings. The desert was dark and lonely. It was like a dead world. I kept wondering if our navigation would work after all, and whether we would ever find *L.G.* V. I could see the glow of a cigarette end wandering about. It was attached to the end of the thin tall figure of Louis. My mind wandered back to an absurd incident in Cairo. Louis, having nothing better to do at the moment, wandered up to a bookstall, and fixing his eyeglass more firmly in his eye, said in a serene voice: "*Have you got Twenty Years in an Air Pocket?*" "Twenty years in a what?" asked the mystified assistant. "*Twenty Tears in an Air Pocket*, by Louis Paget; don't you know the book?" "Well, I'm afraid we haven't got it in stock, but may we order it for you?" "Please," said Louis. Then I came sharply back to reality.

The night was moonless, but I had not bargained for the bank of dark clouds which were now shutting out the stars. We had heard on the wireless that Happy had reached *L.G.* V on his Vernon, where he was to await our arrival. We had sited petrol tins for flares on our landing ground before dusk; but what worried us most was the fact that there were hills 500 feet high within one and a half miles of us, which we should not be able to see in the dark. We should have to climb up off the ground without seeing anything and we should not feel safe until we had reached 3,000 feet, because *L.G.* 8 is already 2,000 feet above sea-level. Luckily the run into wind was fairly clear—just south of Rutbah—and I determined to fly dead straight and climb as hard as I could before I thought of turning.

We took off the ground at midnight. The desert was simply an aching void. When one is flying over a civilized country at night one normally sees some lights; but here was blackness profound. Once I saw two lights away on the starboard bow, which may have been the headlights of two cars out on the track. The sky was half clouded, and I could see an occasional star. We made *L.G.* V in fifty-seven minutes. I was never sure that I saw a rocket until one shot up unmistakably about 2 miles to the north. The great grey mud flat then came into view. It was the first landmark that I had seen. I fired a Very light to show that I had seen the rocket, whereupon Happy lit flares on the mud flat, which he had not lit before because he was rather short of petrol; and the mud flat is about a mile from the tank. We had decided not to attempt to land by the tank because of the camel-thorn, which it would have been impossible to avoid at night.

Louis and I both made execrable landings. We made the mistake of using our Holt wing-tip flares, and the surface of the mud flat is so smooth that the glare of the flares made it very difficult to judge one's height above the ground. Rumour has it that I did a 2-mile bounce: the record for this country. I admit I did not know where I was from Adam; and after I had first touched the ground and had bounced up again, I kept a bit of engine on for fear of dropping from some height. In the end I settled down on the far side of the mud flat. After all our excitement we found to our genuine astonishment that neither of us had broken anything.

I more or less apologized to Happy for intruding on him so roughly at that hour. Handing me a cigarette, he cheerily, if somewhat irrelevantly, greeted me with "*Honi soit*, that is to say, please don't scrape your matches on the blancmange," or words to that effect. He had a good feed ready for us: chai, melon and cold "banger" sandwiches. There were all sorts of things running about on the mud flat, including Jerrymundas, huge spiders about the size of a smallish crab. They fight the scorpions and various other nocturnal prowlers.

All three of us left the mud flat at 2.20 a.m. and we made Ramadi at 3.50 a.m. just as the first hint of dawn was breaking in the east. In the 112 miles from *L.G.* V to Ramadi we made an error of 10 miles, and hit the Euphrates above Ramadi. I think this was due to an error in taking the drift, which was perhaps to some extent excusable owing to the fact that the wind was constantly varying. We landed by flares at Ramadi, for it was not yet light enough to gauge the level of the ground accurately. Fatigue and anxiety disappeared; we felt supremely happy. After the inevitable cup of tea we rose once more into the air in the early dawn, and reached home at 6.15 a.m.

CHAPTER XIII

THE HOSPITALITY OF A SHEIKH

In March, 1926, I was ordered to go to Basrah on duty for two or three days. I was to fly as passenger in a D.H.9a. I went with Flying Officer Farnan, who was an excellent pilot, was doing his third year in Iraq, and knew the country well. I was keen to learn the trip down to Shaibah, the aerodrome for Basrah. Although you have simply to follow the Euphrates, the journey is apt to be confusing because the river has so many branches and little odd tributary streams which are not clearly marked on the map. On this occasion we had a gruelling head wind and took four and a half hours to reach Shaibah, which is a long time for a D.H.9a, although about normal for a Vernon with its lower cruising speed.

You start off southwards from Hinaidi, follow the River Tigris south-eastwards to the Arch of Ctesiphon, and then cut southwards again across the Blue, the real Mesopotamia, that is the land between the rivers. You pick up the river Euphrates near Hillah, about 60 miles from Hinaidi. You actually leave Hillah on your right and pass over Diwaniya, about 40 miles further on. There is a landing ground at Diwaniya. From Diwaniya operations were carried out against refractory tribes at Afej, about 20 miles east. Then you follow along the river past Samawa, and later Nasiriya, close to which are the ruins of Ur of the Chaldees. After skirting some huge shallow lakes you fly across more Blue till you reach Shaibah itself, 15 miles south-west of Basrah. The last part of the flight was terribly bumpy, and we passed through some dust clouds, which did not make it any more pleasant. I felt a bit sick, as I usually do when flying any distance as a passenger in bumpy weather, but consoled myself with munching biscuits.

We arrived at Shaibah at 2.30 p.m., landed nicely and found the squadron commander waiting for us on the aerodrome, having foregone his afternoon's sleep. He had his car and everything arranged for my comfort. He was the most excellent host to have, and in a vague and indefinable way you felt you were staying at a country house with him. The air at Shaibah was bracing, and, owing to the recent heavy rains, the desert was quite green, so that as I looked out of my window I might have been on an English moor. Of course in summer-time it is tremendously hot there, and all the green is scorched up. Hinaidi somehow does not seem "in the country," whereas Shaibah does.

After visiting Basrah next day we drove back as the dusk was falling. You drive along a track across the Blue. In one place the so-called road crosses a great estuary which was once sea. The track runs across it on a low embankment. The desert air tasted keen and sweet. We passed some ruined buildings, one of which was a Turkish hospital in the War. Beyond this were tamarisk groves, or maybe acacia. In the War there was a great battle at Shaibah, and the Turkish general was told to hang on at all costs. When he was defeated, he retired to one of the groves and blew his brains out.

The next day the squadron commander had to go off on a long desert reconnaissance. My work was completed before he returned, so I did not see him before I left, nor was I able to thank him personally for the pleasant time I had had. I left a note thanking him for his kindness.

I started on the return journey with Farnan at 8 a.m. The heavy luggage, such as valises and suit-cases, was strapped on to special carriers underneath the planes. The fuselage of the D.H.9a is not large enough to take the luggage inside. The wind was behind us and it was splendid weather. I asked Farnan to land at Diwaniya on the way back, for I wished to have a look at the landing ground. He accordingly did so. It was a very fair landing ground, although somewhat narrow. There is a road running along one side of it, which is slightly raised above the level of the ground, and which has accounted for more than one wrecked undercarriage. The small town is about a quarter of a mile from the southern end, and at the northern end is a little mosque with a blue dome, which looks like a jewel. The river line is marked by a dark green belt of palms. We had a quick walk round and then took off again.

We proceeded northwards on our way, and had flown for about half an hour, which brought us almost level with Hillah and perhaps 12 miles to the east of it, when without any warning the engine spluttered and then stopped. We were at the moment flying over a foul bit of country, the worst area of the whole trip from the point of view of forced landing; all cultivation and dykes and bunds and ditches. I did not want to worry Farnan, and I felt sure that he would do his best under the circumstances, even if we had to crash. I did

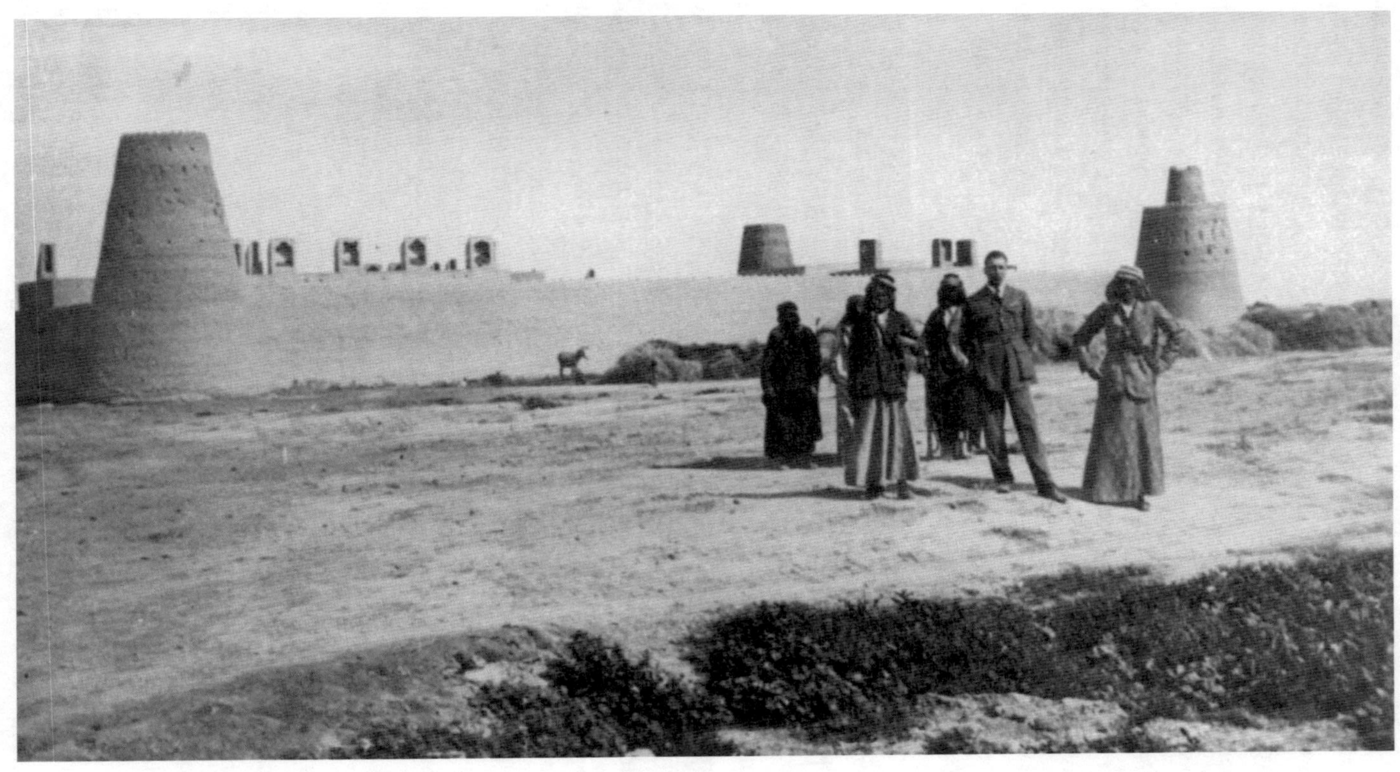

NAIF AL JEREAN'S CASTLE

not see anywhere promising at first, but after a few moments I spotted a tiny bare patch. I leant over to Farnan and said, "What about that?" We were at 3,000 feet and a D.H.9a glides a fair way, so we had a certain amount of time to prepare.

The patch of ground was miserably small, but there was no alternative. Farnan made a good approach. If he did not judge it perfectly, we should, with luck, walk out of a heap of rubbish. I knew there was nothing more to be done and I sat perfectly quiet. In a couple of minutes it would all be over for better or worse. As I had nothing with which to occupy my mind, I was strung up a bit. Farnan just dropped in beautifully and I felt the wheels running along smooth ground. Then I saw a serrated bank coming, about 2 feet high. We were approaching the end of our run and our speed was now reduced to 10 miles an hour or so. But if there were a ditch on the other side of that bank we should certainly go on our nose. Farnan chose the lowest bit of the little bund and swung towards it. I folded my arms in front of my face and waited. Up we went … and … down on the other side. There was no ditch, thank the Lord. Then we ran on for another 10 yards or so, up another bank; and stopped. We got out, both a little excited, but both very thankful.

When I looked round the country, it was ghastly for forced landing; great dykes many feet high, wide ditches full of water, and many other smaller dry ditches, remains of trenches and disused canals. However, I saw we could have had a longer run on our patch, but Farnan did the best he could looking from the air. I was wearing my best uniform and field boots, not a comfortable kit for rough desert life.

In a minute or so, dozens of Arabs shuffled up, for this was a populous area. After a little I heard them saying, "Sheikh! Sheikh!" and a brand-new Ford car appeared round the corner of a dyke. The Sheikh, Naif Al Jerean, and his son, whose name I cannot remember—it reminded me of Goldswil—and their chauffeur, a Baghdad taxi-driver, rolled up. I saluted them and they were extremely friendly. Naif spoke no English, but his son and the driver a little. We palavered about, trying to find common ground in our few words of Arabic and their few words of English. Naif then produced five armed sentries, part of his own bodyguard, I think, and placed them round the aeroplane to keep off the souvenir hunters. We had no wireless with us, so we concocted a telegram, and asked where the nearest railway station was. We took a long time to make them understand. They said "Jarbuiyah." It was not marked on our map, the nearest marked place being Imam Hansa. However, as far as we could make out, they said that Jarbuiyah was beyond. We asked them if they would send off the wire for us and they said they would do so, but begged us meanwhile to come to their "bungalow," as they called it. They assured us that the sentries would guard the D.H.9a.

As we very much doubted whether they would ever send the telegram, anyway till the next day, time being of no consequence to the Arab—I mean that he would call it hurrying if he pushed it off the next day—we decided to risk it and go with them. So into the Ford we hopped and drove off across country over amazingly rough tracks, and along the bottom of a disused canal for some way. As we went along we saw three Arabs galloping on ponies; a wonderful sight. They ride like cowboys, and when they are in the wild open, they look really spanking, jumping ditches with such a dashing air.

Then by and by we drove into the land of yesterday: pure dreams. We came round the corner of a walled orchard to Naif's castle! It simply astounded me, all away in the Blue. In effect it was a fortified farm, but it somehow had a mediæval air. It all seemed unreal, and I just had to give up trying to bother whether it was or no. We went round the further side and found a doorway with antlers over it, and all the retainers and horses and Arab tents in the neighbourhood. Here was a feudal baron, indeed. As a matter of fact, I believe the place really belongs to Sheikh Adiye, Naif's brother, and Naif minds it for him while he is away in Baghdad.

We were shown into a little courtyard and found a garden with a low balustrade round it in which were growing orange and rose trees and oleanders. Then a henchman brought a bunch of keys, real stage keys, about 9 inches long, and Naif opened the hall door. We were ushered into a marvellous hall, perhaps 60 feet long by 20 feet wide, completely covered, as to floor by an Ispahan carpet, one of the most wonderful I have ever seen. The walls of the hall were plastered and covered with green enamel, the ceiling timbered and the beams decorated with inlaid looking-glass in a Turkish sort of design. Tall windows were pierced in the 3-foot-thick walls, and round the sides were chairs and settees. Two oil lamps of the Aladdin variety (made in Austria) stood on a table and two more hung from the ceiling. Naif told us that Sir Henry Dobbs had visited the place once, but I do not think that any other Englishman had been there.

Naif bade us be seated and brought tea (chai) in silver cups and a teapot on a tray, and cream cracker biscuits (Huntley & Palmer's). Splendid tea it was too, without milk. Meanwhile luncheon was being rapidly prepared. Soon it came in on a huge tray, and was placed on the floor. We squatted down Arab fashion, although stiff field boots prevented the action from being in any way graceful, and were careful not to point the soles of our feet towards our host, for that is rude. We made ready to eat seriously. Then they brought in cushions, Naif and his son waiting on us personally, and the retainers in the courtyard outside all trying to see in through the door, through which none but the honoured might enter. Naif's word was law, and at a sign from him someone would appear and do his behest.

On the tray were two whole chickens, probably just killed and therefore a trifle tough, but marvellously cooked; four plates of chipped potatoes, some pickled stuff, and some preserved fruit which seemed like a cross between honey and ginger in taste, rather sweet; and some Arab bread in flat rounds bigger than pancakes. We apparently looked so uncomfortable that they were constrained to bring chairs for the white sahibs—these Arabs have adopted the Indian term—who could not squat at ease. An Arab squats down in one movement as easily as we sit on a chair. The tray was put on a low table, the sort that Anglo-Indian ladies have in their drawing-rooms. A knife, fork and spoon each had been produced as a great honour, but when Naif saw me wrestling with the chicken he could bear it no longer and came and dismembered it with his hands! So thinking it would please him we discarded the cutlery. He then sat just on the edge of a chair and watched us solemnly. He produced one glass of water between us, which we courteously declined. One never knows where the water comes from.

As I looked around, I felt this was all pure romance: just as if we had slipped back four hundred years—the baronial hall; the retainers, the stately robes of the Sheikh and his son; we might have gone to see a film and suddenly found that it turned out to be true. After the repast I persuaded Naif to sit for his portrait. I drew a picture of him and he sent one of his men for a hammer and nails, and nailed it up on the wall. Then I prevailed on him to let me take some photographs. He was rather nervous at first, but in a little while he seemed to enter into the spirit of the thing.

After that we asked if we might go to Jarbuiyah with the telegram. So we got into the Ford complete with two guns. Naif had two men with rifles more or less following him all the time, and he had to give a multitude of orders respecting the *ménage* during his absence. Then he tootled his horn and his Klaxon, just to show what a big bug he was! We set off through the fields, and from time to time he would summon his men, who were working in the fields, and tell them something. By and by we came to the river, and passed quite a

NAIF AL JEREAN AND HIS SON AT HOME

good strip of landing ground which we had not seen from the air. We passed through the village of Imam Hansa, where the driver got some water for the radiator from a little mud building on the outskirts of the village. Another man came out and Naif held out his hand negligently for the man to kiss, which he did.

About 7 miles from Naif's castle we got to Jarbuiyah, a little wayside railway station, and found an Indian Babu station-master-porter-signalman and watchman all in one. He sent off the wire to Baghdad. This was about 3.30 p.m. He spoke English fairly well. Some of these Indian station-masters behaved very gallantly in the Rebellion and more than one was killed after refusing to leave his post. We got the Babu to tell Naif, who had firmly made up his mind we were going to spend the night with him, that the Big Sahib in Baghdad would be angry if we stayed not by the aeroplane (Tiara); He said, "But my sentries, are they not good enough?" We replied, "It is the law, and that we may not break." Then Naif looked like thunder; and when we imprudently suggested sending for Arab police from Hillah you should have seen the look of scorn which he gave us. As if his, the great baron's, own armed bodyguard were to be compared with mere Government police! So we did not pursue that any further.

At last he was persuaded that the Sahibs must sleep beside the aeroplane, and we asked to go to it. He took us back to the castle instead and I wondered vaguely if we were prisoners! It was no good escaping, because I was sure we could not find the aeroplane again. Then more tea was served, and Naif's son asked us if we should like a "little home." This turned out to be a tent. We said, "Of course." Would we like beds? No, we had beds. Still no sign of letting us go. We urged that the sun was getting low and we must reach the aeroplane before dark. I asked Naif's son more or less jokingly if his father would give me a ring as a keepsake. He immediately pulled a little gold ring off his finger and gave it to me. I demurred; but he insisted. Then the taxi-driver butted in and said, "Twenty rupees." But the young man said, "You are my friend; I take no money," thus illustrating the difference between the haughty Arab noble and the degraded Arab who has been polluted by the vices and money-grubbing civilization of the West.

Meanwhile Naif produced a perfectly good bottle of whisky and two sodas, which we partook of, but which he, being a strict Mohammedan, would not touch. He evidently kept it against the day when he might entertain the white man. The young man said he hoped to come to London. We said, "Across the

Sea." But the Sea had no meaning for him. Then the swine of a taxi-driver surreptitiously poured himself out half a glass of neat whisky and drank it. Farnan asked Naif for the bottle in case we were left out in the Blue. Naif immediately gave it to us. At last he let us go just before sunset. We bade him farewell and went in the car with his son and the driver. He begged us to come and visit him again. The driver was now rather under the weather and was singing at the top of his voice. We had the most hectic trip back to the D.H.9a, whizzing round impossible corners and over narrow bridges, only just wide enough for the Ford. We got the young Sheikh to curse the driver and he moderated his driving slightly.

When we reached the aeroplane we understood why Naif had been keeping us—so that he might get a tent erected as a surprise for us! The consummation of hospitality! There was an excellent Arab-made bell tent beside the aeroplane, with two carpets to sleep on. He had also sent out, I suppose on horse, a towel, soap, basin to wash in, and a marvellous hot supper in an aluminium canteen of saucepans which fitted one on top of the other. Rice and curry and a sort of stew, all very nicely cooked. I was flabbergasted. In the West we simply do not know the meaning of hospitality.

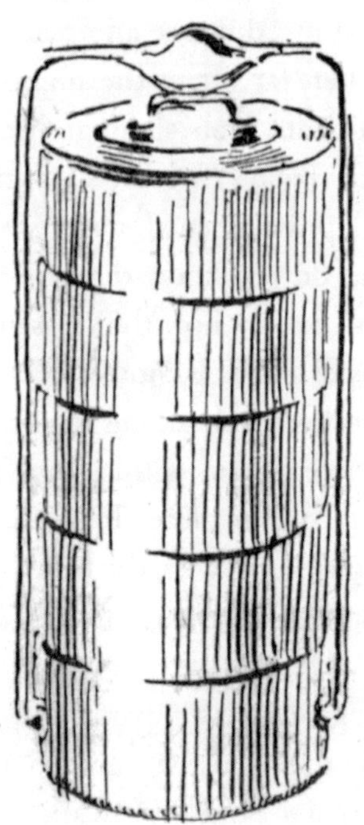

CANTEEN OF SAUCEPANS

And I fancy that under Naif's scowl was hidden the anxiety that every detail for our comfort should be worked out to the pitch of exactitude. His bodyguard had evidently received orders to guard us with their lives; and by Jove they did. Farnan had his camp bed, but I had my valise only, so I took the two carpets. The Arabs made a fire outside the tent door and squatted round it.

After dark I saw the Arabs load up their rifles and loosen their knife-slings. Probably all Arabs do this at night, but it gave me a funny feeling down my back, away there miles from anywhere in the dark with the grim wild figures silhouetted against the flickering fire. Just to show them that we had guns we got out our pistols and ostentatiously loaded them. But I am sure they would never have touched us.

If you are an Arab's guest you are safe, and he is bound to protect you with his own life. When we had eaten our supper and turned in, two of the guard came in with more rugs and asked us if we wanted them, and I accepted one, a great heavy warm one of bright colours. Fancy being tucked up in bed by wild men like that! As the tent flaps did not quite reach to the ground they collected all our gear and placed it in the centre of the tent; presumably lest any marauding hand should reach in in the night. Then we pulled the flap to and one Arab literally sat against it, to guard us, and I fancy never left it; for were we not the honoured guests of the Sheikh, and they his servants? I slept with my cocked pistol in my hand, or rather, did not sleep till about one o'clock, firstly because my mind was turning over and over the impossible possibility of being stabbed in the night for the sake of the hundred rupees (£8) I had on me, and secondly because the guard sang low crooning Arab songs, and chattered to each other unceasingly. Every half-hour or so I heard the almost silent pad of feet round the tent, two Arabs going round opposite ways and meeting one another.

At about 12.30 p.m. I was dozing uneasily when far off in the night—it reminded me of "The Immortal Hour"—I heard an Arab singing. Nearer and nearer came the voice, till our guard hailed. Then, "Salaam Aleikum," and "Aleikum es Salaam." After a pause the tent flap was opened, and I sat up suddenly all alert. "Sahib, Sahib—Telegraph!" And do you know that this was the answer to our wire from Baghdad? Heaven only knows how the messenger found us, or who he was, because the station-master did not know where the aeroplane was. There is a bond of mysterious brotherhood among the Arabs which is incomprehensible to me. Their intelligence system is uncanny. The wire stated that two D.H.9as would leave at dawn for our place. Then things more or less settled down again and I fell into a light sleep, with the little hard metal thing clasped in my hand: not that it would have availed much. The blow, if it came, would fall silently and quickly.

I am convinced that these feelings were quite groundless. Apart from the strict code of hospitality observed by the Arabs, they must have been well aware of what would happen to them if they harmed a Britisher. All the same it was not unnatural to feel rather lonely and helpless out there in the darkness, surrounded by armed men even though their wild exterior concealed the friendliest of hearts.

Dawn came, pale and grey, and filtered in under the tent flaps. We got up and found the guard more lively than ever; the night did not seem to have damped their ardour in the slightest. They boiled up some water for us on their fire, and we had some tea. What the Arabs do not know about making fires in the open is not worth knowing. They can keep a charcoal fire in a little trench glowing almost indefinitely with the minimum of attention.

In preparation for the aeroplanes that were coming out to us, Farnan put out a cloth "T" in the best place to land up wind. Meanwhile a number of inquisitive Arabs appeared on the horizon and wandered up to have a look. Our wonderful bodyguard, two of whose names I gathered were Nasr and Aluard from hearing their conversation in the night, became very excited. Two of the guard opened fire on the intruders, not exactly at them, but close over their heads. When I heard the bullets whistle I thought that things were becoming distinctly unsafe. I shouted "Bass! Bass!" which is the Arabic version of "Cut it out." One of the guard tried to stop one of those who was shooting and struggled with him, meanwhile the two loaded guns were waving about all over the place. I thought that if the shooting went on the opposing party might open fire also and that we might be in the way. However, the guard were soon calmed down, and when the presumed enemies came up they were laughing and in the best of tempers. They did not seem to mind at all.

Probably our bodyguard were merely demonstrating to us how faithful they were and what a great and powerful man Naif Al Jerean was. I suppose that is their normal life, and that they were all quite good friends, but that the guard had to make a good impression. They are odd people and extraordinarily fresh with their guns. Rifles are dangerous toys, especially when they are old Turkish weapons, that have no safety-catches and may go off at any moment. It is easy to imagine how desert scraps arise over odd camels. There is a vast amount of swashbuckling and shouting, but very few people are hurt. On the other hand, the Arabs are devilish good shots when they really aim.

The shooting episode was hardly over when we heard a faint droning in the sky, and two little specks appeared high up in the north. It was a beautiful, fresh morning, although the previous evening there had been dark banks of clouds with stars peeping only faintly through. When the two D.H.9as landed a considerable crowd of Arabs had collected. It was about 6.45 a.m. I was amazed to see how skilfully the D.H.9as were landed and how quickly they were pulled up. They are not so easy to land slowly as in England, for they are heavily loaded with all sorts of desert equipment. Flying in the desert is fine training for a pilot. We made a very careful inspection of our D.H.9a and discovered what we had failed to discover when we were interrupted by Naif's arrival the previous day. One of the rocker arms on the starboard side of the Liberty engine was broken. This would cut out one side of the engine completely and make running impossible. It was a very rare thing to happen. Farnan told me that this was only the second forced landing that he had had in three years. I was flown home in one of the rescue aeroplanes and reached Hinaidi in time for breakfast.

One thing that struck me about our visit to Naif's castle was that we had never seen a sign of a woman the whole time. I suppose they were kept strictly to their own quarters. As a memento of my visit to Naif Al Jerean I still have the little gold Arab ring, with a bird and a flower inscribed upon it. I wonder if he keeps my portrait of him? I felt that the East could teach the West a lesson in stately courtesy.

EPILOGUE

MY DEPARTURE FROM IRAQ

ON BOARD S.S. KAISER-I-HIND

I am sitting on a deck chair looking towards the setting sun, which is making a sparkling pathway on the cool, smooth, blue sea, of the ineffable lapis-lazuli of the Mediterranean. I am leaving the desert and all that it means to me behind, and my mind is surging with confused memories. I am trying to focus the events of the last two years, and I feel the same difficulty that one experiences in waking up from a troubled dream. My spirit keeps leaping at glorious echoes. When they finally pass away I shall be unreasonably sad. I shall then come to myself and realize that I have been a little uncontrolled—and yet—I fancy that no man can come to the desert, endure its infinite moods, and leave it without the feeling of having been mysteriously blessed. Astern the wake of the ship keeps reminding me of the track over the desert.

The squadron on gave me a splendid send off. Although this is quite the usual thing, to me it meant something more than I can explain. When I had packed up I found my car waiting outside the Mess for me, and lo and behold it was decorated with a huge tripod on top of which fluttered a flag, and it was strung with garlands of paper rosettes on sticks. Behind was hung a great bell, and two old shoes trailed on the ground. Surrounded by ardent supporters I was driven to the end of the road between our quarters, where the whole squadron was waiting with two long ropes. The afternoon was hot, about 10 degrees. Undaunted, the gallant men hitched one rope on to each dum iron, and towed the car at a run.

Far away on the other side of the aerodrome were lined up the two aeroplanes as of old—a Vernon and a Victoria—and the men towed us all across the aerodrome, half the way at a run, until they became purple from heat and fatigue. Then they walked, and when near the aeroplanes they ran again. As we progressed across Hinaidi ever the crowd increased, according to Eastern custom, all the coolies running behind and the bearers forming a flank guard on push-bikes. Tenders and taxies joined the throng, and so the motley crowd went forward to the rhythm of my jangling bell. When we were come near to the Vernon we perceived a lorry in which was situated the squadron band complete with piano. They burst out into tunes suitable to the occasion, and, embarrassed by considerable cheering, I attempted to make a final speech. After that I shook hands all round. One man had got himself up in a long white coat with a crook and was driving one of the squadron pigs, a huge sow, and the squadron sheep with a flag tied on its back. I should think that the sow might easily have died after her exertions in that heat; she eventually lay in a recumbent position groaning on the floor of a tender.

I climbed up into the Vernon for the last time. I took the second pilot's seat, and as the engines opened out to a roar, I waved my cap. The last I saw of the squadron was a blurr of waving hands which went misty because I could no longer bear to look at them but I cannot forget the vision of those red perspiring faces; for in them the spirit of the squadron rose to its climax; and it seemed to me to shine out of its setting with an unearthly brightness. For a few moments the sun went out. The ground flowed away like a tide, and the crowd of men shrank to an inconsiderable stature. They were drawn inexorably from me, until they faded like a little cloud into the land of memory.

It is twilight. We have just passed through the straits between Corsica and Sardinia, and the rocks have sunk below the dark horizon. The grey foam is sighing past; and underneath is the throbbing of the screws that are propelling me, revolution by revolution, home—home—home.

INDEX

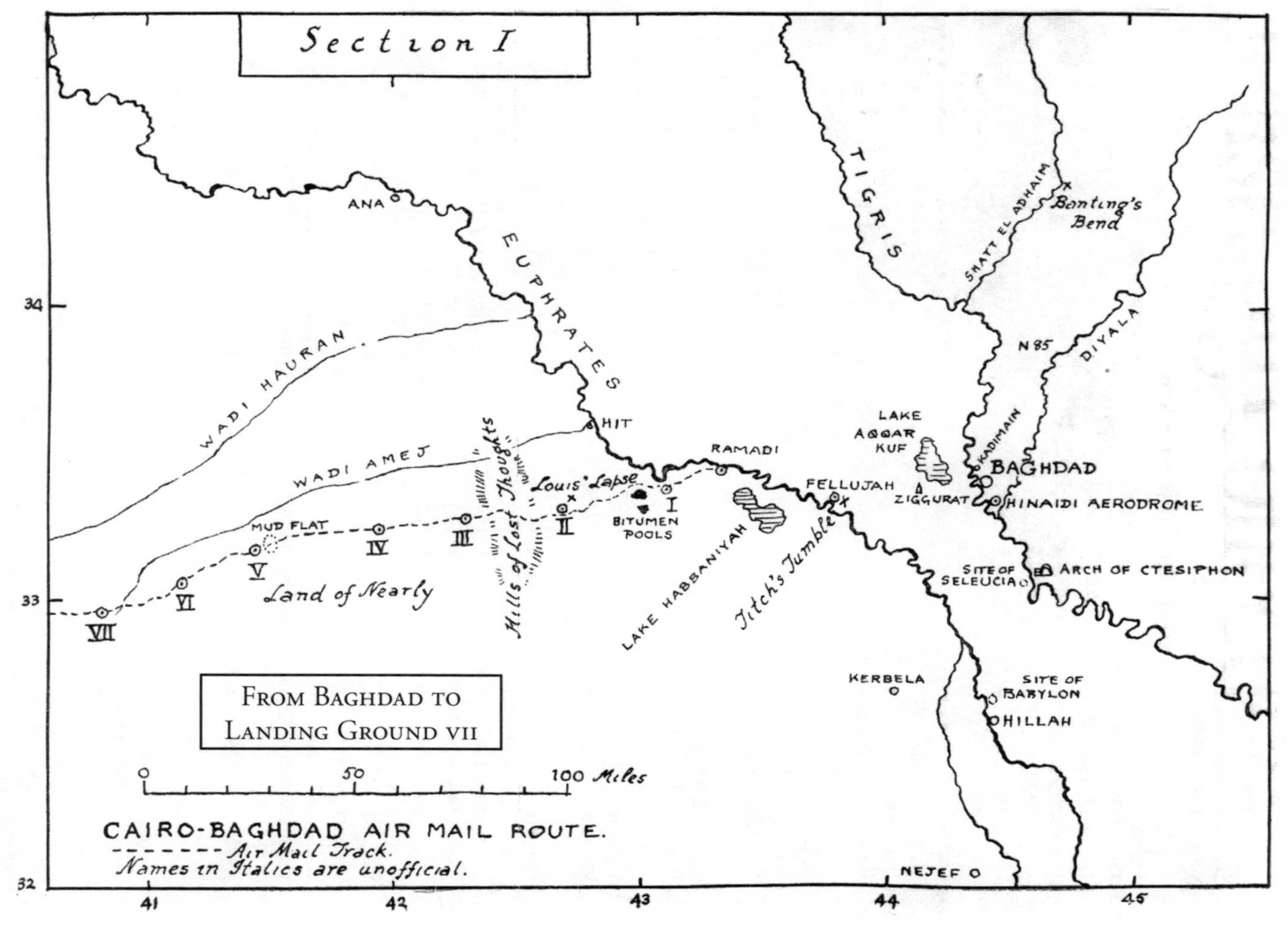

Section I
ANA
EUPHRATES
TIGRIS
SHATT EL ADHAIM
Banting's Bend
N 85
DIYALA
WADI HAURAN
WADI AMEJ
HIT
RAMADI
LAKE AQQAR KUF
KADIMAIN
BAGHDAD
HINAIDI AERODROME
ZIGGURAT
FELLUJAH
Louis' Lapse
BITUMEN POOLS
Hills of Lost Thoughts
MUD FLAT
I
II
III
IV
V
VI
VII
Land of Nearly
LAKE HABBANIYAH
Titch's Tumble
SITE OF SELEUCIA
ARCH OF CTESIPHON
KERBELA
SITE OF BABYLON
HILLAH
NEJEF
FROM BAGHDAD TO LANDING GROUND VII
0
50
100 Miles
CAIRO-BAGHDAD AIR MAIL ROUTE.
Air Mail Track.
Names in Italics are unofficial.
34
33
32
41
42
43
44
45

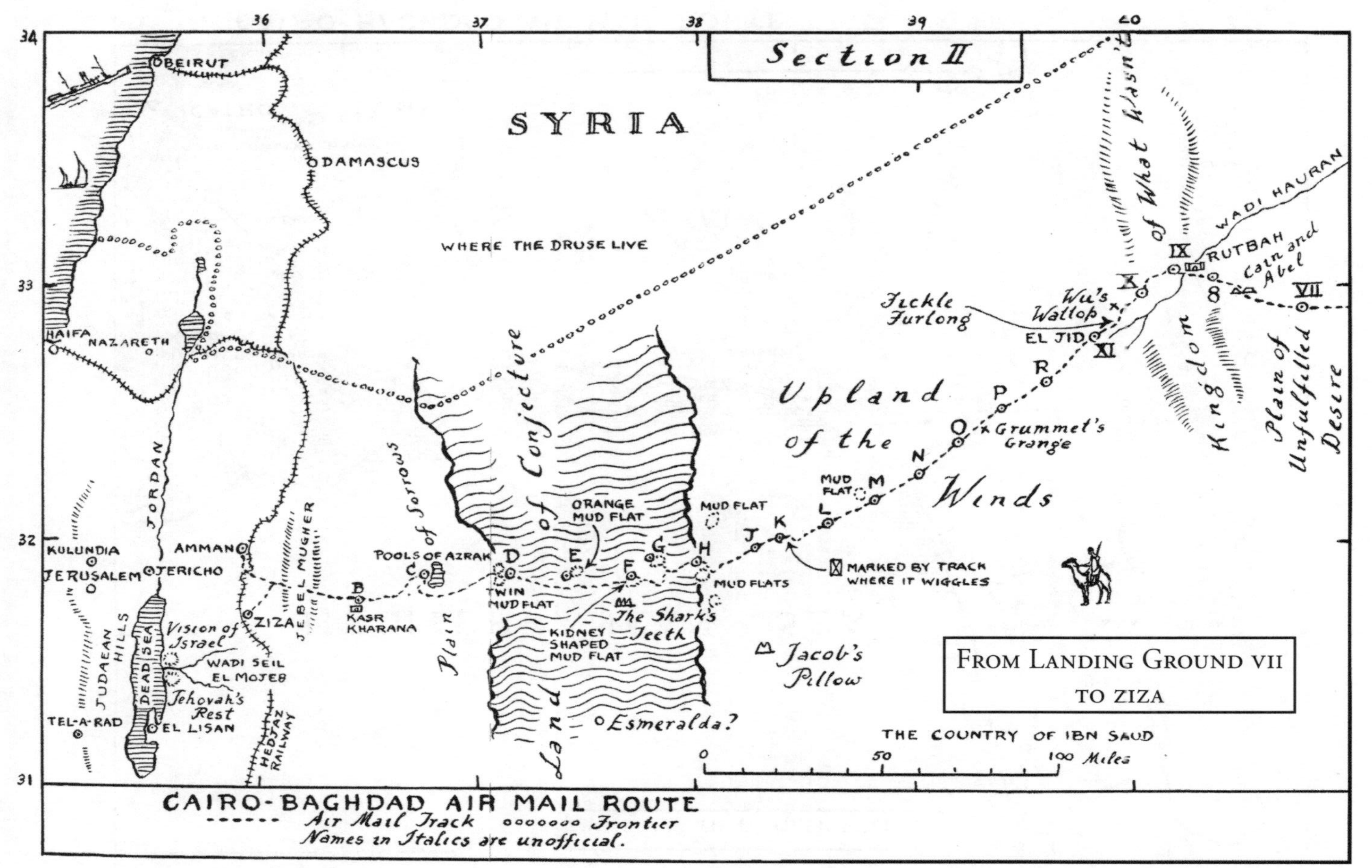
Section II
SYRIA
WHERE THE DRUSE LIVE
BEIRUT
DAMASCUS
HAIFA
NAZARETH
JORDAN
KULUNDIA
JERUSALEM
JERICHO
AMMAN
JUDAEAN HILLS
DEAD SEA
Vision of Israel
WADI SEIL
EL MOJEB
Jehovah's Rest
EL LISAN
TEL-A-RAD
HEDJAZ RAILWAY
JEBEL MUGHER
ZIZA
B
KASR KHARANA
Plain of Sorrows
POOLS OF AZRAK
C
D
TWIN MUD FLAT
Land of Conjecture
ORANGE MUD FLAT
E
F
G
H
KIDNEY SHAPED MUD FLAT
The Shark's Teeth
Esmeralda?
MUD FLAT
MUD FLATS
J
K
L
M
MUD FLAT
N
O
P
R
MARKED BY TRACK WHERE IT WIGGLES
Jacob's Pillow
Upland of the Winds
Grummet's Grange
Fickle Furlong
Wu's Wallop
EL JID
XI
X
IX
RUTBAH
Cain and Abel
8
VII
WADI HAURAN
of What Wasn't
Kingdom
Plain of Unfulfilled Desire
THE COUNTRY OF IBN SAUD
0
50
100 Miles
FROM LANDING GROUND VII TO ZIZA
CAIRO-BAGHDAD AIR MAIL ROUTE
Air Mail Track
Frontier
Names in Italics are unofficial.
34
33
32
31
36
37
38
39
40

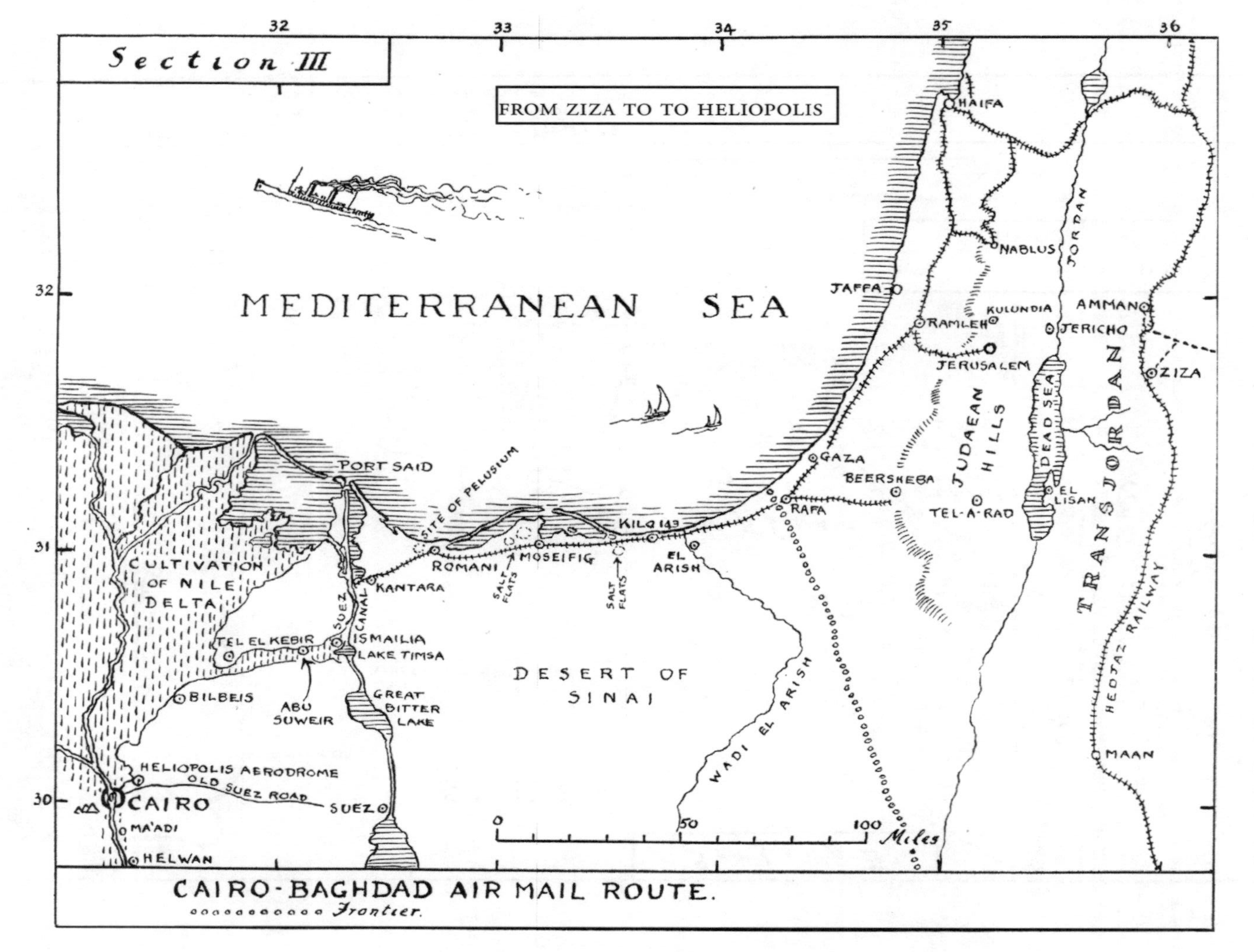
Section III
FROM ZIZA TO TO HELIOPOLIS
32
33
34
35
36
MEDITERRANEAN SEA
HAIFA
NABLUS
JORDAN
JAFFA
KULUNDIA
RAMLEH
AMMAN
JERICHO
JERUSALEM
ZIZA
JUDAEAN HILLS
DEAD SEA
TRANSJORDAN
PORT SAID
SITE OF PELUSIUM
GAZA
BEERSHEBA
EL LISAN
TEL-A-RAD
RAFA
KILO 143
EL ARISH
ROMANI
MOSEIFIG
SALT FLATS
SALT FLATS
CULTIVATION OF NILE DELTA
KANTARA
SUEZ CANAL
ISMAILIA
LAKE TIMSA
TEL EL KEBIR
DESERT OF SINAI
WADI EL ARISH
HEDJAZ RAILWAY
BILBEIS
ABU SUWEIR
GREAT BITTER LAKE
MAAN
HELIOPOLIS AERODROME
OLD SUEZ ROAD
CAIRO
SUEZ
MA'ADI
HELWAN
0
50
100 Miles
30
31
32
CAIRO-BAGHDAD AIR MAIL ROUTE.
Frontier.

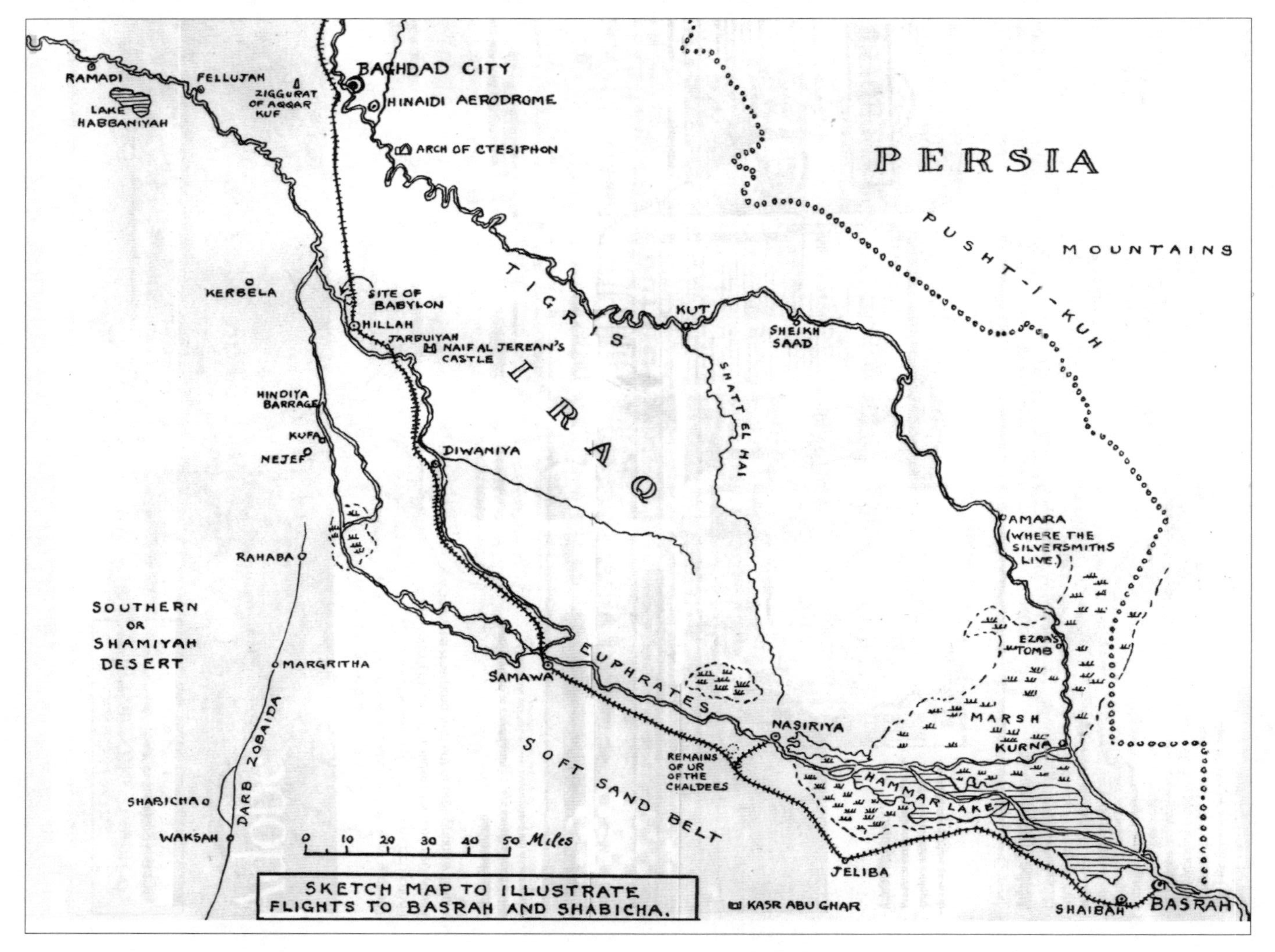

SKETCH MAP TO ILLUSTRATE FLIGHTS TO BASRAH AND SHABICHA.

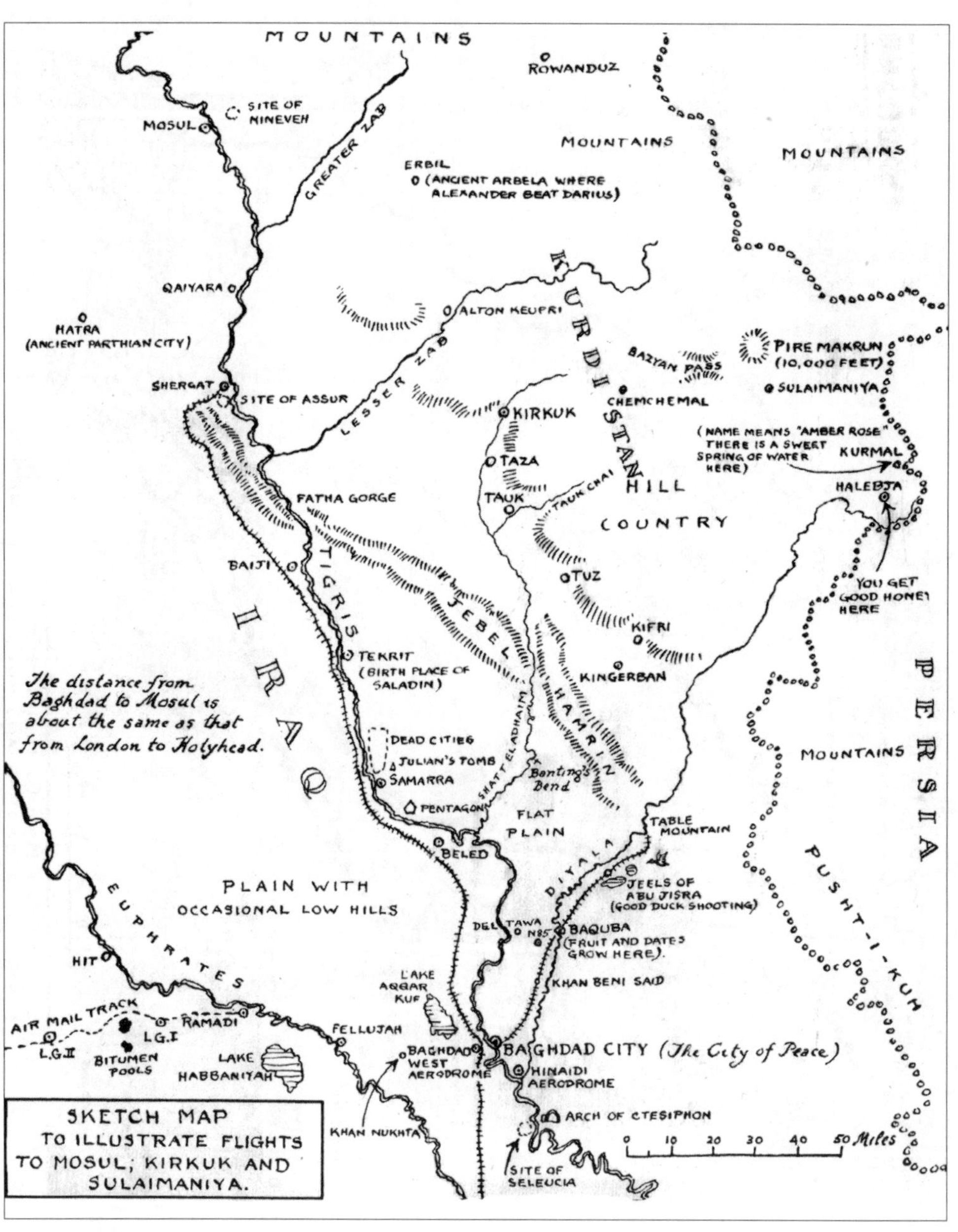

SKETCH MAP TO ILLUSTRATE FLIGHTS TO MOSUL, KIRKUK AND SULAIMANIYA.